Silent Genocide

Silent Genocide

Americans Without Homes

Author

James K. Waghorne

Copyright 2007 ISBN 978-0-6151-5701-6

Dedicated to the over 400 Americans without homes who have perished on the streets in Dallas, Texas since 1999.

Table Of Contents

Introduction:	7
Chapter 1: Social Health Poverty	11
Chapter 2: The Tribe	29
Chapter 3: Miller Time	56
Chapter 4: Americorps	74
Chapter 5: The Castle on the Hill	92
Chapter 6: Silent Genocide	119
Chapter 7: Dark Secrets of the Social club	138
Chapter 8: Homeless Acquire a Voice	152
Chapter 9: Facts and the Numbers	188
Author Profile:	211
References:	213

Acknowledgements

I wish to acknowledge those, whom without their assistance and support, advancement in practical solutions addressing homelessness in Dallas, Texas would not have ever happened.

Advocates and mentors: Clora Hogan, John Fullinwider and Sandy Rollins, Dorothy Masterson, Prince Johnson, Ben Johnson

The National Coalition for the Homeless – Michael Stoops and staff
The National Law Center on Homelessness and Poverty – Tulin Ozdeger and staff
The National Alliance to End Homelessness – Nan Roman and staff
The National Low Income Housing Coalition – Staff

Friendship West Baptist Church – Dallas Texas
Dr. Fredrick Haynes III, Rev. Jerry C. Smith, Curtis Callahan & Staff
Butterflies from Heaven Ministry
Cindi, Todd, Kaye, Benji and Bonnie

Former and currently Americans without homes whose contributions are responsible for this book coming to reality: Hal Samples – Photography, Ben Johnson – Photography, Lowell Smith – thoughts, Ken Flint & Charlotte Webster – Technical Assistance, Hollywood Heinz – cartoons, William Pettet and all the Americans without homes in Dallas for their sacrifice and support. Their courage to fight to be fully welcomed into American society as Americans is a tribute to the human spirit our forefathers endowed.

Musician – Phil Collins

For their reporting:
African American News & Issues
Fort Worth Star-Telegram
Dallas Morning News
Dallas Observer
Associated Press

My Mother and Father for their love and support.

Lastly but most importantly, I wish to thank God. His is all the glory.

Good Morning Everyone,   Jan. 24, 2006

Last night I participated for the first time in the Dallas Homeless Count. For reasons I could not explain at the beginning I had difficulty with the term "Homeless Count". In my lifetime I have counted sheep, pennies and even shoes. January 23, 2006, I counted people.

There were about 200 surveyors divided into 20 teams to conduct inside or outside counts. Those teams assigned outside would ride with Dallas Police Officers to survey encampments, bridges and any other non-sheltered areas. The inside teams were charged with counting individuals in shelters, emergency and transitional housing. I was assigned to an inside team. Please understand I am not naïve to homelessness or its contributing factors. However this night it became a living being.

Like many of you, I have assisted a homeless individual (s) with specific issues, spoke to them on the street and even petitioned for more services. Last night I met individuals as they placed cots on floors preparing to sleep. Last night I spoke with individuals with multiple physical and mental health needs. Last night some did not want to talk while others spoke freely. Those that did speak did not offer excuses, they were seeking solutions. Many were puzzled by our interruption of their routine and its expected outcomes.

After my count I turned in my surveys, my deed done. It was long pass the nightly news when I arrived home, where the doors are secure and the water flows freely. It was 1:00 AM before I settled into bed. You see, I called each family member (four states and the District of Columbia). Glad to report, all safe and accounted for.

As I contemplate my task for today it still shakes me. Lord, last night I counted people.

Vivian Lawrence
Mental Health Association of Greater Dallas
Public Policy Specialist
Criminal Justice

Introduction

Hope should never be compromised as an American luxury, but remain forever the inherited birthright of all.

5/15/04 HUD cuts rental vouchers for the poor
Five days later:
May 20, 2004
U.S. House of Representatives – House Financial Services Committee
Washington D.C.
Newly appointed Secretary of HUD, Alfonso Jackson testifies
"I don't talk about housing for the poor because, being poor is just a state of mind, not a condition."
Shock and disbelief swept through the chamber as Mr. Jackson finished his comment. Representative Barbara Lee from California tried to get Mr. Jackson to clarify and possibly change what he had just said, but Mr. Jackson only reiterated his comment.
"I defy the Secretary to tell all those people looking for jobs in this horrible economy: all those who spend night after night in the cold: and all those working poor and their families who must live in transitional shelters because the cost of housing is so high that 'poor is just a state of mind.'
Representative Frank joined his colleague in denouncing Mr. Jackson obvious belief that the poor economic class in America was solely responsible for their plight.
"Given the assault HUD has been waging on programs that help people in need, your cavalier assertion that being poor is simply a state of mind could serve as a dictionary illustration of adding insult to injury to poor people in America."
"Secretary Jackson, your comments are offensive to millions of unemployed Americans who have been looking for work. There are real economic disparities in this country, and these kinds of comments will do nothing to help us bridge the growing gap between the rich and the poor." Representative Capuano added.
What if poverty and homelessness isn't an accident at all? What if the fact that 25 million Americans including children go hungry everyday inside the wealthiest nation in world

history, has been approved at the highest levels? What if corporate, political and personal greed is directly responsible in the deaths of thousands of Americans every year, using the excuse that capitalism demands such human sacrifice? What if the most dangerous enemy did not reside outside the borders of the United States, but instead resides within; within us.

Dr. Martin Luther King Jr.1967, "Where do we go from here? Chaos or Community? "The curse of poverty has no justification in our age. It is as socially cruel and blind as the practice of cannibalism at the dawn of civilization, when men ate each other because they had not yet learned to take food from the soil or to consume abundant animal life around them. The time has come for us to civilize ourselves by the total, direct and immediate abolition of poverty." During 1967, 10 million Americans lived in poverty and homelessness virtually did not exist. Today the population of Americans, who live in poverty, outnumbers the entire population of Canada and homelessness affects between 2.2 million – 3.5 million Americans every year, victims of devastating natural, unnatural disasters and government public policy; of this population estimates are 1,200,000 will be children, 650,000 will be disabled, 500,000 families and 300,000 will be veterans. 744,313 individuals, according to the National Alliance to End Homelessness latest research, are homeless in America in any given month. Over 325,000 Americans this year; women, children, men, elderly, disabled, veterans, untreated mentally ill, abuse victims, casualties of a lost drug war will sleep at a place known as the "Starlight Motel"; only familiar to those living on our streets, in our wooded areas, parks and under bridges. The American Disability Act has failed to protect the most vulnerable in America, as those who live on the streets are often exploited for profit, brutalized and murdered due to "Hate Crimes". Nationally, a person remains homeless for an average of seven months; in Dallas during this time, a person is 25 times more likely to become a victim of violent crime compared to that of a person with a safe and decent place to live. Only one unit of supportive housing is available for every 25 disabled individuals in need, and the gap of affordable housing in America is at a historic 4.4 million units. Homelessness is not just a tragic economic status but it is a life-threatening event. Reports performed by the National Coalition for the Homeless show alarming increases in crime perpetrated against our most venerable. Since 1999, almost 500 American individuals have become victims of "Hate Crimes" of which 167 have been murdered. Not because of race, sex or religion, but only because they did not have housing.

Homelessness in a nation where it does not need to exist, transcends mans social deprivation to the time when uncivilized primitive communities would take one of their own and place them upon the cold stone altars to sacrifice them to false gods in hope of individual and community prosperity.

Poverty in America is a National shame and disgrace. Homelessness is a National sin. Our homeless; indeed are not like everyone else. For those living on the streets or in shelters, their physical, social, emotional, mental and economic crisis is on public display. No closets to hide the skeletons. No masks to hide their identity as humans living in the worst form of depredation.

The best way to displace compassion and humanity is to dehumanize an individual or population with a label.

William Pettet

Now instead of Americans, instead of individual people, we have been segregated from society to become an "issue". The definition of "homeless" – without a home or haven, has been railroaded into substance abuse, domestic violence, veterans, mental health care, foster care, elderly, poverty; no longer Tom or Jill, a person without a home; but instead a big issue and in America whenever there is a issue, we must have a debate.

Our lack of having a home put aside and placed in the back row with us, while experts of those issues debate among themselves. Denied a voice because an "issue" doesn't have a voice, only people do, and so now stripped of human identity we wait as the sole dilemma in America is the begging question, "Who is worthy of basic life sustaining needs, such as a roof over their head? Who deserves to live and die? Who deserves hope? While the debate rages, more than 744,000 Americans suffer, because an "issue" does not suffer, only the living does. As Mother Teresa would say, "It is popular to talk about the poor, but not with the poor."

No other comment made in recent history exemplifies the gap between classes in America then what former first lady Barbara Bush said after visiting the Hurricane Katrina evacuees in the Astrodome, stating they were "underprivileged anyway" and their newfound shelter "is working very well." An unfortunate comment made by a former first lady, but it goes straight to the heart of the moral question. Can the wealthiest and most powerful Nation in world history, justify the millions of their own citizens suffering in the bondage of poverty when it could be addressed, all the while promoting the moral benefits of democracy around the world? Are Americas homeless the human sacrifices to a false god for capitalistic prosperity? The average life span of a person without housing living on the streets in Dallas is 42; a 30 year shorter life expectancy then someone who has housing. Mahatma Gandhi said, "poverty is the worse form of violence". He was right.

History is seldom recounted from those who were the victims of that history and today is more often a malicious lie in a sad attempt to build fabled legacies for those in power. This book is the result of the thousands of documents and emails concerning homelessness, which were saved dating back to the 1990's. Save so that one day the truth would be told.

There was a story about a young woman desperately trying to get employment but because she was an ex-offender, employers were not willing to take a chance. Her offense leading to a guilty conviction: she did not report a crime, which she had witnessed. I will not make that same mistake.

        This is what I witnessed. This is my report of the crime.

Chapter 1
Social Health Poverty

Only in the 20th century, and only begrudgingly, did we stop treating blacks and women as quasi children. Perhaps in the 21st century, we will extend fully human stature to the so-called mentally ill as well.

Thomas Szasz

Summer 1978

I played the song over and over again, singing and relating to the chorus, "I am the King of nothing". Driving to all the old hang outs where my high school love and I had spent our romantic times, nothing left but the pain of those once happy memories were crushing me. She was the girl I thought I would spend the rest of my life with, the one I would have my last slow dance with. Now gone off to college, she had a new life, new friends and a new desire for something different.

A six-pack of beer and a bottle of sleeping pills rested in the passenger seat of my car. Where to do it? Where should I end all the pain and darkness that had engulfed my being? Near the lake, by the pond where we use to feed the ducks and swing in the chair together, or maybe by the Dairy Queen where I first asked her out? I couldn't think or decide, the uncontrollable tears rushing down, blinding me physically and emotionally. Home…I would end this suffering at home. My parents' house was big and my bedroom was on the opposite side of theirs. They would not hear me. Sleep, permanent sleep would be my savior this night.

I parked the car in the back driveway, not wanting the headlights to possibly wake up anyone. There, my windows rolled up and the music blaring, I chugged the first beer and then the second and third one. I felt relieved that I was finally taking care of the problem. Certain this was the best and only alternative for me, the right treatment for the cruel aliment of heartbreak. I finished the fourth one and took the remaining two beers inside to help with swallowing the bottle of pills. I crept inside the house, quiet as I could be and went straight to the bathroom for privacy. I watched myself in the mirror above the marbled sink as I swallow 4 pills at a time, chasing them down with the remaining beer, until all gone. I wasn't feeling a thing when I climbed into bed for my last night on earth. My mind was numb from the expectation and final end.

The pills mixed with beer, started to curl my stomach and the room became a speeding carousel. Grabbing the trashcan next to the bed, I released vomit after vomit, until only yellow vile came up. The sleeping pills had me in a confused state and after putting down the half full trashcan, I could only roll over and allow the darkness of the night to overcome me.

I would awake to see the morning.

The conversation around the breakfast table that morning was one filled with tears, shock and disbelief as I recounted the night's events to my mother. Frantic calls were made seeking solutions and help, as I went back to my bedroom to lie down, some of the effects still clouding my mind.

My parents kept coming in with ideas of what to do. First I was to go see a Catholic Priest and psychologist, but he was unavailable. Then I was to pack and check into a hospital but first I had to go and see another Psychiatrist. Finally when all the arrangements had been made, there I was sitting in front of a shrink telling my story of what had happened. He sat there listening, not responding to anything I said, only continually stroking his goatee with his left hand and scribbling his notes with his pen on a yellow pad with his right.

At the end of the session his suggestion was to check myself into the Collins Hospital psychiatric floor.

I said goodbye to my parents as I enter into the elevator, five floors up and into the world of "One flew over the cuckoos nest." The doors opened into a small room surrounded by shatter proof glass. Looking towards my left through the plastic glass was the electric shock table in full view, which caused me some second thoughts about signing myself in. The nurse behind the front desk signaled me to the door and she pushed a buzzer allowing me in. I knew as soon as that door shut behind me, I would be theirs to do as they pleased. Already I was planning and plotting for a great escape, my depression replaced with fear.

The nurse motioned me to the desk.

"Are you wearing a belt?" she asked

"Yes" I replied

"Give it to me and also give me the shoelaces off your tennis shoes. Also, hand me your bag, I'll go through it and give it back to you later." She ordered, "Go with this gentlemen and he'll escort you to your room." A big burly white guy showed up behind me without me even noticing.

"This way." he pointed

He walked me all the way down to the end of one of the three hallways and taking out a set of keys he unlocked the door leading into a small room. The furnishings consisted of one padded table with leather straps hanging down towards the floor. There wasn't even a light switch to be found. I could tell that there was a strap for each wrist and ankle and one large one to go around the waist. Another big black man showed up as I was inspecting my padded room.

"Is this our new patient?"

"Yea, this is Mr. Waghorne." The white guy acknowledges.

"Don't worry Mr. Waghorne; we are going to take good care of you." He looked at me with a grin. I had visions of lying on that table being strapped down, Dr. Frankenstein hovering over me, calling down lightening bolts from the sky to zap my brain.

"Take off all your clothes, including your underwear and here's a gown to put on. You're going to stay in our observation room the first night and if you do good, we'll put you into a regular room tomorrow." The black man said as he handed me one of those flimsy hospital gowns. He continued, "Sorry we can't give you a pillow or any sheets, but hopefully you won't be to cold."

I felts tears piling up behind my eyes, but I wouldn't allow myself to cry in front of other men so I stripped down naked and handed them my clothing, putting on my gown, I went and sat on the table.

"If you need to go to the bathroom or anything else, just bang on the door and the attendant will help you out. Have a good night Mr. Waghorne and we'll see you in the morning." With that they closed the door locking me inside my cell. It was around 4 PM. I sat there and let the flood of tears flow, which I had dammed up behind my eyes. My imagination ran wild with thoughts of torture and abuses that I would encounter in the upcoming days. I didn't sign on for this and my priority changed from getting treatment to getting out as soon as possible

That night was miserable. Cold, hunger, fear and the constant flow of adrenaline coursed through my body making sleep impossible. It was the longest 15 hours in my life.

At 7 AM the door unlocked, another large male nurse was standing there at the opening.

"Are you ready for some breakfast, Mr. Waghorne?" he asked

I was starving.

"Yes and maybe a shower if I could?"

"After breakfast, we'll get you into your room. Here are your clothes so you can dress."

I thanked him and went about getting my clothes on as quickly as possible. I was still shivering from the chill of that night.

He escorted me back down the long hallway, passing many rooms along the way. I started to inspect the people who were also confined with me in this hellhole. Most seemed normal but there were certainly those who stood out. Marcus was one of those. When we made it to the cafeteria I noticed a tall young African American was just getting his plate handed to him to put on his platter. He grabbed a handful of grits from the plate and shoved them into his mouth. He then turned to stare at me, opening his mouth wide as the grits slowly drooled down his chin and onto the floor. The large female cook behind the counter giggled.

"Marcus, stop scaring the new people. You know better than that. Now get a move on and sit down at a table." Marcus closed his mouth, his chin still dripping chunks of grits and moved on.

I got my plate of food and found a table to sit by myself. Not because I wanted to be unsocial, but safe.

I studied each person and found two people who looked like the least threat. Tim, a 14-year-old smallish boy and an elderly woman sitting in a wheelchair. To be safe, I would start my socializing with these two and get the lay of the land in this place. I always found that Intel gathering could prove valuable for a person to survive and even succeed in manipulating the system if need be. As I was eating, I noticed Tim by the ping-pong table in the common room. He had Marcus stand at the other end of the table holding a paddle. Marcus never moved a muscle. By the blank look on his face, you could tell he was loaded with medication. Tim would hit the ball to Marcus and it would either bounce off of his paddle or off his body. Tim would go around the table each time, adjusting Marcus's hand to hold the paddle in a certain position and then try again. Marcus grinned each time the ball hit him in the stomach or chest, having no concept of the game and to hit the ball back to Tim. Marcus was more like a two-year-old child than a 19-year-old college student. I noticed the fraternity brand on his arm. How could anyone have a scolding hot branding iron place on their arm to scar them for the rest of their life? I went through hazing as a pledge for Delta Upsilon just like everyone else who pledge fraternity, but being scarred went beyond being packed in ice or having to do setups with your feet on a muddied bank and the rest of your body in a freezing cold stream. Marcus's hazing was pure torture and in the end, put him into the mental hospital so drugged up on Thorazine; he was little more than a zombie. Little Tim on the other hand was a firecracker. Zooming from one place to the next, he had trouble staying still, always in perpetual motion. That's how he ended up here. It seems his mother and stepfather got tired of his antics getting into trouble at school, at home and after he stole their car trying to runaway from his stepfathers' abuse, they thought the best place for him was to be in an institution. Tim was the perfect case of parental abuse. His parents were able to use the mental health care system for their own crutch and lack of parenting skills. Another abuse case was the dear sweet elderly woman.

I was always fascinated by her stories of growing up in the late 1800's and during the early 20th century. Through the wrinkles, which lined her face and the cloudy blue eyes, you could tell she had been a beautiful woman in her younger days. The way she carried herself and in her conversations, it was evident she was also a lady of class and high education. It was only when she talked about her children and how they to gained control of the large estate and monies by placing her in the hospital, did she ever lose composure. She was another example of the dark side in Psychiatry and the mental health system. Individuals would lose their freedom not because of any crime committed but only because someone believed it would be in the best interest to have them confined. The best interest of whom was never debated and the individuals placed in such facilities lost their voice and their choice.

Marcus and I had some great conversations whenever he was coming down off the meds. Both of us in college, we had a lot in common. One day I convinced him to tell the staff he only wanted to take half of the dosage he was receiving. He did and a big argument ensued. 3 large male nurses grabbed him, dragging him back down the hallway where I was placed that first night. The hollering and screaming lasted for about 10 minutes and then came an unnerving silence. About 20 minutes later here came Marcus doing his normal Thorazine shuffle, doped beyond the ability to even recognize his own friends. I spent 40 days in the hospital until I finally signed myself out. My doctor, who also was the same doctor for Marcus and Tim, tried to convince my parents to have me committed. This Psychiatrist had spoken to me once a week during 2 minutes per session, and I knew from our conversations he could care less about my personal well-being. Our normal session went like this every time.

"How are you feeling Mr. Waghorne?"

"I feel fine."

"Are you sleeping well?"

"Yes."

"Okay. I'll see you next week."

"Thank you doctor." His decision to try and have me committed was based on the fact our family had insurance. They had not cured me of my depression. Depression left the day I walked off the elevator and into this nightmare, but they did cure me of not seeking treatment in a mental health hospital and not trusting people with my emotions. No other medical profession, even to this day has such a history of abuse and mistreatment of patients than does Psychiatry.

Endless Choices May/June 2003 – Homeless Author Unknown: Two of Me
A constant battle within

A fight I just cannot win

Could it be?

That there are two of me

How else do I explain?

The ability to stay sane

The battle affecting my mind

No peace of any kind

The two of me afraid to concede

Or admit to need

Hopefully soon it will be

That there is just one of me.

In the recent study performed by the National Alliance to End Homelessness, 744,000 people were found to be homeless on any given night of which 23% met the definition of "chronic homeless". Under this term, 171,120 disabled Americans were without housing and met the "chronic homeless" definition. The number would actually be far greater if it were to include the disabled population thrown away into the prison system.

In Dallas, 80% of our "chronic homeless" were disabled with untreated mental health illness, but the broken homeless and mental health care system also disabled them. Our Nation had rejected and abandoned our indigent living with an illness.

National Center for Injury Prevention and Control:

*Suicide is the eight leading cause of death among men

*Women report attempting suicide during their lifetime at a rate 3 times more often then men

*Suicide is the third leading cause of death among youth ages between 15 to 24 and is the second leading cause of death among college students

*in 2001, 5,393 Americans over the age 65 committed suicide.

By definition, Suicide is an act made by a person with sane ability. These above deaths are a direct result of a disease untreated and not the action of well individual taking their own lives. They are also the direct result of the lack of attention being paid to the needless deaths of over 30,000 Americans every year and over 125,000 attempts due to untreated symptoms. Instead of addressing mental illness, Texas policy is the same as 1800's England. Lock them up in cages!

Sept. 2001 County Commissioner Testifies before Senate – Endless Choices

June 2002 Commissioner Kenneth Mayfield testifies before Senate Judiciary Committee: NACO's President-elect Kenneth Mayfield called on congress to enact federal legislature that would help divert non-violent, mentally ill offenders from County jails. Mayfield has been working for over a year with 30 National organizations in designing a proposal for federal assistance to foster community collaborations between criminal justice and health and human services agencies.

Mayfield confirmed, "Too often mentally ill inmates tend to follow a revolving door, from homelessness to incarceration and then back to the streets. Too many of these individuals do not get adequate treatment and end up being arrested again."

"The nation's local jails have increasingly become the dumping grounds for the mentally ill." Mayfield continued, "Of the 10 million admissions to county jails each year, it is estimated that 16% are individuals suffering from mental illness."

From: judgefinn@davidfinn.com
To: Psyc251@aol.com
Subject: Re: Membership
Date: Wed, 8 Sep 2004 21:40:27 -0500 (CDT)

Dear Pam:

I'll send the Internal Affairs Report to you tomorrow. I'm likely to file a civil rights lawsuit on Friday. Channels 8 and 5 are on it, and the DMN is sending a reporter to interview my client's mother tomorrow. The report is shocking and disgusting. I think that the DMN will do a story on Friday, and 8 will aire the story tomorrow night or Friday. I need you to light them up over this kind of inhumane treatment. Write letters to the DMN Letters to the Editor section and give 8 and 5 kudos for giving a damn about this stuff. The press seems to think that the public doesn't care about the inhumane treatment of mentally ill inmates in Dallas, and your contacts can set the record straight if they are willing to get involved. I've been dealing with this problem for years and in my opinion this is the case to make some major reforms and get an ombudsman in the jail to make sure this is not repeated. When the Sheriff's own report admits that they screwed up royally we need to seize the moment. I've got the FBI and the DOJ Civil Rights people looking at the case and they seem to be genuinely interested in getting to the bottom of this. If a horse or a dog get treated this way it's front-page news, if it's a mentally ill person it's ... We have to get after them on this. Letters and calls to the media will get it done. Please give your friends and members the heads up and strongly suggest that they write letters, emails, and make phone calls to the press to let them know that people do care about this type of misconduct.

Thanks, David

The street homeless in Dallas, primarily African Americans living with Mental Illness have a better chance ending up in the Dallas County jail than they do getting adequate treatment. If you are Black, poor and living with mental illness; sorry, three strikes, and your out. If you are white, poor, and live with mental illness, two strikes but still reference above African American.

Mental Illness in Texas: Executions and Healthcare cuts – Marcia Purse

In Texas, unless a mentally ill person has plenty of money and/or is fortunate enough to have health insurance with decent mental health benefits, the State appears to have the attitude that execution is as good an option as providing care. In 2003, the Texas Legislature slashed millions of dollars from the state mental healthcare programs… Dallas operates under a manage care system. This means that treatment is conformed to a person's diagnosis as oppose to the individual needs. Even worse than placing mental health treatment into a box, veterans in Dallas do not have the freedom of choice when it comes to their primary care for mental illness. Politicians aimed the budget slashing at those who served and many who fought for our freedom by cutting their freedom of choice when they came back home.

March 2003

Clora had been a great source for information on the homeless situation in Dallas for the last three years. With my knowledge of the streets and her inside info, we made a good team. On this day at the Stewpot, she came to me with some distressing news. She had learned of a man who had just committed suicide by jumping off an overpass onto

Interstate 30, and she wanted me to find out more information about the incident. All she knew was that he had been staying at the Dallas Life Foundation, a local homeless boarding facility.

That evening I went over to my friends' apartment to see what they might be able to tell me. Lee, Luke and Carol had each been homeless for three years or longer, but had recently pooled their resources together and moved into a one-bedroom apartment. Lee was a Vietnam Veteran suffering from multiple ailments including P.T.S.D. and needed 13 prescriptions daily just to function. Luke suffered with T.B. and Carol was a victim of domestic violence. Each one of them struggled with their own problems, except now they had a roof over their heads.

I asked if they had heard anything on the news about the death. People throwing themselves off bridges in downtown Dallas should get some news, I thought. Carol gave me an odd look and said she knew about the tragic death. Another formerly homeless person living in the same apartment complex was related to the victim. It was Dominic.

I visited with Dominic the next day. He told me not long before the incident, his brother had been released from jail. He lived with Bi-polar disorder and substance abuse, as did Dominic and others in his family. Their mother had neither the resources nor the knowledge how to help her children when they were younger. His brother was staying at the Dallas Life Foundation waiting for some housing when it became just too much for him to handle.

Endless Choices May/June 2003 - Homeless Author Unknown
Suicide

Misery

Unbearable misery

Few experience

The horror

Of such pain

Laughter increased

Unable to endure

Imprisoned by hurt

Only death

Will end
The pain
Rejection
And total misery
Of your Life

<u>Chronically Homeless 2004 – Letter to Mental Health & Service Providers</u>

Today in Dallas County, over 1,100 individuals qualify under the HUD definition as being chronically homeless, (17% U.S. Veterans) and while the word usage of "Chronic" as to define individuals experiencing long term or cyclical homelessness is definitively wrong, it is imperative to acknowledge that due to their unique experience of cyclical and/or long-term homelessness, status quo mainstream practices have proven inadequate for this relatively (medically speaking) new population. We should review where we are today in services and practices addressing this issue and where we need to go.

While living homeless, within my campsite 4 out of 5 people, we all qualified as chronically homeless and 4 out of 5 suffered from untreated mental illness. Those who suffered from untreated mental illness, 3 out of 4 self-medicated with alcohol or street drugs. 2 individuals were ex-offenders. 1 lived with Bipolar Disorder, 1 with Schizophrenia and 2 with MDD including myself. All individuals had at one time or another used homeless and/or mental health services early on and were treated but not retained.

While one cannot ascertain an accurate percentile population growth of this segment due to the inadequate homeless census counts prior to the summer of 2002, Dallas County has over twice the percentage population of those individuals who meet the "Chronic Homeless" definition, 22% statistically, compared to the National average of 10%. One of the results is currently; Lew Sterret County jail on any given night is the third largest homeless shelter in Dallas (costing tax-payers in excess of $4 million per year) with an average of over 300 individuals locked up for Class-C violations, and an average of 10 individuals locked up in the detention center for public intoxication and when considered, Lew Sterret County jail is one of the largest mental health holding facilities in the State resulting in inadequate treatment and discharge. Some individuals who are citied or detained for public intoxication are not drunk, but suffer from mental illness resulting in false arrest, detainment and criminal records, directly causing additional mental harm, interfering with appropriate medical treatment and affecting the well being of the individual. In addition, eight to twelve hour detainment or incarceration is not a deterrent to these individuals for inappropriate behavior and only hinders the possibility of consistent treatment, which is required for their well-being and to assist them out of homelessness permanently. Also, citing or threatening individuals with citations for sleeping in public, which often is caused by psychotropic medicines used for treatment means individuals must choose between their health and incarceration.

Behavior of this population, which have been recognized but not addressed, is the effects of long-term homelessness and the similarities to those who experience long term deprivation and those who have experienced long term high stress conditions. Reports of increased senses, such as better hearing, eye site, smell and higher energy levels show the body adjusts to the perceived or real dangers one faces while living homeless for long periods. Also, upon exiting homelessness into a housing environment, it is common for individuals to have a hard time adjusting to this lifestyle. The body and the mind have become acclimated to the effects caused by long-term homelessness. It is also common for individuals who have been successful and socially accepted in any cultural environment to resist going to another environment where they have experienced rejection, multiple failures and disappointments regardless of the benefits. In comparison, what the chronic homeless individual can feel or perceive going from homelessness to housing:

Homeless:

Socially accepted by peers

Perceived Success

Unstructured Environment

Hyper Senses

Life on the Edge

Firm belief system

Empathy

Survival-bonding

Versus Housing:

Lost of peers & identity

Support Doubt, dealing with past history Structure

Loss of self

Boredom

Questions

Isolation, loneness

Of course these symptoms and beliefs produce the greatest motivating emotion, FEAR.

False, **E**vidence, **A**ppearing, **R**eal

Within my area of N.E. Dallas, fear of failure was the most common expression when talking about getting back into housing and mainstream society. Housing in many ways is equivalent for the Chronic Homeless as recovery (abstinence) is to the addict/alcoholic. The less support an individual receives the more likely for relapse. Some individuals will simply leave their housing while others will even practice self-destructive behavior so to be asked to leave. The most pronounced physical reaction from being chronic homeless is the lack of ability to sleep in a bed. My own case is not unique, in the fact it took me three months to sleep comfortable in a bed after having slept most of two years on the ground. Some individuals still report sleeping on the floor next to their beds while in housing even after six months. Also, the lack of air circulating and lack of noise (street noise) adds to the problem. Boredom is an issue, which drives many back to the streets. After being successful within a community/cultural setting, becoming housed without specific healthy social engagement as part of the recovery plan to replace that feeling of value or being a part of, leaves a important void in the individuals life, which most likely assisted in some manner as to the cause of becoming homeless initially. Development of peer support/groups and social peer outings are imperative to the full recovery giving individual empowerment, self-determination, fulfilling the human desire to be of value and part of something greater than themselves.

Today, most of the focus in treating the chronic homeless is on obvious illnesses such as substance abuse and mental health. Barriers such as forced abstinence; medication compliance (street therapy) is the norm, while not recognizing that being homeless itself is not just an economic condition but also a life-threatening event and the physical well being of any individual should be first priority. (25 deaths on the streets the first six months of 2004) The entire medical community would agree that a patient should first be stabilized addressing the life threatening event and than treatment delivered accordingly. Ironic that only in the Homeless Community do we view these individuals as less deserving and require that living in an inhumane condition resulting in physical suffering should be part of treatment. While this has its limited success, growth within the chronic homeless population can in part be traced to a failed delivery of service and a "so-called tuff love approach" to a population who are living in a dire situation both physically and mentally. It is my belief that if we addressed their "Homelessness" and the behavioral habits one owns from being long-term homeless along and in conjunction with treatment of their other diseases, our success rate would be far higher, more humane and medically ethical.

Housing First

Can we as practitioners/clinicians truly reconcile our current methods in light of individuals dieing on our streets and justify these deaths by saying they (the individual) did not wish to be compliant and conform with our personal/corporate requirements and ideology thereby removing any burden of self responsibility, placing it squarely on an individual whom we required to overcome today's most devastating form of living conditions before we would give whole treatment. Whole treatment doesn't mean just taking a pill or offering therapy but is recognized also as providing an environment geared towards recovery as part of one's well being both physically and mentally. The question must be asked to what other population in the Medical/Mental Health community do we withhold whole treatment requiring an individual first to exist in a life threatening environment and suffering physical destitution for a specific period of time. If we are to continue on this path and not evolve, then we should have the courage to document this medically as professionals to part of someone's treatment plan and be noted in our own hand writing that those who are the poorest of the poor are to remain homeless and destitute while also being compliant for X amount of weeks or months before we offer to provide a safe and well being environment to the best of our ability; thereby making ourselves both professionally, medically, legally and historically accountable for those individuals while living/remaining and dieing in such a manner as we prescribe. Prolonged prescribed homelessness, as part of treatment will one day be viewed as abusive, inhumane and barbaric as the days when the medical community would seek to permanently institutionalize individuals in cages.

I hope this insight will help the layman as well as the professionals.

Thank you for your support.

Best Regards,

James K Waghorne - President

Dallas Homeless Neighborhood Association

I had wanted to meet with the new Police Chief ever since he was hired but needed to allow him some time to settle in. There was an issue between enforcing the law and some officers stepping over the line. Officer Gordon was one of those who seemed to enjoy stepping over the line and degrading our homeless. I had one meeting with the area

Lieutenant, Jan Easterling, about Officer Gordon forcing our homeless off the sidewalks and into the parking lot at the Day Resource Center. The act not only violated civil rights but went beyond, with Officer Gordon telling our homeless to "get off the sidewalk and get into their cages". Not satisfied with the initial meeting I felt such actions by the police needed to be addressed with the top brass.

I was fortunate having a friend who had served on the DPD, Glen "Hog" Wilson. Glen had over 25 years of service before he retired. I was able to learn the mentality of the force and how it could be just as easily affected by prejudice as any other segment of society. He would tell me stories of how some of the officers on DPD would hunt down Black people walking down the street at night and then finding one, beat the hell out of them, just to kill some time. One of my first speaking engagements was at the Dallas Police Academy during a homeless sensitivity training and it gave me some good insight to what I could be facing in meeting with Chief Kunkle.

Police Academy #273 July 16th 2002 A View From the Tracks "Endless Choices"
I had the privilege to speak at the Dallas Police Academy on June 18th as apart of the homeless sensitivity and awareness classes regularly facilitated by the Director of Endless Choices. The class, made up of young cadets, was very attentive and involved in this issue, which sadly had come to divide more than unite. Their questions were a microorganism of our community as a whole. "Isn't homelessness a choice." or "why should I have sympathy for someone with a drug or alcohol problem."...

It was an honor to speak with these young brave men and women as they embark into the proud and honored tradition of law enforcement. And while we certainly disagreed on some things, the bottom line is when they come across a homeless person they are human beings...

The statement that bothered me most during the training was from one young male cadet, "We'll treat the crazies differently." It's hard to convince some people in law enforcement that outreach into the community and treating people with respect, is part of law enforcement. Police action, like military action is a last option.

At the main Police Headquarters, we entered into a large conference room; there was Sgt. Reese, Deputy Chief Brian Harvey, another Deputy Chief I had never met, Chief Kunkle and myself. Not an idea situation to be in, but it wasn't a meeting in which I wanted to get policy changed as much as it was to learn which way the wind was blowing with our new Police Chief and to let the Department know, someone was watching.

My conversations always focused on the "chronic homeless" population and more directly those living with mental illness. They were the most vulnerable to both predators and police abuse, and the most visible to the general population. As an icebreaker, we opened the conversations with a little background about each other and quickly moved to mental illness since that was my main problem when I became homeless. The unknown Deputy Chief stated he had a family member living with mental illness and boasted how he would arrest that individual on the spot if he broke the law. I wasn't going to debate with him or any officer that exhibits more bravado than human compassion, nor would I allow a bully intimidate me. I only wanted to know where the bullies were located. Then Chief Kunkle really surprised me when he spoke. He talked about his father living with mental illness and the problems his family had getting him the help that he needed. Eventually the family decided it was best to send him to California to get proper care, because the Texas Government was so poor when it came to helping their own citizens in need. If the Chief of Police for the ninth largest city in America could not find quality care for his own father, how could anyone else with fewer resources? It only confirmed what I knew about the system in Dallas, and what was happening to those individuals living both with mental illness and in poverty.

The primitive conditions, the socioeconomic environment, and the stigma surrounding homelessness kill's thousand of Americans every year. No other segment of our society is literally made to suffer before humane treatment is fully given. What other population could we point to, where the physical safety is denied during treatment or even in the beginning of treatment? The "chronic homeless" are often forced to conform while living in the most dangerous environment in America today before offered full sanctuary.

If the predators didn't get you, the weather would and if the weather didn't kill you, the drug dealers would steal your soul. The barbaric philosophy that a person needed to take psychotropic medications in this condition, leaving them even more vulnerable, before receiving full humane treatment, was abhorrent to me. It was throwing the lambs to the wolves. How could Psychiatry force homeless with mental illness to remain homeless until compliance was proven? Certainly this practice is based more on economic status as oppose to medical science where the physical well-being and safety of the patient is as important as the medical treatment itself for recovery. I wasn't sure if the doctors who promoted that homeless mentally ill had to first survive each day in depredation before having security of housing, had not lost all sanity and were not sicker than their patients. The actions of the medical and mental health care system showed that our social health system in our State and Nation had hit bottom.

The results in Texas were astoundingly inhumane and cruel.

2005 Texas Rankings

State Government Taxes & Spending	Health Care
49th Tax Revenue Raised	50th - % of Population with Health Ins.
49th Total Expenditures	50th - % of Insured low-income children
Per Capita Spending on	48th - % of Poor covered by Medicaid
45th Public Health	45th - Rate of Substance Abuse Treatment
49th Mental Health	Health & Welfare
Education	7th Poverty Rate
50th High School Graduations rates	2nd - % of Population goes hungry

Chapter 2
The Tribe

The dark clouds started gathering in late spring 1990. City Hall had ignored the suffering, which was slowly encircling downtown Dallas. The media along with corporate developers started to promote the childhood horror tales about those who had become abandoned by our society; their main goal to drive fear and terror within our community, leading to the abuse, criminalization and even deaths of the least fortunate. Eventually, the economics hardships of others becomes a burden for more than just those experiencing the injustice and it is easier to develop myths, horror stories and fairytales then to deal with the truth especially if the truth was self incriminating.

The Dallas Morning News printed the ammunition that would ultimately be used by a few, yet powerful individuals to launch an all out assault on the homeless. The articles sent to then Chief Mack Vines, were headlined with powerful motivations. Americans without homes were labeled as vagrants and characterized with a cartoon of a homeless man putting a bear hug around downtown.

                              Northrup Properties   May 15, 1990
                              Incorporated

Chief Mack Vines
Dallas Police Department
Police and Court Building
Dallas, TX 75201

Chief Vines –
We are big fans of the Police Department. They are arguably one of the best big city forces in the country. We need your help on a tough problem.
Dallas International Ltd. Has recently signed an agreement for up to $20 million in public improvements to the Farmer's Market District. Part of the agreement calls for approximately $10 million in private development within the District. The presence of roving bands of vagrants in the area make it very difficult to attract private development.

Recent news articles have focused public attention on these problems, copies enclosed. Public intoxication, begging, and theft of copper and aluminum from buildings is an every day occurrence in the District. Most of the crime in our District is committed by vagrants. The City encourages this population of vagrants by allowing illegal soup kitchens and a tent city to operate under I45.

We have removed all blood banks, labor agencies and flop houses from the area. We have hired security guards. We cannot rid the area of vagrants without the City's help. We need the police department to enforce laws against public intoxication and we need the tent cities and soup kitchens cleaned out.

Please help us clean up downtown.

Sincerely,

James L Northrup – President

Reprint Courtesy of the Fort Worth Star Telegram
Fort Worth Star-Telegram - April 15, 1991
The can caper. Fining the homeless? Only in Dallas"

If a homeless guy approaches you and asks for $240 to pay for an illegal garbage-collecting ticket, you must be in Dallas, Texas, U.S.A. Where else in this solar system would the police issue citations to penniless people for rummaging through trash bins for aluminum cans? That's what they did in Big D for a while - until the word got out locally and nationally, leaving egg on the municipal face.

Reprint Courtesy of the Fort Worth Star-Telegram
Fort Worth Star-Telegram - December 20, 1994
Dallas homeless man who sued city found dead. He protested demolition of shantytown

Prince Johnson, a longtime homeless man who found his brief moment in the spotlight when he sued Dallas this year over its treatment of homeless residents, was found shot to death late Sunday near an Oak Cliff house that he was helping to renovate. Johnson was 34. He had been homeless since 1987, he said in a June interview. Dallas police said yesterday that robbery was probably not the motive in the unsolved shooting, which occurred at about 8 p.m.

Mr. Johnson had become the voice and rallying cry for Americans without homes in our community. He was homeless, sleeping underneath the I45 underpass on the eastside of downtown Dallas. This area had been dubbed "shantytown" because of the amount of hooch's and cardboard box homes, which had covered the landscape. With allies, John Fullinwider along with his wife, Sandy; Prince led homeless protests carrying signs condemning the civil injustices "Stop arresting homeless people". Prince became a marked man.

City Hall reacted by criminalizing the homeless, the police attacked their own disabled citizens destroying their habitats forcing them to scatter to find safety from their own government. Even the institutions whose one singular defined mission was to reach out to the disenfranchised turned away to avert their eyes from the injustice happening in their own backyards. Prince, with the help of local advocates filed a lawsuit against the city and won a temporary injunction against the "sleeping in public" ordinance. The 5th Circuit Court of Appeals later overturned the injunction because there was not a plaintiff. The plaintiff, Prince had been murdered and a green light was given for cities across the nation to persecute their own disabled homeless citizens.

After Prince was murdered, Dallas Police took one man into custody on bogus charges, telling the local media the man had killed Mr. Johnson during a drug altercation. He was later released. A female had admitted to committing the murder stating that she was coerced, threatened that her probation would be revoked if she did not carry out the deed and shortly thereafter, she disappeared from the face of the planet. Prince's murderer remains at large.

Prince's life and death was significant in Dallas history. With Mr. Johnson's death, an era passed and a voice for the homeless in Dallas died with him. The issue virtually disappeared from the local media and public attention over the next 8 years.

6/10/94 Publication: THE DALLAS MORNING NEWS reprint with permission
Headline: City prepares to bulldoze downtown shantytown, Homeless face arrest if they stay
Byline: Jonathan Eig
Credit: Staff Writer

2000 The New Millennium

Fluff stories would appear sporadically in the local newspaper and on the news channels primarily during the holidays, stirring some heartfelt charity among our community while the true horrors of homelessness remained hidden from the cameras, reporters and the public's view. The work of the 1990 Dallas Homeless Taskforce was stored away in the back of some filing cabinet collecting dust. Ten years later, Dallas still had the same amount of shelter beds and SRO's, single room occupancy units. Rent had reached a new high, going over 22% of the average median household income. The fair market rent (FMR) for a two-bedroom apartment had ballooned from $501 per month to over $860 per month. Americans would need 3 full time minimum wage jobs just to afford to keep a roof over their head and pay other necessary monthly bills. The local level of people living in poverty climbed to over 300,000 and unemployment was at a ten year high 6.1%. Our future; 78% of the children enrolled in Dallas Independent School District qualified for Federal Assistance and free lunches. The National Housing Trust Fund and HUD numbers ranked Dallas first and second in the nation for the lost of affordable housing. Over $300 million dollars had poured into local agencies to help the homeless in Dallas since 1990. Not one single additional shelter bed or home had been built in that ten-year period. What happened to all the money is still a mystery?

The homeless population had once again swelled in Downtown; new shantytowns had developed further south underneath the main interstate bridges. New media, new hostile politics, new resolve by developers and renewed prejudice. The ingredients for a new assault resulting in human abuses against thousands of disabled and indigent Dallasites without housing were in place once again. There couldn't be a worst time for a person to become homeless in Dallas, Texas.

1/20/2001 Publication: THE DALLAS MORNING NEWS reprint with permission
Headline: City risks losing millions for homeless programs
Byline: Gromer Jeffers Jr.
Credit: Staff Writer

HUD gave the City of Dallas 60 days to fix their homeless programs or face a $12.5 million dollar lost in grant monies but this was just the tip of the iceberg.

"Hate crimes are crimes leveled against individuals because of their "actual or perceived race, color, religion, national origin, ethnicity, gender, disability or sexual orientation," according to the 1994 Violent Crime Control and Law Enforcement Act.

However, in light of a recent report, a new category may someday be added to the list of protected characteristics: homelessness.

In "A Report of Hate Crimes and Violence Against People who are Homeless in the United States," the National Coalition for the Homeless has documented 66 violent hate crimes directed against homeless people last year in 42 cities. Among the incidents listed for 2000, 43 were homicides.

Most of the victims were either beaten or shot and, in separate incidents, at least four were set on fire."

December 23, 2000

The day he left the motel with his menial belongings; the weather sent an ominous forecast of the future. The gray winter clouds settled down capturing building rooftops; constant winter drizzle worked to sap the remaining life out of the green vegetation, everything suffered emotionally and physically from the dread. It was just the beginning of an historical deluge over the next 100 days. People don't have a game plan on the way to homelessness. There isn't a survival guide that can be purchased at the local Barnes and Noble bookstore or a map available pointing people towards the locations offering assistance. A person packs the meagerness of life and goes forward into uncertainty, traveling to what could only be best described as an alien world. The one instinct the man had, go to place where he would not be found; the seclusion of the woods around White Rock Lake could provide that.

The 21-speed mountain bike made travel easy, his belongings thrown into two dark green garbage bags, tied off to the front handlebars. Some ten miles down the back roads staying out of view, hiding his scarlet letter of poverty, 5 hours later he arrived at dusk to the planned destination. With somber resolution and the acceptance of what life had become, the middle age man moved into the clump of woods, which would be home. Finding a trial leading into the ghostly dead swamp forest, he followed the trail of black dirt looking for some cover to hide in. 100 feet in, off the trial to the left, laid some green swamp shrubs and clumps of fallen trees making a semi-circle giving up a small, yet perfect clearing. Worn out, depressed, cold and wet, the solitary figure pulled out his tarp and sleeping bag, unpacking everything else would have to wait until the morning, rest and sleep were the priorities for now. His night was constantly interrupted with worry, every woodland sound made him quiver; he listened intently to the chatter from the local creatures cautiously inspecting him and creeping ever so closer to catch his alien scent which had moved into their neighborhood. Sometime during the early morning hours, exhaustion had finally caught up with him and he drifted away, experiencing his first sleep of the lost and weary. His first day of homelessness complete.

Waking up late morning he gathered my wits and formed a game plan, change out of the damp clothes, get tent up, secure and camouflage the area to keep prying eyes from discovering the homeless domain. That Christmas Eve was spent planning for survival opposed to the last minute shopping, fighting crowded malls, time spent wondering if this gift would work or not. Past joyous times would become nightmares, a hot poker stabbing at sanity, all past happy memories needed to be tossed away for survival sake. His life experiences had educated him to understand both the physical and psychological needs for survival. These days were far removed from childhood. Gone were the freckles that dotted the rosy cheeks, the collar length strawberry blond hair lost, now tan skin was the main hair color. His mother would tell him, "A high hairline is a sign of intelligence." he would joke back saying he was a genius because his hairline went down to his rear end. The past gone now with no future, just the daily plans to be accomplished for survival. Tomorrow on Christmas day and everyday thereafter, it had to be the same. Suffering gives no leeway or compassion.

Snow on Christmas day would be a blessing for most in Dallas, but the frozen white concoction was a curse to those without a home. With thoughts of family, good food, old stories retold for the hundredth time while watching the football games on a large screen, the first homeless Christmas day was held inside a small orange tent all huddled up in a sleeping bag, trying the best to sleep like Rip Van Winkle. Permanent sleep, never waking would make my perfect Christmas gift but Santa Claus stayed away from the homeless, not even he could bring them joy and hope.

Each day brought a new despair. Depression was a constant evil minion always waiting for the chance to steal away any happiness. It knew when to strike to cause the most harm, pain and destruction. What a way to start a new year, a new millennium. New Years' Eve like Christmas came with snow, freezing weather and another prayer for God to take a life as he stayed inside the tent, unfortunately always wakening up to another homeless day. Most of January was spent becoming acclimated to this new alien existence and exploring the neighborhood. The miserable weather was a brutal teacher for the uneducated living outdoors, shivering and the chatter of teeth clacking together became a nightly ritual.

The one luxury in the area was a small park close to the lake containing a water fountain and a portal-potty; prime conveniences for a homeless person. On sunny days, residents would bring their dogs to walk at the park and later the City would gate off the area making a dog playground. People were now the estranged and the new homeless man preferred the nightly visits from the large Barred owls hooting throughout the woods and the roaming little bandit raccoons. Though these animals could not converse, nor could they judge with personal prejudices, far more human than what society had become towards a homeless person, those with wings and four legs made perfect companions for people seeking acceptance and isolation from a world gone astray. The days dragged by during January, primarily life consisted of hanging on to sanity and a futile existence.

February blew in with a vengeance. It was if the Pacific Northwest had moved to Dallas loaded with their Coastal storms and dreary weather. A "green pea" to homelessness, I had not yet learned to dumpster dive for food or "fly a sign" at the street intersections, I still walked around with my head up, stepping over pennies, nickels or other lost valuables that would be picked up by an experienced homeless person. The first month the only common street trade I had developed was "snipe hunting". Tracking down nice long dry cigarette butts in ashtrays outside stores or on the ground made gloomy solitary days, adventurous. The hunt provided some kind of purpose, a mission that could bring a small amount of satisfaction each and every time a cigarette butt was found and the longer butt, the more sense of accomplishment.

A sunny day had become very scarce and soon the food supplies began to dry up. Fond memories of eating at five star restaurants in Highland Park Village and the Sunday "All you can eat buffets" at the Anatole Hotel teased my empty stomach. Black Caviar, Eggs Benedict, shrimp and smoke salmon all for morning brunch. Hours spent nibbling some of this and that, idle conversations while admiring the ice sculptures. Tossing away mounds of food that didn't agree with the taste pallets. A sample here of each offering, leaving the rest on the plate for the waiters to dispose of, now all I could think about was how delicious a .99-cent fast food hamburger would taste. Desperate, I rode the bike to a pawnshop, selling my transportation and used the money get some much-needed supplies.

The continuous rain was ever becoming a serious problem. I had lived in Dallas since 1964 and could not remember a time when so many storms had hit during the wintertime. Inclement weather murdered homeless Americans every year both directly and indirectly. The clothes I wore everyday were now damp. How I longed for the days of a closet full of dry clothes and hot soaking wrinkled-toes baths. The almost daily storms compounded the untreated depression. What is major depressive disorder? It is the disease born of the darkest deepest pit in the bowels of hell, cut off from all positive emotions and goodness. The value of life totally depleted, replaced only by pain and grief. Here is the place where your very soul resides. The thousands of old dieing marsh trees surrounding the campsite formed a shield between a misunderstanding world and me. The greatest paradox of depression is starving for understanding while seeking isolation from anyone who could offer such. I would work so hard every minute to stay alive, yet pray just as hard for the misery to end. As a teenager, I had tried to take my own life, but now my faith would not allow it regardless of the extreme pain. I would never travel down that path again. Only God could take my life. In addition, the ideal of a lifeless body left to the whims of creatures that lived in the woods made me cringe with disgust.

A natural devolution when faced with living in a life threatening condition, my primitive survival habits started to form over time. The campsite was at the highest ground level possible for the area, a vantage point to watch the coming and goings of strangers. A small foot-deep creek bed ran near the homestead making it easy to check the water level in my area; the main channels of creeks feeding White Rock Lake kept the bed dry normally. I had never seen more than a couple of inches water streaming through it and as long as the spillway did its job on the lake, I thought I was safe.

February 7, 2001

The day started with promise, instead of the gloomy low hanging clouds that had become customary, bright blue clean skies greeted me. During one such day, I had spotted some anglers at the lake. They always came down after the heavy rains hoping catch a big catfish. In better times, I had enjoyed many hours trying to hook an elusive monster from the depths and if a pole were available, certainly I would have joined them. That experience of being an angler gave me a great idea and so on nice days I would walk to the .99-store, purchasing knives, packaged with a fishing stringer and resale them to the anglers for a nice profit. All anglers can use a new fishing knife and an extra stringer. It was a full day of work, walking two miles to the store and then around the lake, but I was happy to have something to focus on other than what life had become. Going back to camp that afternoon $10 richer put a smile across my face. Rush hour traffic was just beginning, dinner needed to be cooked before nightfall, to hide the small firelight from unwanted eyes. Chicken Noodle soup was one of the diet staples accompanied with a potted meat sandwich to round it off. After cooking and eating a hearty meal, throwing a few slices out to the woodland friends, it was nice to get some early sleep after a long day of walking. Sleep had become a dear friend and silence was golden. There is a comforting, also hypnotic aura sleeping outside once a person gets over the fears.

This particular night's quite though would be shattered minutes later by the sound of sirens coming down the street. There isn't a siren in the world, which is welcomed by a homeless person. Somewhere from deep within, I knew that the police once trusted, were now enemies. Instinctively, I knew that today as a homeless person, I was in danger from the police. Panic grabbed me and only knowing what was happening in the neighborhood would settle the unwanted anxiety. Putting on some clean clothes, masking my homelessness, I would look innocent of poverty and leave the safety of my adobe to investigate. At the edge of the trail what I witnessed something, which caused the blood to raced from my face as a flood of water was crossing the road, down the hill, along the jogging trail, making a beeline right for the encampment. Up on the road, a fire truck was rescuing three people out of their trapped vehicle while police were blocking off the intersection. "Where was all this water coming from?" Walking away from the highway towards Mockingbird Ln, I crossed the road past the town homes and walked to the side of the topless club. At the back corner of the town homes near the fence, which separated it from the DART train tracks, a four-foot high wall of water gushed up into the air. Old Faithful could not spew as much water. Millions of gallons were flowing down the hill into the town homes, topless club, and two convenience stores on its way to my homestead. Of all the things that could happen, a broken water pipe could wash away my supplies and put me in danger of becoming discovered. Running back into the woods towards my home, over the next few hours, I sat and watched the water rise in the small creek bed. Evening was coming and that comforted me until the media helicopters started to circle the area to catch all the commotion, their spotlights glaring down. An 84" water main break was big news. There was a circus hovering overhead and quickly I threw as many dead limbs as I could gather over the tent to camouflage it and after fifteen minutes of hiding inside my tent, the unwanted guest finally left. I had escaped being discovered and the site was secured but the rest of the wetlands did not fare as well. Any future rain would be rejected from the over saturated ground meaning soon catastrophe was coming. The lightning flashed across the night sky towards the south like some disco dance floor strobe light. The towering walls of threatening clouds were easily viewed with each flash, exposing the thunderheads reaching into the very heavens. It was not going to be a restful night. Goose bumps rose on my arms as I watched the inevitable approach, like watching a slow motion car wreck, I could not avert my eyes away from the sight. It held me almost trancelike until the rain started to pelt the top of my head.

Jumping inside the tent, the visions of the devastating destruction caused by tornados kept replaying in my head. The train sounds people say they hear before the whirling giants snatched their homes was something I was expecting to hear from this monstrosity but the sound I heard was nothing like that of a freight train.

I thought someone had stepped onto a twig snapping it, in far off distance. Then another twig snapped and another, getting closer each time. The thunder gathered with a continuous boom as it approached; and then I heard what sounded like the snapping of ten twigs, than fifty twigs and hundreds breaking. A giant monster was tramping through the woods heading right for my site. Frozen, I listened as the evil closed in. It wasn't death that held me, but the thought of the pain that would lead to that final exhale of life. It was soon obvious that the noise I was hearing wasn't twigs breaking, but full size trees being snapped like toothpicks by the oncoming straight-line winds and downbursts. The ground was soaked; the roots of the trees were giving way while other deadwoods trying their best to hang on were shattered in half. Run an inner voice said, run for your life. Never had clothes and shoes been put on so quickly and unzipping the tent opening, I stuck my head out ready for flight; but it was too late. The tree across the trail near my tent was over 16" in circumference at the base and rose to over 20'. The wind caught the top and the tree exploded five feet up from the base. "Oh God", I yelled as the monster tumbled downward to crush my life. Throwing my arms over the back of my head I waited for the impending pain of being crushed and the accompanied death. The limbs started to hit first, shooting tiny pieces of bark into my face and eyes, the sting making them water instantly. Putting my hands back over my face to try and protect it, I ducked back inside the tent to hear one final "Boom!" it was suddenly over; my entire body was shaking as I listened to the storm travel north on its destructive path. The tree that had sought my life had been in the shape of a "Y". On the way down, the major part of the trunk fell short; the two large limbs fell harmlessly to either side of the tent. Still alive at least for now, I accepted that my safety wasn't in my control any longer. Homelessness steals away that kind of security.

February 2001 would go down in the record book as fourth wettest month ever recorded in Dallas. Without sunny days to make money from the fishermen, it wasn't long that a small can of potted meat and a loaf of bread purchased at the Tom Thumb for about $1.25 was a 3-day meal. Soup was too expensive now and sometimes the potted meat had to be left on the store shelf and the meals during those days became "make believe" sandwiches. "Make believe" there is something in-between the two slices of bread your eating.

Many times during the last weeks, I had watched the water rise and fall quickly in the little creek bed near my site. Last night a heavy rain had hit again and this day the rain was causing the water to rise faster than normal. Throwing on my raingear, I walked east towards the main creek channels that flowed into the lake, knowing I could now read the water and how full the channels were to get an idea of what was happening. I traveled often to the main channels, as they had become a nice outing in the past. Spending the day exploring the grounds, scavenger hunts, looking for items washed up by floodwaters and I enjoyed watching the two Nutrias play around, slapping their paddle tails hard against the water whenever I was too close for their comfort. I knew they were oversized rats, but they looked more like big brown beavers. Halfway to the main channels was a medium size creek bed, much larger than the one by the camp. Approaching it, I saw what I had feared since moving into the area. The floodwaters had already crested over the banks and were coming westward towards the campsite. There's nothing quite like the cold empty feeling you get in the chest when panic starts to arrive. I had plenty of luck up to that time just surviving the freezing cold temperatures and hunger but a flash flood was a different beast altogether. Getting back would take fifteen minutes, which was enough time to form a plan. The rain made it impossible to move everything without getting it all wet so I would have to load as much as I could, stacking my belongings inside the tent and place it high up in the trees; then with the sleeping bag, a blanket and my winter coat, escape to higher ground finding another place to sleep for the night, waiting out the rain. I worked quickly once back at the site noticing the water in the small bed had breached its banks.

I finished securing the belongings, placing them high up in a tree and started to walk towards the normal exit where I was greeted by a chilling horror. The highest point of land had become an island and my island was being engulfed completely under a flood of dark, lifeless water. Feelings of being completely vulnerable and unable to control the situation, like many others had done, I did the only thing I could, and put fate in God's hands. Nightfall had taken hold. My only two choices available was either to stay and climb up a tree to outdistance the rising water or try to venture through 100' of cold, deep treachery.

What does it truly mean to walk by faith? I found out with every step as the freezing death continued to inch its way up around my body, seeking to drag me under. Drowning wasn't exactly the top choice I had in leaving this world. Fifty feet out, my body started to tremor, the chilled February floodwaters seeped into my bones.

Every step was challenged, painful and as frightening as the first step. The bottom floor was littered with unseen hazards, trees and branches, which had been knocked down by the earlier storm. The strong current pushed against me, working hard to throw off my balance. Struggling to hold the gear above my head and keep it from getting soaked, the travel was at a snails pace. Coming from an upper middle class background, I never knew complete total misery; but we were introduced this night. Making it out of the woods was the first barrier. A small gully waited between the paved jogging trial and myself. 20 ft. from the sidewalk, the water reached over the waistline.

Most of the strong current was focused towards the center and once to the outer areas and smooth ground, I could walk easily and the anxiety started to subside. The cold and the waterlogged blue jeans adhered to the skin and my wet clothes were now a threat, so pulling out a pocketknife I cut my jeans into shorts. I then used the knife and poked holes into the edges of my blanket. Removing the shoelaces from my boots I was able to wrap the blanket around my waist and used the shoelaces from my boots to strap it into place.

It made a quick kilt to help keep the northern chill off my now naked legs. The thick winter coat and sleeping bag would have to do through the night.

Within the next hour, the campsite was underneath three feet of floodwater. The rain had conquered every piece of dry ground even under the street bridges and as long as the rain continued, there wasn't anything that could be done. I had never tried sleeping under a bridge before. The large crossbeams where the bridge met the road were wet and muddied. There were a few dry spots left on the slope so putting the head of the sleeping bag facing upwards towards the girders, I crawled inside hoping to stop the chills, which had enveloped my body. The outer shell of the sleeping bag was like butter against the steep cement slope and immediately I started to slide downward, flapping out my arms to grab a hold of something to stop Newton's' Law of Gravity, but it wasn't until I went knee deep into the channel water, that I finally came to a stop. Lightheaded and shivering from the freezing cold; I picked up the soaking wet useless gear and went to the only secure walled in shelter close by. Maybe God was retelling a modern day version of the Prodigal Son, because the next place was truly the pig pits of earth. A blue colored portal-potty. I had used this portal-potty many times in the past because I abhorred defecating in public and using newspaper to clean with. It was nice to have a "pot to piss in" as the saying goes. Toilet paper, much like clean socks and underwear, is a luxury to homeless people and given an opportunity, a homeless person with access to clean privacy, would gladly use it. Unfortunately, homeless are given limited access to both public and private facilities so like any other animal or person living in third world primitive conditions, they would have to make do with what they had, or didn't have. This portal-potty would become my temporary housing facility that night and I was grateful it was available. The foul stench hit like a hammer as it was evident this one hadn't been serviced in sometime. The fear of freezing though, made the most intolerable smell bearable. Finally in a safe place out of the rain, the weight of despair from my situation began settled down upon me. Everything covered in filth and mud, I didn't know if the belongings I placed in the trees had survived. Uncertainty is a cruel tormentor.

It is always during the darkest times when the nightmares come calling. As the tears started to well up in my eyes, I heard a small weak audible cry for help outside the door, each one louder than the one before so wrapping the kilt around my waist; I opened the door to discover the source. To my surprise, a tiny calico kitten crawled out from underneath the portal-potty, his little body soaking wet, shaking and trembling as he turned to look up at me with his desperate blue eyes. Certainly, in this kind of foul weather, homelessness does not suffer humans alone. Reaching down, I scooped up my new small friend and immediately set out to dry him off with what was left of the toilet paper. The kitten was a ragged skinny little thing, his ribs clearly visible from the ordeal he had suffered in his brief life. Wading up a ball of toilet paper, a soft dry bed for him was made in the corner and both exhausted, we hunkered down next to one another and were fast asleep.

What little sleep I got was restless at best, as I tossed and turned in the cramp quarters, trying to find a comfortable position and someway to keep the stench at bay from intruding my nostrils. Urging my eyelids to open, I was heartened by the sight of light coming into the portal-potty. The sound of pitter-patter, which had cursed my ears these many days, was gone. Today would be a better day for my new friend. A big smile crossed my face at the thought of the cute ragged kitten. His body wasn't any bigger than my hand. Rolling over, I reached out to poke him tenderly in his side, waking him up to a new brighter day of promise. He didn't move.

Late February 2001

It was one of the few Sunday's this year blessed by clear skies. Desperate for help, barely having survived the last two months and nothing to eat except for bread for the last three days I started to walk to church. No one ever knows how God might answer their prayers and the answers sometimes come in very strange forms.

The trio were sitting down in the grass behind the Tom Thumb grocery store, sharing a bottle of gut wrench whiskey called Kentucky Deluxe. Weary of talking to strangers, especially other homeless people, I struggled with the idea of saying anything to them. This was their land after all and I was the new intruder in their realm. The last thing I needed was trouble but understanding I couldn't remain isolated forever; the need for socialization would help with sanity and survival. Any form of human socialization would find gratitude. With anxiousness swelling and filling my gut, I shifted course off the path towards the small circle of men. The three watched intently as I approached. The one on the right looked the youngest, dark hair shoulder length, unremarkable facial features with a small amount of whisker growth around his month. Sitting cross-legged same as the others, his pale blues eyes betrayed some deep sadness, I thought. The one with his back towards me looked as if a strong stiff wind would blow him away, still, underneath the ragged black coat and black jeans, I could tell there was hidden muscle to be weary of. His long black hair and facial coverage showed he was a veteran in this world. The last one starring a hole through me was far grungier than the other two and it was hard to tell exactly where the clothes ended and where the dirt began. His long white beard revealed hints of red from days past. A large crooked red nose, wry little mouth, and a face lined with every year spent in hardship, I knew instinctively this was the "man". Best to introduce myself to the least threatening, I mumbled to no one in particular as I walked over to where they were sitting.

"Hi, my name is James and I'm homeless staying down the path there." Sounding like some naive kid.

The young man grabbed my outreached hand shook it, "I'm Don." He said with a nod. Next reaching out towards the skinny man, "My name is Billy but they call me Little Billy."

"Nice to meet you" now moving my hand towards the leader.

He glared up at me with bloodshot eyes squinted, as if searching for something and then looked at the hand with disdain. In his gruff whiskey voice, "I'm Bar-B-Q Bob. Do you have a free-world?"

"A what?" I asked.

"Do you have a free-world? A cigarette!"

Bar-B-Q Bob epitomized the perfect portrayal of horror stories profiling the homeless. He was vile, nasty, crude, selfish, dirty and drunken most of the time and when he wasn't drunk, he was working store patrons for money to get drunk. Bar-B-Q was an old remnant left over from the days of train jumping Hobos. Born Steven Collins, for over a decade, he had become the most infamous homeless person in the area of Dallas known as "crack hill", given that name for the amount of illegal drugs sold on any given street corner. If ever there was a mentor to show me how to survive the cruel reality of the streets, Bar-B-Q Bob could. The only question; how does an upper middle class, green pea homeless person become a pupil of the most despised hobo in north Dallas?

"Sorry, I'm out." and before another syllable proceeded from my mouth, "Well then. Have a nice day." Bar-B-Q growled. A clue taken that this monumental occasion in life had come to an abrupt and swift end. Stun for a moment, slowly lifting my abandoned outreach hand to a wave, "O.K. then, See you later." I could feel Bob's piercing eyes in my back until well on my way. Still, important information had been gathered; names and next time bring cigarettes.

Bob would later tell me that he didn't trust me because "I was too damn clean". Laughing at the image, gray slacks, shiny black shoes, dress shirt with a vested sweater pulled over it. Maybe I was just a little to clean for telling these people I was homeless, but I remember looking good wearing my fine threads of ignorance.

Above: James Waghorne, Eric, Bar-B-Q Bob

March 2001

I was lost. The first encounter with the area homeless ended disastrously, but with each new encounter over the month, I started to slowly breaking down the barriers of mistrust with Don and Little Billy. Bar-B-Q was a different story. One day behind the Fina gas station I would find out just how hard it would be. The three had just purchased some emotion and hope killer. Sitting down in their customary positions, I asked Bob. "Where do you sleep?" trying to strike up a conversation. Bar-B-Q leaped to his feet, his face inches from my own, "What…are you writing an "F-in" book or something?" he snarled. Lucky for me, Little Billy and Don came to my rescue. "I was just asking." I spurted out. "I didn't mean anything by it, just talking." "Yea, Bob, he was just talking." Don added as he pulled Bar-B-Q back down and handed him the bottle. "I don't like anyone asking about my business. What is he, a snitch? He needs to mind his own "F-in" business." "O.K. Bob, don't worry, he's doesn't know." "Yea, he doesn't know better." Little Billy chimed in patting Bar-B-Q on his shoulder. As I walked away, I knew it was going to take something extraordinary to gain Bar-B-Q's trust.

The Fina gas station had an old broken down carwash off to the side. It made a great place to stay out of the inclement weather. The forecast spoke of more rain that day, and if I were to get any dry "butts" now would be the time. After the earlier meeting that day, I really didn't want any part of Bar-B-Q for the time being, but it was evitable I would run into them while snipe hunting and sure enough there they were at the carwash. Clifford had scored two quarts of KD, (Kentucky Deluxe Whiskey). Bar-B-Q was slumped up against one of the walls, passed out with an empty bottle lying to his side, his hand still firmly gripped around the neck. Clifford, evidently gravity too much to handle, had slid down to his side on the cement floor. Little Billy was nowhere to be found. Don was outside doing his best imitation of why severe drunkenness and walking does not mix. His legs would go one-way and his torso another, looking more like a wet noodle than a person. Don didn't drink when I first met him. His brother had succumbed to Wild Irish Rose, a cheap sweet wine, and died of cirrhosis four months earlier. Life on the streets and hopelessness has a way of changing a person and it had done so to Don. Seemingly, finally admitting defeat, he got down on all fours and tried to crawl. Where? I didn't know because Don was heading towards the cliff leading 20' ft. downward towards White Rock Trail. Crawling though was just as challenging for him because he couldn't get all his parts moving in unison. A last ditch effort, Don pulled his body upright and then with all grace, went head on into the side of a curb with a sickening thud. Heads make a strange dull thud noise when colliding with cement, sounding much like a rotten watermelon hit with a baseball bat.

To my amazement, Don wasn't knocked out cold by the collision but a pool of blood started to gather at the base of his head, caused by the gash in his topside. Don had come to my rescue earlier and I couldn't bring myself to leave him just lying there.

At 5'9", Don still carried the muscles developed while serving in the Army, weighing in the neighborhood of 185lbs but drunk he might as well had weighed the same as 250lbs of wet sand. As hard as I tried, I couldn't lift him to his feet so grabbing him around the armpits, his head dangling in air, I dragged him into the carwash, posting him against the wall next to Bar-B-Q. Bob awoke just long enough to see the blood now pouring down

Don's face and asked in a slur "What happened?" before passing out again. There wasn't going to be any extra help found here.

Going inside the gas station, the attendant allowed me to get a large cup of water and some paper towels after I explained the situation. When I arrived back at the carwash, Don's face was covered with streaks of blood; the gash on top of his head had slowed to steady thick ooze. Having put some ice in the water to make it as cold as possible and maybe help congenial the blood in the wound, the freezing cold-water pour into the wound seemed to sober Don up for a brief second, trying his best to move away from the new pain and he fell sideways. Holding him down, I was able to wash the wound and clean his head and face off; I compressed the paper towels over the wound. The gash was as thick and as long as a ring finger. I stopped the bleeding by applying pressure. Taking Don's hand, I placed it on top of the paper towels to hold it in place. Bar-B-Q and Clifford now up, out of their blackouts said they would look after him and that under no circumstances should emergency be called. I clearly understood that would mean police, and possibly a night in detox.

The next morning I stopped by the Fina and found the trio sitting on the embankment between the creek and storage shed company, out of view from the streets and pedestrians. They were sharing a 40 once bottle of painkiller called Bud Ice. They greeted me with friendly hellos and smiles. Even Bar-B-Q. I sat down on the ground with them, asking Don how he felt and if I could check his wound. It was still clean and there were no signs of infection starting. We carried on with some small talk, recounting the previous day's events as they continued to pass the bottle around. Bar-B-Q always got the last swig from any bottle so when it came time to finish it off; the bottle was passed to him.

"James, what you did for Don; you are now officially in the "tribe". Bar-B-Q said as he passed me the bottle. I didn't drink and really hated beer, nor did I care to finish off something that had the backwash of three men, but still, till this day, it was the best thing I had ever tasted.

October 2001

I checked into the Salvation Army on October 9th, a day after my 43rd birthday. Two-thirds of the boarding dormitory was dedicated to court ordered drug offenders, part of a million dollar contract with the County. They received the cream of services; three meals per day, caseworkers, job assistance and placement through contracts with employers. Like the rest of the community, I was misinformed about what the local Salvation Army truly did and believed their 500-bed facility was dedicated towards helping the homeless. I was even more shocked when for the first time in my life I was treated less than human and more as a criminal. The homeless had to pay a cost of $7 per night for boarding, regardless if you were able to get one of the few beds to sleep in or had to sleep on the floor. You were homeless, therefore defected and not worthy of compassion and care. This was my first direct experience with the arrogance of class-ism attitude. We weren't guest of the Salvation Army. We were victims of power egos and control.

At 4:30 AM, every morning the lights would cut on and an employee would march down the hall shouting orders to get up. Six hours of sleep would be average and not nearly enough to help recuperate from depression. The showers were intolerable, cold water and if you didn't have water slippers to wear, fungus and other health issues could be a problem. One individual with obvious untreated mental illness had fungus so bad; his toes had fused together, the dead white skin continuously falling off. Twice, a bridge troll, (hermit living under a bridge) suffering from "wet brain" had been discharged from Parkland Hospital across the street to the Salvation Army had released his bowels in the shower room. "Wet brain" is the result happening to those individuals who drink and drug their brains to mush, and one of the first signs is the lost of bowel control in the form of diarrhea. Even under threats from the staff, I would take my whore bath everyday in the sinks as I did when I lived on the streets at the local Exxon. The homeless were thrown out at 5:30 – 6:00 every morning after breakfast with all their belongings regardless of the weather conditions. Picking up day labor at the auto auctions, I was able to rent a small closet at a Storage Company nearby, but the cost of nightly board and rent to secure my belongings easily devoured my $300 per month income. It was easy to see how individuals became trapped in these types of places, institutionalized for life. Firsthand research studies found that shelters at best, met basic needs and at worst, perpetuated homelessness. Cities were correct shrinking their homeless shelters and instead started focusing on building temporary and permanent supportive housing units, which had shown an 80 –85% success rate. While many individuals complained about the restrictive rules in shelters and dormitory boarding facilities, they never bothered me. My issues came with the theft and degrading treatment from staff members and also the lack of help. Today, many Dallas shelters are designed to proselytize to a captured audience, keeping people in the constant state of homelessness. In foreign countries they would be known as reeducation centers. The horror stories of individuals being trapped in such places for 15 years and longer, is not uncommon. As a Christian, I enjoyed the church services, but I could clearly see why others might not because of the guilt message preached most of the time. Those who chose not to attend the nightly service were forced to sit in a time out chair until services were over, not able to talk or read. Some shelters and boarding dormitories even went as far as throwing people out if they did not conform.

The four days per week I wasn't able to get work, Duke and I would scour the city for services. Duke was aptly named. A true cowboy, slim and tall as the sky, we made for an awkward sight as he towered over my 5'8" frame. Duke was streetwise and the fact he didn't drink or drug made it comfortable for me to hang around with him. On one of our trips, Duke and I were walking downtown on our way to the only soup kitchen in Dallas. Just a block away from our destination, a late model blue colored foreign car pulled along side the sidewalk. Four young black males inside, the passenger inquired if we had a driver's license and if so, would we like to make twenty dollars each. Duke immediately answered no, even though we both had our I.D.'s. I took my queue from him. "No", I answered and kept walking ahead. The guys left off in their car down the street as I gave Duke a puzzled look. "I didn't think you wanted to go around to Home Depot stores returning stolen goods or going to banks trying to cash "wash checks", he smiled at me. "I've done business with those types before." He continued. They steal from places like Home Depot and use homeless to take back the merchandise for store credit or they have stolen checks, wash them, taking the ink off after first copying the owners' signature and rewrite them. The homeless go inside the bank and try to cash the phony checks. If the cops show up, the real crooks take off and leave the homeless holding the bag. There are a lot of con games out here for the homeless to get snared in. The predators know they're desperate and many are mentally ill. These are just two of the more popular scams in Dallas. Never tell anyone you have a driver's license." He warned. I just shook my head in disbelief as we continued walking. There is more to homelessness to learn than just survival, I thought as we got in line for lunch.

I was getting ready to go to work with my street newspapers when a car pulled into the parking lot where Eric and I were talking. An elderly Hispanic woman was driving with a beautiful young woman in the passenger seat and a young Hispanic male sat in back. The young women signaled us to come over and asked if either of us if we had a driver's license. Eric didn't, but I had mine and answered yes. She got out of the car with the young male and approached me asking if I could help them.

"My mother is moving here to Dallas to stay with us. We can't help her move because of our jobs and were looking to find someone who would help. She lives south of San Antonio and we'll pay you $200.00." Pointing to her mother, "She doesn't speak English very well and we need someone who does. We will pay for everything"

These people were very well dressed and if I didn't have my papers to do, I would've said yes but a red flag went up in my mind.

"I have a friend, just around the corner who had a license, maybe he would like to." I replied.

I went and got Bobby and he agreed to do it. Bobby had always been a worker. It wasn't until about three weeks later after Bobby left with the trio that he came back. He was clean cut and had on new clothes. A reward for a job well done I thought until I heard his story.

They got down to a small town in south Texas and sat around for a few days. That's when he started to realize this wasn't about moving furniture to Dallas but instead moving illegal aliens. They told him he would be paid $200 a load if he agreed, which he didn't. Bobby escaped that same night and had to hitch hike his way back to Dallas. Using the homeless as "coyotes" to haul illegal aliens to the U.S. is a common practice. It keeps the ringleaders out of harms way while if anyone gets caught, it's the homeless person doing federal time much like my friend Lee did. He got scammed in the same way. He was hauling a truckload of people while another truck was following miles behind full of drugs. The people in the truck behind him called the police to catch Lee and the illegal aliens, so while the police were busy with their capture, the truck full of drugs could pass on by unnoticed and untouched.

Duke and I became good friends but I couldn't tolerate being treated in a 3rd class citizen manner from the Salvation Army staff. After asking to meet with the only caseworker for weeks without success, I decided it was best to move back onto the streets. I was a "river rat" and would never become a trapped "shelter rat". I couldn't stay any longer at the shelter.

December 2001

The Fina Station had become a target and the police would frequent the location regularly harassing everyone; Bar-B-Q and Don moved their site behind a shopping strip-center near the old Katy Trail railroad tracks. Little Billy had gone back home to his father's house. It was rumored that he was dieing of stomach cancer. Probably welcomed by him, Billy could never forgive himself. His life shattered that day in the car when years earlier he and a friend were driving to the store with Billy's new little girl riding in the back inside her car seat. The little baby crying, Billy's friend asked if he could hold her, and comfort her. Billy agreed and as his friend was bringing the baby to the front seat and Billy turning his head for just a second to inspect the transfer of his precious package, he turned back around and it was to late for the brakes to do anything. The image of his baby girl going into the windshield would haunt him forever. Billy didn't drink because he was an alcoholic; he drank because he had sentenced himself to death that day.

The woods provided cover and the location was further away from the main street, Skillman, and the area provided a treasure of dumpsters close by. One mans garbage is another mans treasure and for the homeless on the streets, sometimes it meant the difference between eating something and going hungry. I was happy to find the two tribe members after leaving Salvation Army. Bar-B-Q was right; charity did cost to "damn" much in this city.

The first night back on the streets, Clifford, a part time homeless, came down to our site bearing gifts of alcohol. Clifford was an American Indian. He had suffered a severe head injury as a child and was living on disability pay with his father. I was surprised at how many people with homes would visit with the homeless just to party. Unlike the others who would go back home, Clifford would stay around for days and weeks, which I didn't approve of. He always brought trouble; making matters worse, he was a kleptomaniac and since I was the only one that didn't drink, I had to carefully watch the belongings whenever he was around.

They chugged their liquid feast down, always arguing who was drinking too much during their turn at the bottle. It was late night when the alcohol ran dry and people started to sleep or pass out. It's hard to tell the difference between the two. Bar-B-Q waddled on the ground, trying his best to make it inside the tent and he found himself in a pickle, having to relieve himself but not able to stand up, he cried out for my help. There are not a lot of people I would hold up while they did their deed, but Bar-B-Q was the exception, if not for him I would had never survived, so picking him up off the ground from the backside, I wrapped my arms around his chest, walking him to the nearby tree and held him up as he took care of business. It was an awkward moment and I didn't pay close attention to the runoff leading to my shoes and with a short curse, I dragged him back to his tent, allowing him to plop through the opening onto his blankets, giving a small chuckle as he groaned when he hit the ground. He muttered a few cuss words at me before passing out. Lying down on my folded cardboard boxes, I thought how nice it was to be back home with the tribe.

February 2002

There were many ways for death to capture the homeless. Hit & runs, muggings, homicide, insects, disease, drugs, alcohol and the weather. Summers cooked you to death; spring and fall storms swept you away into a murky death while winters could freeze your eyeballs so hard they would literally crack. Tonight would be like that; it was supposed to dip down to 14 degrees. More than year had passed since my first day living the life of homelessness and now I was a veteran, having acclimated to the existence of primeval survival. I had four blankets, a sleeping bag and candles inside my hooch. Still at night sometimes, I would have to take my winter coat and wrap it around my feet to keep the toes from getting frostbitten. In case Mother Nature called, there was my 44-ounce cup beside me to empty the bladder into. It wasn't wise to leave ones covers and hooch once your body heat was tramped under the blankets. Mornings I would wake up to find my sleeping bag frozen at certain spots from my breath, due to the condensation. This night would be hard, and not just because of the cold.

I had gone downtown to pick up some extra copies of "Endless Choices". The local street newspaper used by the homeless to earn income. For the homeless on the streets when it came to money opportunities, "rain means gain" and "cold means gold". Bad weather meant good revenue for those of us on the street corners. Clora, the editor, had three people in her office when I arrived at the soup kitchen called the Stewpot. Being courteous, I introduce myself to the three strangers. I knew all the normal vendors and these individuals were new and one of them really stood out. Most homeless wear the look of despair; it can be seen in their eyes. Moses had a beaming face that just lit up the room, so I decide to engage him and find out what his story was. He told me he was a victim of a bad divorce and an abusive relationship; he had come down with his family from Oklahoma to escape the situation. All the money was gone and the family had to sleep inside the car because the shelters wouldn't take them in. It was 17 degrees last night and they needed to earn some money to get a room to keep from freezing to death this evening, so they had heard about Clora and "Endless Choices" and were getting some papers to work the rest of the day to earn what little they could. A smile crossed my face as this ten-year told me how he would help out his sister and mother by standing in the freezing cold to help earn some money to survive.

I hated that our shelters would turn away women and their children when they were fleeing from a domestic violence situations and instead of giving the kids a safe place, throw them out into streets in harms way because the parent didn't bring enough identification. Sadly, it wouldn't be the last time I would witness such tragedy.

I laid comfortably inside my hooch that evening, all bundled up, wishing that I could've helped somehow, but life and death was a constant visitor for all of us this night, with no victor assured. I could only pray for them and all of us.

March 2002 - Homeless man found dead in Dallas; hypothermia cited as cause

It was nearly three o'clock in the morning. The nights were starting to become pleasant since late March had arrived. I sat in the gray leather chair Don had gotten from his boss while Angry John sat on the piece of board that we had placed on two empty plastic soda bottle cases. It made for a nice bench in our homeless campsite for when visitors came by, like John who camped just across the railroad tracks with Luke and Carol.

I enjoyed talking with Angry John. Ten years younger than me, John was 34 years old and had an Aaron Flynn look. He was intelligent, having studied in college with a background in theology, which we always discussed at some point in our talks. He was called Angry John because when he was drunk he would bully others and became violent, often shouting at anyone who would upset him. I never experienced his anger myself due to the respect I had earned among the tribe. I was considered by many to be the voice of reason since I did not drink or do drugs. We often talked into the wee hours of the night since the effects of his day's intake of alcohol had diminished and his depression had surfaced, which I truly believe was the reason we enjoy our conversations so much since I understood depression.

"James, I going to tell you something I have never told anyone else." John looked up at me from his bench with watery eyes. I was taken back a little since I had never seen the visible signs of his depression before. I sat silent and just nodded my head in acknowledgement.

"I don't remember at what age I realized my mother was doing tricks to take care of her coke habit. Somewhere around eight or nine years old, I guess. By the time I was twelve, I was dealing the stuff myself helping cut my mother and her Pusher. I felt pressured and was not sure what would've happen if I had said no. It was a good business since Waco at that time was small and there was only one other competitor. By the time I was eighteen, my friend and I had become the biggest dealers in town making tens of thousands of dollars. One day there was a knock on the door at my apartment and my friend answered it. Standing there was a guy with a shotgun waiting. As soon as the door was opened, the guy from the Bandito's unloaded both barrels into my friends stomach." John's eyes were now tearing as he went on. "The guy ran off as I pulled a pistol out from the couch. My friend screamed falling backwards to the ground and I ran over and knelt beside him." John now looked directly at me as tears flowed down his cheeks as he raised his hands as if to show me something. "I tried to put his insides back. They were spilling out all over the floor and I just grabbed them in my hands and tried to hold them back into his stomach. Blood had soaked up to my elbows and the ground around us was soaked as I watched my best friend die." There was a moment of unsettling silence, then John's facial expression change. "I took the gun and went to the Banditos' place looking for the guy. The Banditos told me that this was not a sanctioned hit and that I could do anything I wanted without interference. So I found the guy and took care of business."

We sat there in silence, each lost in their thoughts. Nothing else was said that night because nothing else could be.

I not sure to this day what did it for John. Maybe it was to have someone who cared enough not to judge but to just listen to what ghost haunted him. That's the time when the truth about the homeless really comes out. When the ghosts come to visit.

That was our last real talk. John left the camp soon after. The next time I had seen him; John had quit drinking and was working for a plaster company. He came to the camp to visit and I chided him for doing so. "Don't you ever come by here to visit again? You're not homeless, stay away." Once a person leaves their homeless friends behind they should never come back to visit, because a visit becomes a sleep over and sleep over a weekend and so on.

Our tribe at any given time consisted of 30 – 40 homeless in a two square mile territory. Many would come and go. Bar-B-Q headed towards Garland City limits with Cajun to escape the 5-O harassment. Kent, Jason and Cornbread moved into Carols and Luke's old tent. The illegal immigrants stayed under the bridge down the tracks and the refugee Sudanese stayed across the tracks near Luke and Carol's old site. Even further, down the tracks, three new homeless to the area had set up.

I had often seen Dawn flying her sign at the intersection. Knowing she was camping with two guys, I never spoke to her for my own safety. Homeless women normally hook up with guys, giving them survival sex in repayment for protection. Don and I were planning on scourging up some food from the dumpsters, 7-11 would normally throw out the day old sandwiches at this time, a great meal, second only to the Williams left over fried chicken thrown out nightly.

When Dawn appeared at the top of the hill, overlooking our site, a trash bag in her hands, blankets and other belongings with her, I knew something had gone wrong and invited her down. It was the first time I had a good close-up look at her. Short, filthy blond hair clung to the sides of her head. The right side of her face and jaw had swollen to the point of disfigurement. There wasn't any visible chin. Homelessness obviously had not been kind to her as most street women. Weather beaten, it was hard to tell her true age, her body was gaunt, a sign of drug use. The druggies were bones and the alkies were swelled. Of all the deaths I had seen since becoming homeless, drugs, cirrhosis or AIDS, I'm not sure which one was the most gruesome.

"Do you mind if I stay here for the night? My friend just got arrested and the other guy left. I don't want to sleep by myself. I've been roughed up good lately as you can probably see." Dawn asked, sitting down on the bench.

"Sure, you can stay here." Don answered. "That is if you drink." Don had become a true liquor whore, always looking for a cheap way to get drunk.

She reached into her small knapsack and pulled out a small bottle of liquor. Opening up the bottle, she downed a swig and passed it to Don, now her best friend. "You can sleep in my hooch. If you want to place your belongings over there, you can. They'll be safe." I told her. We all shared the food she brought with her and while she and Don got loaded, we talked into the night.

Dawn was from Houston. Unlike most homeless, she was raised in a middle-class family and all indications were that she had a good childhood. It wasn't until she left home getting married to a spouse-abuser and drug addict that her life would take a turn for the worse.

"Did your boyfriend do that to you?" I asked, pointing to her face.

"No, I just met him three weeks ago after I got out of the hospital. I was staying over by Bachman Lake 2 months ago and a Hispanic guy jumped me. He hit me on the side of my face with something and shattered my jaw. I went down and he climbed on top, choking me. I passed out but woke up watching the rest of my clothes being torn off and he was on top raping me. Each time I came to, he would choke me again unconscious. The last time I woke, I just kept my eyes closed so he wouldn't choke me anymore. I stayed still and just let him finish raping me. I thought he was going to kill me. I don't remember how I got to the hospital but they had to wire my mouth closed. I cut the wires myself when I got out. It still hurts like hell, but I can drink now." She said taking another swig.

That night I was awakened by the screams coming from inside my hooch. "No, don't beat me anymore. Please don't! Stop! Don't hit me!" Dawn made a small crying noise, then went back to sleep.

Chapter 3
Miller Time

"If liberty means anything at all, it means the right to tell people what they don't want to hear."
George Orwell

There was danger growing in the community and the country. Hatred and intolerance was becoming acceptable and even fashionable. Politicians would target the minority poor homeless, igniting a small group dynamics into a mob mentality while building a like-minded following. Hatred is a powerful elixir.

February/March 2002 – Homeless Census count nears 4,000 – Endless Choices
March 2002
A small donation of just $1 for a copy of "Endless Choices" would be split between the homeless individual and the non-profit 70/30. The money earned helped the people pay for dormitory boarding fees, buy food, pay bus transportation and additional basic human needs. I never could figure out why some days I would earn only a $1 while others, as much as $40 for eight to ten hours of work. Human compassion was a fickle acquaintance from day to day. The money I earned was used primarily for two items. Food and Dr. Pepper. I had two rules that everyone knew among the tribe, I didn't buy alcohol for anyone and I would not share my Dr. Pepper.

My game plan was to consistently move around to different intersections, hoping to build a customer base and a regular steady income. Today's location at Preston and Royal Lane would be a familiar place. Growing up in North Dallas, this was my old area, nice homes and nice cars, upper middle class income.

Three hours later walking up and down the median, I had only earned enough for bus fare, but at any red light, that could change and lift my spirits. Seeking donations is like fishing; it is the hope of hooking a big one that motivates the individual. With the homeless, it went even further. It meant the difference between having or going without for another day. With a stack of papers in one hand and my erasable signboard in the other, I was wondering if my written message needed changing. "$1 feeds two – Endless Choices nonprofit". I didn't like leaving the intersection to change my sign because you never knew when that one person would come by with a blessing and it was nearing lunch hour, a nice high traffic time so I decided to stay with it.

I had seen Laura Miller on billboards but I didn't ever expect to see her driving up in the white S.U.V. plastered with "Elect Laura Miller" bumper stickers coming in my direction. I'm not sure why, but when I saw her, a feeling of hope started to rise up in me. Maybe because she claimed to be a Democrat, or that her platform was blue collar, or just that a politician certainly would show some kindness to the downtrodden. I was hoping for the great Kennedy replacement. Luckily, she got caught at the red light and I started my walk towards her direction, her Sports Utility Vehicle stopped in the middle lane. I could clearly see her face, not more than ten feet away, I stood still; making sure she would see me unless purposely ignored. Homeless can read people's faces inside their cars and when they don't wish to be bothered by giving. Normally I could pass by 20-30 cars during a red light before it changed but I stayed right in her view and when the light did change, she had never once glanced my way but instead stared straight ahead never acknowledging my existence. Disappointed, feeling like some piece of dirt, I hopped on the next bus, went back to my home and my small patch of woods.

Intolerance historically is achieved with fear tactics, inappropriately blame for problems, promoting hatred and ignorance by generalizing an entire population based on the actions of a few and thereby avoiding the whole truth. Domestic Violence victims were blamed for their abuse done by others. Our black population in America also suffered from this type of campaign. Even today, a network media outlet recently categorize black people as thieves getting supplies from damaged stores versus whites just trying to survive doing the same thing in the wake of Hurricane Katrina.

Starting with Laura Miller's victory for Mayor, in 2002 the media campaign in Dallas had officially started to dehumanize our homeless. Searching to segregate a population, certainly this meant slanted stories, highlighted with acts, which would be viewed by mainstream society as publicly immoral and obscene. The pen is mightier than the sword. Jim Schutze, a man I came to respect, likely was inspired to write a article in the Dallas Observer, a free weekly publication, by the revelation that Mayor Laura Miller with downtown businesses had plotted and conspired "to ethnically cleanse downtown of homeless people", and, "to move the bum population out of downtown". The big plan included forcing the service agencies out of downtown along with the homeless population to a small area, advertised as a campus style facility. A concentration of human misery and depredation, as Ft. Worth Texas had done to their homeless. Hidden away, thrown away and forgotten, Dr. Martin Luther King Jr. had warned against this inhumane tragedy during his Noble Peace Prize lecture.

Born in Baltimore, Laura Miller became a journalist. In Dallas, she worked for the now defunct Dallas Times Herald and later she would write for the Dallas Morning News and The Dallas Observer, where she gained popularity for attacking Dallas Politicians. She served a single term as council member before becoming Mayor, taking over when the sitting Mayor Ron Kirk decided to try and become the first African American U.S. Senator from Texas. Her campaign based on blue collar mainstream promises of better pay for police and fire department personnel, cleaning up City Hall and fixing potholes, won the election for her. Laura would say on visits to Dallas, it was like the Emerald City, a city on the hill and she would work for it to be that way again. Instead of the Emerald City where four homeless were welcomed by the citizens with opened arms, services and eventually even jobs and housing, City Hall became a castle and she wanted to get rid of Dorothy, her three homeless friends and all the other homeless.

October 2002
Proclamation
By Mayor Laura Miller
Dallas, Texas

WHEREAS, the United States has lost well over 250,000 units of government subsidized housing since 1996; and

WHEREAS, since 1997, the minimum known homeless population in the City of Dallas has grown 240%, from 1,800 in 1997 to 4,458 as of

August 25, 2002; and

WHEREAS, the City of Dallas has lost at least 5,692 units as affordable housing as owners pay off their low-interest HUD-insured loans early—the highest number of any city in the country; and

WHEREAS, the number of public housing units in the City of Dallas has decreased by almost one-third from 7,374 units in 1978 to 5,031 units today; and

WHEREAS, Dallas has lost at least 1,760 subsidized housing units as owners choose not to renew project-based Section 8 subsidy contracts—the second highest number of any city in the country; and

WHEREAS, there is a 31% failure rate when tenants try to use Section 8 housing vouchers and vouchers are not a secure form of housing assistance; and

WHEREAS, the City of Dallas struggles with its shortage of affordable housing for very low income people; and

NOW, THEREFORE, I, LAURA MILLER, MAYOR OF DALLAS, TEXAS, in honor of UN World Habitat Day and International Tenants Day, do hereby proclaim October 5, 2002 to be Save Our Homes Day, and I urge our citizens to express support for saving and building more low-income housing, replacing all public housing that is demolished on a one-for-one basis, re-regulating owners of HUD-assisted housing, and treating all tenants and homeless people with dignity.

Signed

Laura Miller, Mayor of Dallas Texas

November 2002

A week before Thanksgiving, the National Coalition for the Homeless, the National Student Campaign Against Hunger and Homelessness co-sponsor National Hunger and Homeless Awareness Week. Clora Hogan would organize a big event every year. Clora at the time was the primary advocate for the homeless in Dallas. A lone voice among a city filled with hypocrisy.

Over 500 people were served brisket, turkey, fried chicken, soup, veggies and desert. 500 gift bags were handed out, Parkland Hospital gave out almost 200 flu shots and 225 people received haircuts. Entertainment was provided by a host of organizations but the surprise guest was Mayor Laura Miller. The crowd booed as she approached the stage to speak. Clora half-heartedly raised her arms up and down in motion to quiet the crowd. What the Mayor said was very interesting. She opened by saying her message would be short and simple. "Dallas has not done a very good job at addressing the homeless issue." She stated.

The Mayor admitted the city had been irresponsible, she admitted the city-ran day shelter was inadequate, she admitted the homeless didn't have storage, she admitted the homeless and poor didn't have access to affordable housing, yet it would be the homeless and poor under her leadership who would be criminalized in our City. Laura and her opponent for Mayor, Mary Poss, would both oppose the initial $3 million dollars bond monies for a new 24hr center for our homeless. At the end of the public hearing for the upcoming bond, Councilwomen Veletta Lill said, "We live in a state that puts very little value on human life. Spending very little on social service programs." While certainly true, the City of Dallas was using resources and monies instead to do additional harm against the least fortunate.

Voters of Dallas overwhelmingly approved the bond, passing it with 79% of the vote and suddenly Laura Miller along with Council Members started to change their tune concerning the homeless. That's the flip-flop nature and lack of character in politics today. Oppose something one day and then after hearing the will of the people, pretend to be the champion of the cause. Laura Miller would later take claim for being that champion but actions always speak louder then words.

To: Honorable Mayor Miller
From: James Waghorne
Subject: Homeless Summit
Sent: 11/7/2002 2:04 PM

My name is James Waghorne and I am a homeless survivor. I also work for the Metro Dallas Homeless Alliance.

This will be the first winter in two years I will have a roof over my head. Today we made many proposals at the Homeless Summit because the need of the homeless is easy to identify, just hard to implement.

I can use many success stories for examples from other cities.

But honestly, whatever programs we come up with to help the homeless is doomed to fail if two issues are not addressed first. "NIMBY-ism" The "Not In MY Back Yard" syndrome and the lack of education about homelessness are the biggest uphill battles for homeless people, service providers and communities face in their effort to end homelessness, as we know it today.

As Mr. Don Williams of Trammel Crow recently said at the Enterprise Foundation Conference here in Dallas, the City "Dallas is short 30,000 affordable housing units.

Housing, Centralized Services and new (funding) legislature are certainly needed. Though there are many varying success stories out there such as Pathways to Housing in New York, which targets the homeless on the street with an 85% success rate since 1992, they all had one thing in common and that was winning these battles through partnership and community education…

Fw: Mayor Miller's response

Thanks for the info- we are going to make something happen

Laura

May 2003 Bond Package Leaves Homeless people out in the Cold – Homeless Animals to get $12 million, Homeless humans cut down from $6 million to $3 million

November 2003 - Mayor Miller targets panhandling in her first State of the City address even though the City Council and Mayor would be warned by city staff that the new ban would hurt charities such as MDA and others.

2003 in Dallas could only be classified as the beginning for an all out malicious assault aimed at the homeless poor in Dallas. New laws under the disguised terminology "Quality of Life Laws" equated to new Jim Crow laws based not on race, but class-ism. Corporate interest had control over City Hall for years. As one lobbyist told me after a meeting in the City Council Chambers, "money runs City Hall. If you have the money, you get your needs met, if you don't, get in line with the rest of the beggars."

March 2003

Dallas City Council passes City Ordinance 25213 effective April 15th. The new solicitation ordinance makes it illegal, a Class C misdemeanor, to solicit donations at intersections, and on or near certain properties.

It was called the "Panhandling Ordinance".

It was the City's first step to outlaw compassion and charity in Dallas, targeting the poorest class of American citizens. Homeless caught would be issued a $500 fine or taken to jail. To keep within constitutional boundaries, charities such as the Shriners' for Children Hospitals, and the annual Easter Jerry Lewis MDA fireman fund raiser would also be outlawed from the streets, costing them over $250,000 in lost donations for the children and less fortunate. Laura Miller would later state this ordinance was one of her greatest achievements as Mayor.

With the victory on panhandling, politicians had a green flag to move forward on the ultimate plan to remove all homeless from downtown.

A New Step On The Part Of the City to Address the Problems – Endless Choices

Friday, November 1, was a cool and rainy day, but it didn't deter homeless people from gathering at the Stewpot before marching as a group to city hall. This was the first real opportunity for them to speak to the Mayor. And speak they did.

A second room was set up incase the attendance was more than the 150 seats allowed in the briefing room used for the summit. Many were surprised that it was indeed necessary. The Mayor opened the summit stating that this meeting was not a grandiose scheme to validate a plan already in the making. Contrary to all reports, from the City Manager's office and some Council Members, she said that getting the homeless issues on the bond package may still be possible.

Though not obligated to be there, eight council members were in attendance. John Loza, whose district covers part of downtown and the Cedars areas, said he would give the city a "C" grade at best on how it has handled homeless issues.

Leo Chaney, whose district is near Fair Park and made up of working class people with low to middle incomes, said he entire community need to address this issue of homelessness. He stopped short of repeating what he stated during a council briefing on the need for a new Day Resource Center: NOT IN MY BACK YARD! During that meeting he agreed that housing and programs to help the homeless are needed but he did not want them in his district.

Everyone agrees that the County must take an active role in any plan developed to help homeless. Betty Culbreath Lister, Director of the Dallas County Health and Human Services, became emotional speaking of the need for legislation to deal with people who are dual diagnosed and won't follow a treatment plan.

The law states that a person can't be committed unless that person exhibits a threat to himself or to others. "A threat means if someone threatens to stab or shot themselves. A person refusing to be medicated or committed to treatment programs are a danger to themselves," said Lister.

Lister was the first, but not the only, speaker to mention a centralized intake facility; a place where social service providers would be there for assessment only. Clients would then be referred to agencies with the resources to help them. Ideally a central intake facility would be open 24 hours a day, unlike shelters that have limited intake hours. "The need for street feeders would go away if we had a centralized intake facility. Meals at the facility could be prepared and served by the faith based ministries currently feeding the homeless," said Lister.

Mayor Miller kept her promise to hear from the audience who signed up to speak by keeping planned presentations to a minimum. The first person called a homeless man who told the Mayor he stayed at Dallas Life Foundation the night before. He was very articulate in describing the conditions there that sometimes cause people to choose to sleep on the streets instead. To many, homeless shelters are not the answer. They do not provide the help needed to return to mainstream society. There is no dignity in shelter life he told her.

Another homeless man, William Pearce Autry, said the problem was not homelessness but hopelessness.

A need for housing was the refrain heard throughout the summit. A refrain spoken by the advocates, the homeless, and business people as well asking for low income housing, transitional housing with supportive services, Single Room Occupancy (SRO) housing, and safe haven's for people with mentally illness.

Speaker, D.D. McDonald, introduced himself as someone years ago was known as a slumlord. "I provided cheap and clean housing," he said. "It was a safety net for the poor and it kept families together."

He told Endless Choices that at $12 a week a family could always get a friend or family member to help them out if they couldn't pay the rent.

He described today's homeless situation as a disaster. He believes people left homeless in this disaster could be helped in the same way as other disasters; by giving them a mobile home to live in. The homes would be placed throughout the county, not all in one place.

"Give them dignity," McDonald said. "The city says it can't provide public restrooms for them and businesses won't let them inside."

Street feeders, most of them faith-based ministries who come downtown to feed food and spiritual nourishment to the homeless, where well represented at the summit. They countered the city's argument that it needed to restrict street feeders for the health and safety of the homeless.

"How healthy is it to have people hungry enough to eat from a dumpster?" asked several advocates when addressed the Mayor.

Street feeders asked to be seen as part of the solution to helping the homeless. They want to work with the city and they want to continue their ministries.

Mike Anderson is an Attorney for Chevez Properties and a member of the Mayor's In the Loop committee. He admits that three years ago when he started talking about homelessness and how it affected downtown businesses he was ignorant about the complexities of homelessness. Now he educates other business people, telling them, "If you help the homeless you also help your businesses."

Children are the youngest victims of homelessness. Although they are not as visible as adults, the population of homeless children is also growing. Barbara Landix, Director of Vogel Alcove, a daycare for homeless children, told the audience of a 4-year child hording food out of the trash because she feared not having anything to eat later.

"Stop the cycle by moving children out of homelessness first," she pleaded. "Children need a safe and nurturing environment."

The Mayor ended the summit saying that her mind was reeling with ideas. One of her character traits is to act quickly. "This was an eye opener," she said. "I will discuss a 24 hour centralized intake facility for all providers, including faith based organizations with the council." Before conclusions can be made, I hope to find a way to hear from more of the homeless people."

People left the summit with the promise that the city will get their act together and do something about the problems of homelessness in Dallas.

November 2003 Next step in Mayor's crackdown on homeless

"It's one of the first things that police officers told us in the weekly crime meetings, is that when they see a guy going down the sidewalk with a shopping cart, chances are, it's full of stolen merchandise." said Miller.

It was a typical false statement made to try and justify their actions against the homeless. How many police chases are there in the U.S. tracking down a person with a shopping cart full of stolen goods?

Since 1998, Dallas has been the number one city in America for crime eight years straight, and the "Most Wanted" individual was a homeless person pushing their belongings around in a shopping cart.

Fine for shopping cart: $500

Interdepartmental City Hall Email

From: "Dave Hogan"
To: "James Mongaras"
CC: "Carol Webster", "MacArtur Gilmer", "Ron Cowart"
Subject: A thought about the Mayor's upcoming meeting
Date: Fri, 09 Jan 2004 12:54:12 – 0600

Re: MDHA question about the Mayor's meeting w/just the Homeless coming up. I think it would be a good idea to include formerly homeless folks, too. They bring a unique perspective about their life as being homeless, now as again self-sufficient, and what it took to get back there. If the Mayor could see some folks successfully coming out of homelessness, then maybe she wouldn't have a burning urge to lower the window of her passing luxurious carriage and yell @ them?!

November 2003 Dallas Police records show 450 citations issued to homeless for solicitation

The Mayor of the ninth largest city in America, Laura Miller, "For a while I would roll down my window and yell and scream at them (the homeless) to get off the streets"! Jim Schultz, from the Dallas Observer, wrote an article titled "Lysol Miller." In the article, he uncovered not only the movement to segregate homeless individuals from Downtown Dallas but also revealed the prevailing feelings that civil rights were secondary to the revitalization of downtown and the interest of the developers. Advocates had to confront what was not only immoral, but dangerous.

From: Rebecca Troth
To: James Waghorne
Subject: Homeless Assistant Center
Date: Fri, 24 Sep 2004

James -- Tulin forwarded me your e-mails about the city's efforts to move the center away from downtown. Depending on the actual comments made by members of the council and other decision makers, we may have what is called "direct" evidence of discriminatory animus based on race or disability. There also may be evidence that the efforts to move homeless people have a disparate impact based on race or disability. This would depend on the number of people we're talking about and how many are members of a minority group and/or people with disabilities. Another relevant fact would be the racial composition of the area they want to put the center in, compared to the downtown area. Unfortunately, I don't think the income disparity would not be a sufficient basis on which to bring a case.

Anyway, assuming you could get some specific statements showing discriminatory intent based on either race or disability and/or statistics showing that this action would disproportionately affect people with disabilities or minorities, we could probably help you try to find a law firm that would be willing to help you make a case.

It's going to be somewhat problematic because a lot of firms don't want to antagonize the city government, but it's worth a shot. Let me know if you have questions.

Rebecca K. Troth

Legal Director

National Law Center on Homelessness & Poverty

November 2003

In my new position as outreach and peer support counselor with Dallas MetroCare Homeless Services, formerly Dallas County Mental Health Mental Retardation, I would often find my friends and help them get into services. Our normal campsites now had completely wiped out by the Police, most of the gang now hung out behind a small strip mall near Lovers and Greenville Ave Eric and Clark did some work as "flyer hangers", putting advertisements on peoples doorknobs and also kept the parking lot clean for the owners of the strip mall. Ellen, with her husband Mike and "floppy" Bobby. Luke, Carol and Lee slept inside an old 90's conversion van in the parking lot, purchased after Luke had received a $2,000 inheritance. Bar-B-Q would stop by when in the area, which meant trouble would be close by. Bar-B-Q was a magnet for police.

One particular cop just hated him for hate sake. The Officer would virtually hunt Bar-B-Q down, even going out of his normal cruising areas, leaving behind citizens in danger, just to arrest Bob. He had arrested and abused Bob so many times; the officer had an outstanding warrant opened so he could pick him up whenever there was a chance. Today was one of those days.

Bar-B-Q had just acquired enough change from panhandling for a bottle and was on his way to the store to claim his prize. We were all in the back of the building talking and watching as Bar-B-Q was making it to the side of the building on his way to the liquor store down the street. Officer Bailey swerved into the lot, almost sideswiping Bar-B-Q. The rest of the homeless made a b-line and jumped into the van to hide, not wanting to experience the forth-coming wrath. Not being homeless any longer, but still weary of this type of person and the small fact he carried a gun, I moved to the side, near a bridge pillar out of sight. The Officer towered over Bar-B-Q as I listened and watched. "Thought you could get away from me? My buddies told me you were over here."

"Man, why don't you just leave me alone?"

"Not today." as Officer Bailey grabbed Bob's arm, bending it behind his back, slamming his face into the cruiser trunk and slapping on the "iron bracelets".

"F you man." Bob yelled out.

Bailey then picked him off the ground and slammed him again against the police car. Some blood appeared on the side of Bob's mouth as he was thrown into the back seat, cussing as loudly as possible going in.

Bar-B-Q would be out in less than twelve hours and the game would start all over.

Whenever the police have the blank check to use "zero-tolerance", civil rights fly out the window and the City of Dallas had given our police a whole book of blank checks concerning the homeless.

It was my opinion our Mayor was following in the footsteps of former New York Mayor, Rudy Giuliani, where multiple civil rights violations aimed at Americans without homes resulted in lawsuits against the City. What truly was our Mayor's commitment?

February 2004: Homes and Communities HUD quarterly newsletter Dallas

It was an historic day February 25 when the City of Dallas unveiled a preliminary draft of its 10-year plan to end chronic homelessness. The ceremony at City Hall made Dallas the first municipality in Texas and the largest community in the Southwest to formalize a long-term commitment to its neediest homeless citizens.

Unfortunately, the HUD newsletter didn't report on what happened later that very evening.

Late that evening, Mayor Miller along with full Council support, denied a family shelter, The Annette Strauss Family Gateway Center, to apply for tax credits from the State to build housing apartments for homeless children and their mothers. 150 homeless children and their mothers. Council Member Maxine Thornton Reese stated that "almost" twelve people complained about the area in which the gated community would be built. The unanimous vote killed the project and along with it, the hopes of those it would serve.

I found that politicians love making resolutions and commitments, only to not back them up with action.

March 18, 2004

The Honorable Laura Miller

Dallas City Hall

Dear Mayor Miller,

The National Law Center on Homelessness & Poverty (NLCHP) has learned that the City of Dallas is close to completing its 10-year plan to end homelessness. While we commend this effort to address the problem of chronic homelessness, the plan is missing some crucial components needed to truly end homelessness.

Your proposed plan reveals that there are 933 individuals experiencing chronic homelessness and 4,200 individuals experiencing transitory homelessness in Dallas. Approximately 33 percent of renters in Dallas County are unable to afford a one-bedroom apartment at the fair market rate. In addition to new permanent supportive housing and transitional housing, your plan calls for 1,334 new affordable units to alleviate the shortage of affordable housing. However, the plan allocates only percent of those new affordable units to very low-income households. While any increase in affordable housing is a step forward, the plan should dedicate more affordable housing to very low-income individuals to achieve the goal of ending homelessness. Without an adequate, consistent supply of affordable housing, Dallas will not be able to bring about a permanent end to homelessness in the City, no matter how many shelters, transitional housing, and services are provided. If people have nowhere to go after receiving services, they will remain homeless.

Creating more affordable housing for very low-income individuals and families would not only help alleviate the problem of homelessness for the 22 percent of individuals experiencing chronic homelessness, but would also help solve the problem for the remaining 78 percent of people experiencing homelessness in the City. Dallas should seek out broader solutions to address the needs of all individuals experiencing homelessness, including families with children, as the homeless population in Dallas would undoubtedly tell you. Any plan to end the problem should incorporate the voices of people who have experienced homelessness themselves. Their perspectives can serve as a valuable resource, as they can help identify solutions for homeless person's most pressing challenges. We therefore urge you to include homeless and formerly homeless people on the task forces and outreach teams that will help carry out the plan.

NLCHP would be happy to serve as a resource to help Dallas develop its plan to end homelessness in the City. I am enclosing a copy of a report that NLCHP released this year that highlights some of the constructive approaches to homelessness around the country.

Sincerely,

Maria Foscarinis – Executive Director

Mayor Miller didn't want any outside interference. She was on a personal mission.

Dallas City Code Food Ordinance – for those serving homeless

Ordinance adopted June 8, 2005 Chapter 17–1.6 (a) (5)

DEFENSES FOR CERTAIN TYPES OF ACTIVITIES

(5) a church, civic, or other charitable organization serving or distributing food, without charge, to homeless individuals on public or private property, provided that the organization:

(a) was conducting that activity at a location approved by the director;

had a written consent from the property owner to conduct that activity on the property; was currently registered with the director (on a form provided by the director that is required to be completed on an annual basis) to conduct that activity on the property; conducted the activity in accordance with all terms and conditions of the registration as required by the director; and had met annual training requirements for safe food handling as required by the director.

(b) A person commits an offense if he violates, or fails to comply with, a term or condition of a homeless feeding registration issued pursuant to Section 17-1.6(a)(5)

During the dark ages, also known as the time of godlessness, food and the threat of starvation would be used to control the suffering peasants. Using food against a segment of population is the ultimate act of class-ism. Not allowing people to practice their religion is the ultimate act of tyranny.

Driving the point home, City employees handed out the copies of the new ordinance limiting freedoms at the Martin Luther King Jr. Center and enforced training sessions to be done at the Center.

When it comes to the Black Perspective, African American News & Issues is the States' widest circulated and read newspaper.

"Big D Dissing of Homeless" – A Damn Shame!!! By Darwin Campbell

The innocent homeless in Dallas are sacrificial lambs and clear victims of Mayor Miller and a greedy city council drunk on dollars and cents.

With potential billions at stake for entertainment venues, downtown renovations, beautification and development and competing for future tourism dollars, the city is casting the homeless out and writing them off. Just last week, police stepped up enforcement on a September 2005 ordinance that penalize charities, churches and other organizations that serve food to the needy outside of city designated areas. The city is also considering Mayor Laura Miller's suggestion to ticket people who donate money to panhandlers, because a blanket ban on panhandling has proved largely ineffective since its inception two years ago.

Imagine that, Dallas is now in the business of legislating simple human, heartfelt compassion of people wanting to reach out and help the less fortunate. The law is intended to prevent people from giving money or feeding the homeless without proper credentials or facilities.

Dallas is becoming more like George Orwell's award winning book, "Animal Farm" Wikipedia, the free encyclopedia, nut shelled the satirical novel written and published in 1945 at the height of World War II. The book is about a group of animals ousting the humans from the farm they live on (Manor Farm) and run it themselves, only to have it corrupted into a brutal tyranny on its own. Animal farm is a thinly veiled critique an satire of Soviet Totalitarianism, but can clearly compare to the kind of growing control and rule-bound structures the city council "horseshoe" is setting up for people living in Dallas.

The homeless can no longer go to the Resource Center and even spend the night. Last May, one of Dallas' most elaborate homeless camps, with cardboard shacks, tents, porta-potties and a microwave powered by electricity tapped from a billboard was raided. The City declared war on the encampment bulldozing the camp several times. Homeless people fought back rebuilding their homes.

Running off 10,000 homeless people or selectively screening them out of downtown and penalizing the compassionate to remake as image to build some version of the "Emerald City" is wrong. This kind of attitude is making a strong statement that tall skyscrapers, downtown lofts and condos are more important than human life. Its cold shoulder to the homeless is only the beginning and mirrors its attitudes and fate of any other ethnic and minority group that gets in the way of progress. No wonder The National Coalition for the Homeless ranked Dallas 6th meanest city in the nation to homeless people and the meanest in Texas.

Does that make Laura Miller the 6th meanest mayor in the nation? Huhummm? Instead of acknowledging and talking about the root causes of homelessness, Miller and the city's new laws only make matters worse and spur homeless people to become more creative. That in turn led city officials to declare war on the homeless and seek them out…

The homeless are not our enemies. They are our brothers, sisters, fathers, mothers, cousins, nephews, aunts and uncles. How much compassion does each of you on the Dallas City Council have for the homeless? Not much, according to the coalition for the homeless…

We call on the "Animal Farm" at Dallas City Council to change the rules and stop being mean to the homeless. Have a Heart!!! ...

My piece of advice to Dorothy and her three other homeless friends, carry a bucket of water with you while in Dallas and especially while visiting the Castle on the Hill. Dallas is no Emerald City.

Chapter 4
Americorps

"…to protect and defend the Constitution of the United States against all foreign and domestic enemies."

April 25, 2002

I raised my right hand and swore to protect and defend the constitution of the United States. It was the proudest moment in my life. I had regretted not joining the Armed Services when I was younger but now through the Americorps program, I could serve my nation and community as a VISTA, Volunteers in Service to America. It would be challenging having a full time job while living in a clump of woods in N.E. Dallas. While 26% of the homeless in Dallas had an income, the monthly income average was less than $350. Americorps gives its volunteers what is known as a subsistence allowance, set at the poverty level for the area they served in. My allowance would be less than $900 per month.

The mission of a VISTA is to develop sustainable projects to help impoverished communities or peoples. My particular job was to help with the consolidation of homeless service agencies and stakeholders into a new single coalition in Dallas. Promote the new alliance, build a web site, investigate all the services in Dallas for the homeless and Nationwide practices, attend all meetings concerning homelessness and assist with the Continuum of Care process by working with the City on the HUD mandated homeless census count. It was a big chore but homelessness gives a person a lot of free time. As I sat down to lunch with other VISTA trainee volunteers, I couldn't help but reflect back on the most recent events.

A month earlier, the police razed my site. They used their knives and slashed everything in sight and then threw what was left in the mud. An all too common malicious action. I was sadden that I couldn't salvage the Bible which Todd and Cindy had given me and that I couldn't find my pocket radio to listen to my Christian station, KLTY. The Bible and radio station brought me through many dark times of suffering. Kent, Jason and Cornbread were nowhere to be found. It was evident by a quick inspection of the area that they had been forced to pack up and leave. Super Dave left a note for me, written in red ink as a warning on the 4x8 plywood I had used to go over the two pallets, "James, come see me, Dave." I had to gather what I could before the police return; the usable items not destroyed were placed into my converted carrying bag made from a pillowcase. I packed remnants of my slice tarp, rope, and a few heavy clothes I could wash. Not wanting to take too much or the police might figure out I was still close by; it was best to leave the destruction undisturbed as much as possible. Climbing up the hill to the top of the Katy Trail and down the other side, I went to where Michael and his cousins were staying.

The World Church had brought Michael and his 3 cousins to the U.S. from Sudan. At the age of twelve, Michael along with his cousin James became fighters in the Sudanese civil war. The Moslem's had slaughter most of Michaels' family and his 3 cousins were the only ones he had left. Michael killed his first man when he was thirteen and went on fighting for nine years with the Christian resistance. Such an experience, one could've easily assumed that these people would act barbaric; instead, they were the most regal people I had ever met in my life. Untouched by the leprosy of materialism and greed, highly intelligent each one was able to speak four or more languages. Still though, they had a very limited knowledge of America and once they lost their support system and their employment in the busted Tech Industry, they became lost.

While the Sudanese certainly knew poverty, the culture of homelessness in America clashed with theirs. In fact, they had no concept of begging because where they came from; everyone shared what they had for survival sake. People would work together for the common good of the whole community. They could ill afford to abandon any individual because that could mean the lost of the entire community. Every person and life was as cherished as his or her own life.

I was amused that I had to ensure our refugee friends that there weren't any lions in the woods here in Dallas. I moved in and stayed with the Sudanese, finding their sense of morals and community comforting from the days when I grew up. Dallas at the time was considered the friendliest major city in the southwest and was why so many flocked to live here in the 1960's and 70's. It was the atmosphere of a small town with big town shopping and dining but fear and greed replaced that reality. The popularity hangover left over from the notoriety for being home to America's Team and a popular television series named Dallas, depicting oil wells and horses in every backyard, had done severe damage. Before the early 80's, Dallas didn't have any homeless to speak of nor did America except for some hobo's living a life left over from the great depression and the original homeless, Vietnam Veterans.

I earned the Sudanese respect and they in turn watched my back, making certain that no harm would come to me by day or night. These were my Christian angels. They called me Jay-mesh, finding James hard to pronounce and they stayed near the entrance to the path while I stayed further down so that I was safe. I didn't take the normal precautions this time like I had in every other camp. The most important one I had learned while being homeless, always leave a back way out.

After having been ran off from the last campsite, my hooch was very small this time. A small tarp 3x6 strung from a tree to a bush, covered me in case of rain and two couch pillows the Sudanese had given me for a mattress.

Ever since November of last year, the word had come down from City Hall to wipe out all encampments even though there were only 2,100 shelter beds in the city of 6,000 homeless people. It was a trend Dallas leaders had adopted. Bully the weaker and much like any abuser, blame the victims.

Every morning I would get up at 7 A.M. and go downtown to get copies of the street newspaper "Endless Choices" so I could earn some money. In three weeks, I would be in Tulsa for Americorps training and be sworn in, but for now as I had done for the last 7 months, I needed immediate money to help the others and myself. This is what "Endless Choices" the street newspaper provided.

The days were starting to get warm and it was taking longer into the night to cool off. Sleeping through a winter was hard, but adjusting to warm weather takes some time and I was not good at sleeping in the heat. Also, the nasty little spiders that stayed away during the cold were starting to make their presence known. A little bite from a Brown Recluse would rot the skin and could even cause death. I tossed and turned that night sleeping through my watch alarm and it was around 8 AM when I started to hear the commotion. Loud orders were being shouted and I could hear the Sudanese speaking in their native tongue. I knew immediately that it was the police and with no way out, I covered my head with my coat and hoped that they wouldn't come down all the way to the end of the path. I heard them getting closer, all the while yelling and screaming at my friends and then I heard one of the officers let loose a barrage of cuss words as he had stepped into someone's feces. A grin crossed my face but was soon gone as I heard the words, "We have another one down here." They found me.

"Come out, show your hands." "Let me see your hands!" peeking out from underneath my coat, I saw the worst sight possible. This wasn't the ordinary DPD, but the Dallas Transit cops. Dallas police were uncivilized, but these DART guys were ruthless. I put my hands out and then slowly crawled out from underneath my small hooch. Keeping my hands in sight as the cop started to question me.

"Do you have any weapons?"

"No sir." I answered.

"Let me see some I.D."

I pulled out my license and gave it to him. He got on his radio and called it in. While we were waiting to hear back, again he started to question me.

"Why you're here?" he asked with a bumbling Texas draw.

"Sir, I became homeless due to a bout of depression," I explained, "and soon I will be going to work for Americorps." I answered.

"I bet you do drugs and have AIDS, don't ya?" "Most likely ex-offender aren't ya?"

"No sir. I've never been in trouble with the law before and use to work at Prestige Ford before I became homeless."

His eyes widen and then he asked about a couple of retired officers who worked there to see if I was telling the truth.

"Yes sir, I know them. You're talking about Bill Peace who was with the Garland Police Department or Glen Wilson with DPD." Actually, both Glen and Bill were very good friends of mine and if they knew that I was living like this, most likely they would've came got me. He knew Bill Peace because he had also served with the Garland Police before moving over to DART.

Satisfied after my license came back clean, "Well get your stuff and get out of here." The officer ordered.

I was packed in 1 minute as he handed my license back to me. He followed me back out the trail and there at the end near the side of the road, Michael and the others were in handcuffs. One of the transits cops was berating them,

"I was one of those Rangers who jump into your Country to help train you guys to fight and them you come over here living in my woods…"

The officer who knew Bill turned to me and told me to go; I didn't think a second before heading off. As I was leaving I heard him say, "That guy is not the typical homeless." How wrong he was I thought as I started to plan where to spend the night. Super Dave would certainly welcome me down to Dave's Cave and it was close by.

Two days later I went back to see what happened, certain that Michael and the others had also found a new place, but there sitting down on top of the hill was Michael. His kneecaps were still swollen and crusted with dried blood where the former Ranger and now DART police officer had taken his baton and whacked him repeatedly, splitting them open. Michael was made an example of in front of the others because he told the officers he wouldn't go. He had been run off from his own country by such prejudice and he wouldn't let it happen again, he told me. Now he was physically unable to go.

2/04/03 Dart Police accused of brutal attack on homeless. Downtown Librarian, Rebecca Brumley, who witnessed attack threatened by police. Endless Choices

I wondered if I could make any difference against such hatred. I wondered if one voice could still make a difference in America.

Michael holds up two fingers showing how many days he has gone without food.

I was truly blessed to have this opportunity and a dream fulfilled. It was awkward holding up my right hand and giving pledge to my country, all the while knowing that after my three days of training in Tulsa, I would be returning back to Dallas, back to living at

Dave's Cave to begin my work as a VISTA. I hoped that my current living arrangements on the streets while serving my country and community would not only inspire others in my situation, but also bring positive attention and media to the plight of us without homes in America. I wanted people to know that if given opportunity, homeless can make a beneficial impact on society.

6/01/02 Bridging Two Worlds – Homeless VISTA Volunteer Wages Personal War against Poverty – Endless Choices

Most Federal representatives have more important things to do than reveal personal details about themselves. But James Waghorne's story is unique. While he's currently serving as a local VISTA volunteer, busy researching homelessness in Dallas to help local organizations and city departments address this problem more effectively, James Waghorne is also homeless. Right now, in fact, though he's loath to reveal the exact location of his residence, he's living in the woods.

Come on. You've got to be kidding. What on earth is a government volunteer doing living in a hutch somewhere in a local park? Does this mean that downsizing government has gone to far? Is the fact the government is currently setting up in a park, beneath a makeshift tent, reason for fiscal conservatives to take to the streets and dance?

As with any homeless person, it takes plenty of small talk to get Waghorne to explain the method to his seemingly madness. He's not absolutely forthcoming about what some might consider 'alternative lifestyle." What's important about his odd position, one straddling two worlds that often collide, is that he's waging a personal war against poverty and homelessness, he says.

"When you look at how best to do your job and actually get through to the homeless population here in Dallas," Waghorne says, "it's good to remember that you suffer from homelessness and poverty everyday. Being homeless really helps me stay in touch with the issues that surround homelessness and poverty, bit I also hope to get out of this inhumane condition, just like everybody else who ends up on the streets."

Without intending it, Waghorne's obvious commitment to advocating for the homeless in Dallas is like the conditions Civil Rights era "Freedom Riders" deliberately put themselves through, in order to bring a maligned and ghettoized population back into the fold of the American Dream. The only difference, really, is that Waghorne advocated for homeless rights long before it all became official for him. Living homeless for almost two years now before VISTA, Waghorne has helped some of his homeless friends get off the streets.

Currently, Waghorne receives what VISTA refers to as a "subsistence allowance" in consideration for his volunteer work. In other words, his government paycheck is almost tiny, only $722 each month, but such allowances to VISTA volunteers, he says, are designed by the government to insure volunteers are living at income levels commensurate with those of the communities they serve.

"The fact I'm living in a campsite right now isn't an issue for the people I work with. They understand there are not enough beds in the city to house 4,000 people," Waghorne says. "When I first became homeless I decided not to live in a shelter because I could save my money – as oppose to paying to stay in one of those places."

Of the four largest Dallas homeless shelters, two charge their residents fees for meals, a bath and a bed. For Waghorne, part of the largest segment in the homeless population, (Male – ages 18 to 45), only 250 free shelter beds exist in all of Dallas. Not a lot of options for the estimated 2,300 homeless men in our City. The Dallas Life Foundation, for example, charges clients $5-$8 per night. Many of these homeless can be seen in Downtown Dallas, panhandling for the money to get in before the Foundation's seven p.m. intake deadline. The Salvation Army also charges its clients $7 a night for food and lodging.

The money charged to stay in the shelters is not called a fee but donations. If a client is paid up for a week or more and leaves before the time paid for is used, the remaining monies are not refunded. After all, it was a donation not a fee for services.

Waghorne is currently looking for a room and has been checking out dozens of boarding houses, mainly because his income doesn't allow him more luxurious quarters such as a one-bedroom apartment. This, he points out, isn't unusual for many low income Dallasites, and the problem's he's having finding suitable lodgings illustrates in a personal way a much larger problem: "I find it extremely frustrating that there's not enough low income housing in Dallas to help anyone who wants to have a safe and decent affordable home." he says, "New housing needs to be built to accommodate people a my income level. This means a rent level of approximately $200 -$250 per month. Federal assisted housing has a two year or longer waiting list, leaving the 26% of our homeless with an income out in the cold."

Waghorne adds, however, that a consistent income is a good thing. For him, it's more a perk than anything else. He's been working to bring homelessness-related issues to the eyes of the powers-that-be for over a year. More importantly, he's been doing it for free.

The wiry tan VISTA volunteer's personal story of his run in with homelessness, he says, is fairly typical. The 43-year-old, raised in Dallas, attended W.T.White high school in north Dallas and spent time in college studying business. He worked in his family business and also in the automobile industry where he rose to become one of the top salespersons for Park Cities Ford.

"After my experience with homelessness in 2000, I left knowing that there had to be solutions. What I couldn't understand was how to get those solutions to the people who befriended me and helped me survive during that time. I was like everybody else at first. Frighten and ignorant, I thought homeless people were just drunks, drug addicts or severally mentally ill. When I got to know a few of them, I realized they were just like everybody else struggling with some serious issues, but they were having to do so in front of the public while also trying to survive in the worst form of poverty in our world today. That really changed the way I see what is happening in our country today."

Like many homeless people, Waghorne's story actually began due to a serious run-in with depression. One day, he says, he just walked off the job, feeling downright suicidal, waited for the money to run out. Soon, not able to defeat his major depressive disorder, he discovered he was homeless. Ultimately he set up camp near White Rock Lake, and befriended several homeless men and women. "These people obtained blankets for me, watched my back and cared of me the first three months I was homeless. They helped me survive. I believe the least I could do was return the favor."

It's been nearly two months since James Waghorne began officially advocating for Dallas' homeless population as a VISTA volunteer. But, two months is an eternity away from the twilight period in his life when helping the homeless meant calling the hospital to help a friend enroll in a drug and alcohol rehabilitation program, attending Dallas Homeless Consortium and DASH meetings where he could give caregivers an on-the-streets view of homeless concerns, or selling Endless Choices.

By Gordon Hilgers

I was the first person assigned to the project to help the new organization Metro Dallas Homeless Alliance to collaborate and become the expert authority on homelessness in Dallas. Two more teammates would come on board in June and the last one in December. I worked those first two months alone, building assets before the others arrived to ensure they could jump right in. I started to research homelessness, both locally and nationally. I also started to plan a summer census count and structure goals, which could make a meaningful impact on our homeless and myself. It kept me busy 14 hours a day and then it was back to Dave's Cave to rest.

Dave's Cave was not a cave at all. Next to the broken down car wash at the Fina gas station, a steep hill overlooked the White Rock jogging trail. Two semi-circles were dug into the side of the hill and were reinforced with cement bags. Two pieces of plywood were placed at each end of the circles, making firm walls and a stable roof. It was big enough, that Dave used six pallets to make two rooms and then went so far as to build a porch. The only downside to the hooch, it faced eastward. Seldom was there ever a breeze to blow away the stench from the sewers located nearby. We also had to burn mosquito coils constantly, to keep the West Nile Virus laden pest at bay.

I was most at risk because my crohn's disease gave me a low immune system. Also, whatever the reason, the mosquitoes seemed to enjoy people without alcohol in their system, which meant I was their main target, but every night my biggest worry was not the damage a small mosquito bite could do to me but instead, it was being discovered, attacked and brutalized by the police or transit cops.

The negative media and hostile actions from our politicians had created an environment for abuses. City Hall was textbook in the psychological process to unjustly persecute a segment of society. The process starts first with a demeaning label, then rumors and dehumanization. The rumors always generalize the entire population creating a culture of suspicion, fear, blame and finally judgment.

We believe we had learned from history, and today, we were too superior intellectually to fall into the snare of societal prejudice. Segregation of the past was born by such immaturity and much of the causes of homelessness today is a direct result of the prejudice birthed in such a social weakness.

Any solution to end homelessness had to first target this physiological warfare.

Step two would have to address the ego-filled, dysfunctional homeless service system. The amount of homeless suffering and dieing needlessly because agencies refused to work with one another in collaboration, was in the thousands across the nation. This would be as challenging, if not more so, than turning around the media and politics. There was a lot of prestige and money involved in what I call the "human suffering trade business." Over $60 million dollars annually.

I would never be able to prove agencies purposely perpetuated homelessness, but I could show how the systems in place prolong the amount of time a person suffered in such a condition.

Step three would be the hardest of all. Bring real solutions to fruition.

If there was one thing I learned about sympathy and understanding. It seldom equates to nothing more than talk. Hatred rallies all kind of people, bringing them out of the woodworks and can be sustained for decades, passing down from one generation to the next but compassion has short legs in today's society. Compassion is stamped with an expiration date.

It would be a challenge to see homelessness actually end in our community. Many battles had to be fought.

August 27, 2002

All the odds were stacked against us and our adversaries were to many to count but physiologically speaking, Dallas City Hall had developed into a "mob mentality" and presented the greatest threat. I never thought that such words about my own fellow Americans and local Government would be written but articles in the paper would prove these correct. Dallas City Hall had an undeclared war against fellow Americans based on wealth and health.

I had written a few articles for "Endless Choices" and from that experience I knew how to get attention. "Blood leads", the saying goes in the media world.

Past homeless census counts in Dallas were not accurate and proving this became my top priority as a VISTA. Conquer untruth with truth; so proving the annual census was undercounted would be the tip of our sword.

Every year cities across America need to conduct a homeless census count if they wished to participate in applying for the HUD super N.O.F.A., (Notice of Funding Availability) homeless assistance funds. The census count, along with a listing of services available, would be used to create a service gap analysis showing where funds were needed in the community. Agencies and cities use this analysis to apply for millions in their Continuum of Care application to help fill those gaps and address the homeless needs. The City was purposely undercounting the homeless population and misleading our community about the amount of human suffering happening in our town. It also had an affect on the amount of HUD funds available to the city and non-profits. The last census count the city held in January 2002, only accounted for four individuals of my tribe members living in the area of N.E. Dallas. Investigating their census and tactics, I found the city had refused to work with the County getting their numbers and left out 16 agencies. Still, using a summer count would be a gamble and prove tricky.

Most homeless census counts are done during the winter because many homeless will seek shelter indoors. During the summer time, many leave the two shelters and three boarding dormitories in Dallas to sleep outside, enjoying the freedom and saving money. For the largest segment of our homeless population, men between the ages of 18 – 44, only 250 free beds existed and none of the facilities dedicated medical beds for mental health individuals to take medicine and recover. It was primarily these individuals who were the victims of the system, tossed out into the streets like lepers to once again become victims of crime and abuse. Our county jail had become one of the States largest mental health facilities and third largest homeless shelter in Dallas. These numbers also were hidden away in the dark. Accurate numbers would place political pressure on the

City, exposing their apathy, class-ism and unwillingness to address the issues with concrete solutions. It would also give the new Alliance power, which could be used to start taking control from the City.

Since this was my first census, Dave Hogan of the City, would still be in charge of the outside count and I would oversee the inside count. I researched other cities and patterned our count after Boston and Ft. Worth developing an anonymous survey that would give us information and data for a gap analysis. As a VISTA, I had to be sure that this count would set the foundation for all future census counts.

The city lead January count yielded 3,989 homeless individuals during the seven-hour census. I knew that the outside count would not be accurate again, not only because City Staff would lead it, but also because Dallas was 384 square miles of territory. 7 hours in the dark, I'd be happy finding 25% of those outside. It was imperative that the inside counts came through with some big numbers. The P.R. campaign was almost just as important as the truth in numbers. The VISTA's sent out emails to organizations asking for volunteers and press releases were sent to the media. This count unlike others previous would be done with the public watching. The Mayor and Council members were sent invitations also, inviting them to participate. I hoped some would show up, but it was just as good politically speaking if they didn't. It would prove their disinterest in the suffering happening in their backyard. City Hall's campaign was to make people without homes the "bad guys"; mine was to expose the truth.

Advocates, like prophets are not welcomed in their own hometown, the weapon of truth to bring about change is despised by the status quo and humane humanity is not viewed as economically or politically beneficial. As one Council Member said, life now has a monetary figure next to it in the accounting books and in Dallas that equated to .03 cents per homeless individual per day, as the City of Dallas only dedicated 3% of the City's general fund.

The biggest challenge of the census would be trying to get the jail count. Our homeless are locked up for unpaid fines and trumped-up charges, cycling in and out of jail. Getting the jail count would subvert the City efforts to hide away as many homeless as possible during the count. Police activity always increased immensely before a count, rounding up homeless for outstanding warrants and razing known campsites forcing the homeless to go elsewhere. Along with the police escorts purposely taking volunteers to old abandoned camps, the outside count would forever be sabotaged. One of the more profound examples of the police joyriding volunteers around came during one census when a Council Member had to start showing her police escort where the homeless were. One certain way to overcome the city's efforts to undercount our homeless was to get the jail count. Even with the severe thunderstorms that morning, washing away many campsites pre-identified for the count, on August 27, 2002, 4,658 homeless individuals were accounted for. Twenty-seven of my tribe participated, ten others had their campsites washed away and I couldn't find them in the seven-hour time frame. Almost 700 more homeless were counted than the City stated in the January count. It was a clear victory and each additional census count the numbers would increase, putting City Hall on the spot. Next we needed to expose their unwillingness to help the least fortunate.

Year	2001	2002	+/-	2002
TOTAL	2,909	4,658	1749+	%
Male	1,623	2,621	998 +	56.3%
Female	661	1,865	1204 +	40.0%
Youth	721	1,111	394 +	23.9%
Mental Illness	481	894	413 +	19.2%

Any community can tie their crime rate directly to the quality of social services in their area. Instead of quality services for the homeless, the city criminalized them effecting all citizens. And according to the citizens of Dallas, in the National Citizen Survey concerning social services for the entire community, Dallas was below poor; it was failing at a score of 32 for consecutive years. It would only make common sense that the 9th largest City in America would hire a Doctor to oversee the Department in charge with the well-being of citizens, but common sense is not the strong point of Dallas City Hall. When it came to the homeless in Dallas, the Director for Environmental & Health Services in my view best compared to former Michael Brown of F.E.M.A. and the Hurricane Katrina victims. Karen Rayzer would complain to our VISTA project manager, long-time advocate Dorothy Masterson, about our census findings, demand meetings, challenge every count, even bringing in their own city statistician to challenge the outcomes, but he couldn't find fault with the methodology I had developed and the resulting numbers.

Hiding the truth about the amount of individuals suffering, the city could keep status quo. I couldn't out power these people, but with my passion, I could outwork them.

I knew more than 6,000 individuals experienced homelessness on any given night and using Dr. Martha Burt's methodology from The Urban Institute, it showed over 11,000 people in Dallas experienced homelessness during a one year period. These numbers would be supported with other documentation from Parkland HOMES mobile medical units, J.P. evictions notices and DISD estimates. Naturally it would be easier to demand all shelters and dormitory boarding facilities to give yearly numbers and cross reference them for duplication using an identifier, but that would require cooperation among all agencies. During this time, cooperation among agencies was nonexistent as each worried more about their own money, as opposed to what would be in the best interest of the suffering.

Our census counts started to show success as we receive media and public attention regardless of the barriers we faced getting the truth out. HUD chipped in a record $11 million, a 113% increase in federal funding (still a record increase today) even though the City of Dallas and homeless agencies had been found guilty of misleading in the past. Donations to charities and nonprofits would start to increase.

1/20/03 Time Magazine speaks to Dallas Homeless, abuses reported, Police harassment cited. – Endless Choices

800 individuals living on the streets were disabled. Their substance abuse was a form of self-medication but also a form of solidarity within the community they had been rejected to. Not having the capability to control their thoughts and without appropriate services available in the shelter system, like myself, I preferred counting on the kindness of others or finding a meal in the 7-11 store dumpster. There was enough food thrown away every night in Dallas to feed the homeless a meal ten times over. To help degrade those living on the streets, the term "service resistant" was used to define them; except in Dallas the services and beds weren't available to these individuals. We weren't service resistant; we were service failures caught in a system designed to fail eight out of every ten individuals.

The warm weather count went better than I could have hoped for, the winter numbers for the January 2003 census count still needed to show improvement. This time I would co-chair the entire count, inside and outside. I had 55 agencies committed and most importantly Dallas County was completely on board, after threatening the Director of the Health and Human Services Department with filing a complaint with HUD if they didn't participate, putting their federal funds at risk. Knowing I couldn't completely overcome the City's sabotage efforts, the inside count would once again be the primary focus, where the city had no control. A lesson learned from the first count was the dramatic information we had to obtain, which would strike emotional and intellectual chords in our community. Debunking the myths surrounding homelessness with hard facts and having the faces of homelessness speak would be keys to the struggle.

Americorps VISTA Report
January 21, 2003 Head Count

	MEN	WOMEN	CHILDREN	UNIDENTIFIED	TOTAL
Total -	2023	842	711	1605	5181

The survey found over 2,435 people in Dallas became homeless for the first time. 48% had high school diplomas and 13% had college degrees. 29% had income but couldn't afford housing. Over 37% of the homeless had disabilities. The main purpose of the census count and survey is to report to HUD about the gaps in our services and is a required part of the application for Federal Funds. While it is impossible to get an exact count due to logistics and the limited time to conduct the census, it is known for certain that 4 agencies refused to participate and that the street count was low. Based on this information and first hand knowledge of those not counted during the event, it is fair to say over 6,000 individuals are homeless on any given night. It is the intent that our report will not only be used to raise much-needed funds, but also to educate the general community about homelessness in Dallas.

April 11, 2003

My term with Americorps was coming to an end. I had the option of serving another year, but felt confined by federal laws. The constraints didn't allow me the freedom needed to achieve the ultimate goals for grassroots organization, housing solutions and addressing

NIMBY-ism head-on. The media, although almost all negative was reporting on the issue. In my position, I couldn't launch a true P.R. campaign to counteract it. My presence was known in City Hall and among the agencies, but I had to get the public support and that could only happen if I started punching the bullies in their noses.

To: mdha@mail.com
Subject: Thank you
Metro Dallas Homeless Alliance – Members

As of the 24th of this month, I will have finished my 1-year service as an Americorps VISTA (Volunteers in Service to America). It was an honor and privilege to serve you and my community in this capacity. As many of you know, I was homeless living on the streets when I accepted to become a VISTA. One of the goals for any VISTA is to put into place sustainable projects, which will remain long after their service has ended. It is my hope that the permanent web site for MDHA and recently, the 3,000 "Helping Hands" pocket pals distributed to the Dallas Police Department will serve as reminders that with opportunity and support, a homeless individual can make a positive impact, be it large or small, on their community. When asked about what a new 24-hour Resource Center needed, Sergeant Reese of the DPD answered "Compassion".

During the last year, I have made it a point to learn everything I could about homelessness and our services here in Dallas as compared to those available in other cities. I had the opportunity to travel to Boston for a conference, and there spoke with homeless individuals from across the U.S. and Canada. While the lack of low-low income housing, permanent supportive housing and CFDS (Client Friendly Driven Services) are the most common reasons given for homelessness today, I believe Sgt. Reese put it into one defining word.

I will continue to advocate and attend speaking engagements for the homeless, serve on MDHA committees and also hope to serve as a "formerly homeless" representative on the Board. I look forward continuing to work with everyone and thank you once again for your support this past year. I would like to especially thank Dorothy Masterson for all her hard work on the VISTA project and my three co-volunteers, Paula Melvin, Manuel Carrasco and Kit Lowrance for their unselfish dedication towards improving the lives of others.

I had one more count to perform (2004) and because of the harassment I received from City Hall due to past counts and the numbers revealed, I recruited help from Ken Martin, Executive Director for the Texas Homeless Network.

From: James Waghorne
To: Dave Hogan (City of Dallas)
CC: Ron Cowart
Subject: Re: census count
Date: Mon 27 Oct 2003
Hello Dave,
It's getting to be that time of the year again. I hope all is going well with you.
When I was down in Austin for the Texas Homeless Conference, I asked for T.A. from HUD for this count and they will be sending a representative (Ken Martin) to help us. Certainly I would wish for him to meet the main people and agencies involved in the count so we can ask him any questions, which we might have. Email me or call me when you think would be the best time for Ken to come see us.
Hi James,
This sounds good – how about Oct 30 or 31st? Also early Nov is adjustable for me. Ron Cowart & I were talking about another recent issue you may be interested in- Let's talk.
Thanks Dave

If there were 6,000 homeless on any given night in Dallas, it was important to get that number accepted by both the media and City Hall. This would be my last shot as co-chair for the Dallas County census count because the new Executive Director for the Metro Dallas Homeless Alliance would take over for the 2005 census count. The final tally for 2004 – 5,936. Our first hurdle of truth was behind us.

Why is Dallas behind other cities addressing homelessness?

Historically since 1990, Dallas has had many committees' and task forces try and put together a plan to address the growing social problem of homelessness. The results of these actions have proven inadequate primarily due to lack of funding, not following through or faulty procedures and an unwilling political climate to get the job done. Over

$80 million dollars is spent or lost every year due to the inadequate practices addressing homelessness. During a one month period this year, 20 chronically homeless individuals where track for misdemeanor crimes such as public intox, sleeping in public, etc. The individuals were ticketed/citied 86 times during this one-month period.

Dallas is very unique compared to other cities when it comes to the structure of service delivery. This also adds to the problem of addressing homelessness and in many cases has added to the growth of homelessness in our community. Currently today, 48% of this socially and economically disadvantage population has been homeless for more than a year. An incredulous 12% increase from last year. The longer a person remains in the state of homelessness, the more resistant, unwilling or unable the individual becomes toward services. Currently the City of Dallas has over 1,181 individuals who qualify under the HUD definition as to being "Chronic Homeless" and another 2,000 individuals on the edged of becoming chronically homeless. The delivery of services has become clogged.

The Problems

1. A shelter system not designed to move people out of homelessness.
2. Dallas leads the nation in lost of affordable housing under HUD guidelines.
3. Social Security benefits are taking 18 months longer to receive than in other parts of the country. (Presumptive benefits)
4. A service delivery system aimed at keeping people homeless while being treated.
5. Lack of Government leadership and funding.
6. Stigma, NIMBYism, prejudice, etc…
7. Lack of exit plan to integrate ex-offenders back into mainstream
8. Lost of labor skilled jobs & outsourcing
9. Poverty wages

Chapter 5

The Castle on the hill

"Attitude reflects leadership" - Remember the Titans.

Headline: September 21, 2001
Office of Inspector General: Audit Case Number 2001-FW-1006:

Our audit concluded the Consortium has a broad-based membership that provided fair representation of the community. However, the Continuum of Care applications filed by the Homeless Consortium contains inaccurate information and overstates its achievements. We also have concerns that in its role as lead agency of the Consortium, the City of Dallas did not provide the organization with the leadership and guidance necessary for the Consortium to become successful.

Findings:

The Consortium Mislead HUD and Did Not Effectively Evaluate or Provide Meaningful Feedback on Grantee Performance.

City of Dallas:

Overall, the City did not implement its grants in compliance with grant agreements and federal regulations. Specifically, the City:

Failed to provide $250,980 in supportive services required by its Shelter Plus Care grant or adequately document the services it did provide;

Was behind projected spending for its Shelter Plus Care grant by $259,295 and $39,572 for its Supportive Housing grant;

Submitted inaccurate and inconsistent Annual Progress Reports;

Included $52,977 in ineligible and $2,261 in unsupported cost in grant draw-downs;

Did not monitor the participants and their supportive service needs sufficiently; and

Did not perform yearly Housing Quality Standards inspections for apartments inhabited 1 year or more.

OIG (Office of Inspector General)

OIG Evaluation of Comments:

Considering the evidence, the use of the word mislead was appropriate. The applications were prepared in order to make the Dallas Homeless Consortium appear as a well-run organization that had made significant strides in its efforts to help the homeless. However, there was little evidence to support this. HUD also recommended that the City of Dallas be removed as lead agency.

June/July 2002 Endless Choices ask National Coalition for the Homeless to investigate city's homeless actions aimed at limiting homeless on public property - Endless Choices

There were many beachheads from which City Hall was assaulting their poor and each assault had to be confronted. Their effort to "ethnically cleanse downtown of homeless" and their propaganda campaign of prejudice. In addition, the direct abuses needed to be documented along with the hypocrisy and lack of action.

Keeping track of what was happening inside the Castle was frustrating and very time consuming. It's equivalent to watching two-year-old triplets. One child gets into something and while you're getting him handled, another one is busy messing up things and so on. In the Castle, there were the Politicians, City Manager and Department heads. Karen Rayzer, head of Environmental and Health Services and her cronies were up to their old tricks; they had even more devious plans.

September 22, 2003

Donna and I went to the library to discuss outreach efforts with Carol Webster. She was a city employee working under the Department of Environmental and Health Services. Her job was with the City Crisis Intervention team, a small group whose focus was primarily working with the homeless. This was going to be Donna's and my first opportunity to go with the City and Police to conduct what is known as a "sweep". A reference politicians and city employees used as in sweeping the dirt away, even if they were humans, their actions justified by blaming those they're victimizing. Sweeps entailed going to known locations where our homeless had made campsites and local residents had made complaints. The objective was to virtually wipe these sites out. The City hid these actions from the media and up to this time had denied conducting sweeps. Later, they would publicly sanitize their actions stating that the sites enabled the homeless and therefore stepping on them was justified. The sweeps are done without any offer of assistance and used primarily to harass homeless and arrest those with outstanding misdemeanor citations. I was hoping that these next two days would start a change of this practice and lead to a more sensible approach as sited by research and endorsed by the federal government under what was called "evidence based", or "best practices". I had never found any good abusing another human being, especially those living with disabilities, which happens to be the individuals a person will find most common living on the streets of America today. Unfortunately, the bully tactics and abuse disguised under terminology such as "zero-tolerance" is the course of action our City and police used, even to this very day.

We met Carol at the wall in front of the Downtown library, located directly across from City Hall. Like in most major metropolitan cities, those individuals who weren't receiving proper services tend to hang out in the Downtown areas and near the major libraries. It's a good place to do outreach and start initial contact. Building trust had proven to be the best and most effective way to help people get into services.

We went down the wall, talking to people asking them what their immediate needs were and the common responses such as clean socks, water, food, and bus tickets would always be the answers. Long-term solutions and answers come only after immediate survival needs are met. This is common for every human being. After an hour or so we worked our way around to the back of the library where Carol had parked her city vehicle and it was there where she told us of the City's plan.

"Now you can't tell anyone I told you this." She started off. "The sweeps set for Thursday and Friday are going to be used to arrest people. My supervisors came up with a plan to have the police purposely provoke those living with mental illness and addictions to arrest them on the spot and take them to jail."

I looked at my coworker Donna who was a License Chemical Dependency Counselor and I believe the look of disgust on her face could only be matched by my look of disbelief. They planned to purposely violate the civil rights of disabled citizens of who over 95% would be African Americans and their mentality was that this action would help our homeless problem.

Even though Carol asked us not to tell anyone, what was the purpose of telling us? Carol is a best friend to our homeless and the most qualified city employee when it came to working with them, but she was caught in the worst job anyone could have where she had to make the decisions of not saying anything in hopes of still helping a few, while others were being sacrificed by her employers. Regardless, I felt I had to tell my supervisors of their plans, and so I did.

Jessie and Hope could only shake their heads as they listened to what had transpired. The Dallas MetroCare employees who were to participate the next two days of sweeps were told not to do anything in which they felt would be unethical. I was hoping for more. I was hoping they would call the City and condemn their plan but because Dallas MetroCare worked with the City on different projects that was not going to happen. Jesse had warned me about the corporate politics before I was hired and much like Carol, he too was trapped with what could be done. That night before the sweeps I remember one thing, praying for a miracle.

That morning we all met at the Martin Luther King, Jr. center to organize and go over the different sites chosen for that days sweeps. I thought how ironic to meet at a center named after a man whose life was dedicated towards ending injustice, prejudice, promoting equality, and the end of poverty. Laura, another mental health caseworker and I had been assigned to ride together. We hadn't made it to our third stop when Laura told me that the conditions she was seeing which our homeless were living in had made her ill to her stomach. I knew first hand what she was saying having been off the streets for only eleven months now. It was hard to visit my past suffering through the eyes of others who had found themselves here, but it was even harder participating with these city bastards. If only God would answer I thought, as we were getting ready to head out to our third location.

As I got into the old blue Ford Aerostar, my cell phone rang.

It was Scott Sayers, a news reporter from channel 4, a Fox news affiliate. He had asked me to do a story about building a new Homeless Assistance Center and wondered if I would do something that day. Because of what I was doing at the time, I tried to convince him that it wasn't a good time but I let my tongue slip that I was doing outreach and after that, he wouldn't be put off. So, I let the rest of the party go on and waited for Scott and his camera crew to find us. About 15 minutes had passed until Scott caught up with us but during that time, Laura repeatedly made sure that I knew her opinion of having a news crew here and it wasn't positive. Scott was the first film media person I had met. His high energetic personality and friendliness gave me an assurance that this person would do the story justice and so we to find the rest of the group, 4 police squad cars, a city attorney and 4 outreach workers including Dave Hogan and Ron Cowart from the Crisis Intervention Department. We found them in a parking lot across from a vacant field. In the vacant field 6 homeless people had set up their hooch's. It was this lot they were targeting. Scott pulled his news crew across the street to film; Laura and I went to talk to the others. It didn't take long for them to notice the camera being set up and all hell broke loose in the group. Carol asked what was happening and when I explained that Scott just wanted to do a story about building a new center, it didn't go well. All the City employees jumped into their cars and vans and sped off; even two squad cars left, not any of them wanting to be seen on the T.V. nightly news while doing their vicious actions. It was my prayer answered and even today, I like to think Martin Luther King Jr. had put in a good word.

Scott changed the story to focus some on outreach and a plan for a new Homeless Assistance Center (HAC), while still capturing the other squad cars of police questioning the homeless on the vacant lot. I never mentioned to Scott what was really happening, so mention of the "sweeps" weren't reported. Still that afternoon, the City had called my employer to launch a complaint; it wouldn't be the last time. The City also told them that they decided to cancel the sweep planned for the next day. Jesse, my boss, decided even if the City hadn't canceled, Dallas MetroCare would not put its reputation or mission on the line. The story which aired on T.V. that evening gave a positive message, one that City Hall couldn't even complain about, but I now knew exactly the depth our City Hall, the Mayor, City Manager, the Director of the Environmental & Health Services Dept., all the way down the City Hall chain would stoop to, when it came to a person without a home. I also knew now, they feared me.

December 2003

City of Dallas study and report is uncovered. The report concludes Dallas homeless likely to become victims of crime at a rate 25 times higher than that of the National rate.

I have never found out who my angels were at City Hall, but I was privy to information, that was meant to be secret and kept from the public. The above report was denied to have existed for months. After persistence, Karen Rayzer had to relinquish a copy of the report. In the study, 1 out of every six people surveyed, (312 surveyed) had become a victim of violent crime since becoming homeless. Making such studies public would hamper the City's effort to criminalize the homeless and their P.R. campaign of prejudice.

Maybe it was the fact that eighty percent of the victims (people) in this report are disabled as to why Karen Rayzer and others in City Hall didn't want the report released. According to the F.B.I., Dallas is the number one city in the country for crime. Under Laura Miller, Dallas has consistently ranked in the top five categories for: murder, assault, burglary, robberies and rape. This was their idea of solutions:

November 2003 Dallas announces 4 initiatives to reduce crime. 30-day police crackdown on panhandlers, enforce shopping cart ordinance, put signs up to remind people to lock their cars – City Hall

The cost to put a homeless person in jail was $32 per day or $960 per month. This didn't include the cost of officers transporting and court cost. It also doesn't include the personal safety cost to the citizens of Dallas. While Dallas County tries to address overcrowding and civil rights violations inside the County jail, 300 homeless are being locked up for begging, sleeping in public, pushing a shopping cart or other life sustaining practices at a cost of over $4 million per year. Discrimination doesn't only cost those whom it is aimed at, it cost everyone regardless and for the homeless individuals, when they get out for these Class C misdemeanors, after taxpayers pay the bill, they will still be homeless on our streets.

From: James Waghorne
To: "Vincent Golbeck", Dallas Police Department
Subject: Re: Crime statistics
Date: Fri, 06 Jun 2003 09:12:13 – 0500

Hello Vince,

I know that you were busy during the last homeless association meeting dealing with Exxon and the protesters. In light of the recent murder of a homeless man last Sunday, I would like to get a report on crime against the homeless here in Dallas. I know it has increased in recent months. I would like to give the report to the association and MDHA. Also, it was discussed that it would benefit our community if a Female Officer would volunteer her time to teach self defense and build a rapport with the female homeless population so we can develop a trust where female victims will be more apt to report crime. Also, was the victim whose remains were found at N.W. Hwy and Skillman ever identified and cause of death? Hate crimes against the homeless needs to be addressed before we have a situation like Denver did.

From: Vince Golbeck

Subject: Re: Crime statistics

Good afternoon James,

We don't keep crime statistics against the homeless or committed by the homeless. We only track hate crimes at this time.

To: Vince

Thank you Vince. Question? My understanding that under the current definition of Hate Crime, that crimes against the homeless are not considered by some Cities. Is that true about Dallas?

<<<Vince Golbeck>>>

That is true James.

Vince Golbeck is currently a Deputy Chief for the Dallas Police Department. I could always count on him for honesty.

Interdepartmental City Hall email: 1/08/04

From: Jill Jordan (Assistant City Manager)

Subject: Re: Homeless on the Plaza

To: Karen Bradford (Rayzer), Karen Boudreaux, David Hogan

Cc: James Mongaras, Ron Cowart

Jill Jordan 09:08 AM

Mr. Griffith (Council Member and Mayoral candidate) asked if we could continue the move of homeless to a more suitable area. He suggested the Day Resource Center but I told him that we have homeless who like to stay outside. So, he asked that we find another temporary spot for them to hang out until the new intake facility is build. Could we/should we approach Oncor again about making their lot the temporary spot? We'd need shade, benches, tables, etc. How could we do this?

From: Karen Bradford (Rayzer) 10:16 AM

Jill,

I think this is a bad idea for a couple of reasons. At least with the (City Hall) Plaza you have trees and such, which kind of camouflages the gathering. There are no additional cost with them being on the plaza. With moving them to the Oncor lot, we (the City) will now have the expense of maintaining and cleaning the plaza and the Oncor property. If we can manage to get them to move over to the Oncor lot, we will need to fund for some type of security. The difference with this and the feeding is the feeding was an attraction, what will serve as the attraction to get them to move to the Oncor lot. But these are just my preliminary thoughts. I am querying my staff as well.

If the directions are to try again for the Oncor lot, I will, but I think it is a bad move.

David Hogan 12:02 PM

Karen,

I agree with you. Besides, we can't MAKE them go or stay anywhere. Is the entire Council having a problem with homeless folks on the Plaza or just Mr. Griffith? Is he willing to toss some $$$ for additional outreach to these folks, or is he looking for a trail boss to herd 'em?

What happened to passive-resistance methods that was going to be done – classical music, etc?

Somehow we gotta get the politicos to understand that these folks are people who are homeless, not cattle to be stampeded around the City at will! "Rollin, rollin, rollin, keep them doggies movin....Rawhide'

Drover Dave

It just seems that these people in City Hall wanted to draft their own Constitution. The City evidently did rewrite the Constitution and Bill of Rights, because our homeless are not allowed to assemble on City Hall property and are repeatedly driven away from other public areas. Police threaten the homeless poor with criminal trespassing citations for gathering on such property or for standing on sidewalks outside service agencies.

To: Kim Horner (Dallas Morning News)

From: James Waghorne

Sent: Thursday, January 15 2004

Subject: Article

Hello Kim,

Enjoyed your article on the shopping carts. Over at the police front on Bryan, they already had a 'lot' full (starting a little early). Last night the police harassed "Hunger Busters", bet Phil is hot today. I understand everything is being pushed back as far as reports and Site selection until Feb. 9th. After I finish with the Census Count, I will make sure that the Council members will get the results of the Homeless signature vote on site choices and contact you before I present them with it.

James

I had learned there were four primary statements in City's Hall propaganda campaign, which would come from the mouths of those in the Castle on the Hill to justify their inhumanity. The homeless are responsible for crime, the homeless have shelter if they choose, we are not targeting the homeless and lastly, we are trying to help the homeless. Every year City Hall reported to the federal government the City not have enough shelter beds therefore getting their $4.4 million from HUD in federal grants, yet told the general public just the opposite to promote an atmosphere in which they could justify their actions.

April 1, 2004 MDHA Board Meeting:

City disbanded Site Selection Committee. City Hall was keeping tight-lip on possible locations for a new Homeless Assistance Center, but rumors still surround downtown location. Mayor wants to appoint a "Hometown Hero" such as what Atlanta did to raise money. A list of names was suggested to her but the Mayor wants to choose her own. People such as Herb Kelliher (Southwest Airlines) and Mark Cuban (Dallas Mavericks) were mentioned. A criteria from the Mayor, is that the person chosen cannot be female. Five months would pass by.

9/1/04 Mayor Laura Miller chooses former adversary, Tom Dunning to become the city's 'homeless czar'

After the first Homeless Assistance Center site selection circus ended, having been exposed as a plot to exterminate the homeless from downtown, the Mayor and City needed another distraction to keep the citizens eyes off what was actually happening on the streets and promote an image of caring, moving ahead on the issue. Tom Dunning was chosen to lead a new Task Force. Mr. Dunning, a former Mayoral candidate and prominent local business leader who had served on a committee to address homeless issues for Dallas back in the early 90's; now 14 years later, he would do so again.

From: "Karen Boudreaux" KBOUDRE@ci.dallas.tx.us
To: James Waghorne
Subject: Re: panel
Date: Thu, 30 Sep 2004
James,
This panel will be first and I have allocated them 1.5 hour. Thank you
Karen

I was asked to put together a panel of homeless and formerly homeless to address homelessness with the new Task Force because not a single homeless or formerly homeless individual was asked to chair one of the seats. 7 homeless representatives were given 1.5 hours before the Task Force to talk about the issue they were suffering from. It was an insult but also the main underlying reason why homelessness had not been solved. Not seen as good enough to have a seat at the table, we were reduced to dogs looking for table scraps. Only one member of the Task Force brought the discrepancy to the attention of others, an African American, the Honorable Judge John Creuzot.

A majority of citizens in Dallas have a good and compassionate heart; it just needed some CPR to jump-start. Exposing what was happening in their backyard and allowing our City Hall to shame itself, along with some of the politicians for their abuse and class-ism would have to be an international campaign to have an economic impact. Tourist, businesses and conventioneers, don't want to travel or relocate to a "Mean City". Heartlessness is not a popular destination point for vacation and until it is either eliminated or no longer tolerated in Dallas, it would have a negative effect and impact on everyone.

December 1, 2004

This day; a day of promise and new beginning for many disabled homeless who had been forced to sleep outside on the sidewalks in the freezing cold; the City ran Day Resource Center was to open into a 24hr facility because of the public outcry surrounding the deaths of two homeless men in October. News crews were there early to report the event to the community about the positive changes for the homeless. At approximately 5 AM Police and City Employees set upon hundreds of disabled homeless asleep on the sidewalk under the orders from the Castle on the Hill.

What was supposed to be a day of new hope for the less fortunate should go down in history as Dallas's Tiananmen Square. Rousting the homeless, police and city employees started a campaign to destroy all their belongings, leaving them freezing in the cold.

Women ran crying after City trucks, which were hauling away their life saving medications, pictures of family, winter coats, shoes, and blankets. Even an elderly mans dentures were trashed with all his other belongings. All the gifts the homeless had received at the annual Veterans Stand Down; trashed. Christmas presents for children; trashed. Bibles trashed. Hope trashed The horror on the morning news was shown from household to household on TV's across Dallas and North Texas, as viewers watch the assault in disbelief. By the time I arrived, those from the Castle on the Hill had completed their ambush, leaving hundreds in despair. The news reporter seemed to be in shell shock after having witnessed the event. I not only had seen it before but also was a victim myself of such evil. There isn't any other term for human abuse and the actions of a City government against their own citizens.

Mayor Miller on the evening news would mislead the public stating, "The homeless had been warned." She never apologized, not even till this day.

National Coalition for the Homeless: A seizure of property violates the Fourth Amendment when a governmental action unreasonably interferes with a person or his/her property. Courts have found that police practices of seizing and destroying personal property of homeless individuals violate these constitutional rights under the Fourth Amendment. In addition, some courts have also affirmed homeless persons' right to be free from unreasonable searches even if their belongings are stored in public spaces.

Within a few days of the heartless ambush, during a meeting hosted by Pastor Haynes at Friendship West Baptist Church, City Manger Mary Suhm stated it was her who made the decision that day and vowed to pay and replace everything the homeless had lost. Without Friendship West church and its leaders involvement, I am certain nothing would've been done. Many at the meeting wanted the Mayor's head but they would wait, being able to exact their revenge against her in an upcoming bond election. The comment, which rang loudest but was the one barely audible, "We have to start taking care of our people." Rev. Haynes stated to others. He was right, because City Hall was poisoned beyond seeing their own abuses against their own citizens. I would meet with the City Manager to negotiate new practices by City employees and police to protect our homeless. I knew though that the City Manager would never live up to her agreement.

From: James Waghorne

To: Michael Stoops; Tulin Ozdeger

Subject: Update; DRC and Sweeps of Homeless

Date: Tues. Dec 07, 2004

This is the latest surrounding the vents on Dec 1st. Still working on other issues and individuals to address the underlying current, which lead up to this human tragedy. If you have any suggestions, please let me hear from you.

To: James

Thanks for this update. It sounds like your meeting with the City Manager went well. That is good that they will be reimbursing people for their lost belongings. It would be nice to get more than 24 hours notice for the sweeps, but I guess that is better than nothing. The extra storage space at the resource center also sounds like a good idea.

Best

Tulin

From: "Scott Sayers"

To: James Waghorne

Subject: Hey James!!

Date: Fri, 03 Jun 2005

Hey James,

Great to hear from you!! Sorry in the delay in getting back to you (I was off for a few days), but Yes!! Would love to do the story and would definitely love to see the video esp. if it shows DRC staff throwing drugs away that others can get. If you're friend has anything like that – or can get anything like that, call ASAP and I'll go "dumpster diving" to recover the medications for our story

Thanks for thinking of me!

Scott Sayres – Fox 4 News

As donations poured into the city ran Day Resource Center; food, blankets, coats and clothing, the City Staff would have the first pickings, taking whatever they wanted or could sell to make a little extra money. Someone donated boxes of new "Starter Jackets" not one made it to a homeless person. Even the City Police on security would take their choice of food donated.

In addition to the rampant theft, employees were taking peoples belongings and throwing them away or just placing them outside the doors for anyone to rummage through. Often times, these belongings had psychotropic medications. It wasn't people without homes that the City were abusing and stealing from; it was disabled individuals with mental illness. Alzheimer's, Parkinson's, Bipolar, Schizophrenia, Major Depression Disorder. Included were those with diabetes. The conditions had to be reported.

7/24/2005 Publication: THE DALLAS MORNING NEWS reprint with permission
Headline: Giving them shelter Stench, heat, crowds endured for a place to rest their heads
Byline: KIM HORNER
Credit: Staff Writer

Kim Horner's report along with the photographs by Mona Reeder of the Dallas Morning News provided a detail representation on the conditions surrounding the City ran shelter. Kim and Mona came to the Day Resource Center at dusk and stayed the entire night. City employees at first tried to stop the Dallas Morning News from doing the story and from entering into the building, without success. The story made the front page of the Sunday Edition. A photograph captured a young women lying on the pavement, the look on her face said it all. The article stands today as the testament of the abuses by City Hall, which had claimed our homeless.

From: James Waghorne

To: Tulin Ozdeger – National Law Center of Homelessness and Poverty

Subject: Article: Night on street is far from restful – Dallas Morning News

Sent: Monday, July 25, 2005

Hello Tulin,

I thought you would find this interesting. I've been harassed because of the media attention to the point a City Dept. head and the manager of homeless services demanded a meeting with my two supervisors for the company I work with and try to force me to stop talking. Any Suggestions?

James

The compliancy of City Hall was never more evident than when the lease for the Day Resource Center was running out. Without any options for the City, the property owners held all the cards in the deck. To sign a new lease, the City would agree to only open the center during normal business hours, seven days per week and would have to do approximately $300,000 of improvements for the owners. This meant finding a new location for the 300 who slept at the center. No one could even imagine what the City chose to do.

January 31, 2006

The City had told the homeless and others that new arrangements were to be made for the upwards of 300 disabled homeless staying at the Day Resource Center. Discussions about a warehouse on the property where the new HAC (homeless assistance center) was to be built; could provide for all with $95,000 in renovations and improvements. Everyone had been placed at ease.

Tyrone, a formerly homeless and city employee at the Day Resource Center had been a great ally. Often times he would relay to me what was said during meetings regarding the Day Resource Center. He had a tape recording of a meeting held at City Hall concerning what would become the eviction of the 300 disabled homeless out to the streets. No place to go. As I listened to the recording, I felt sick to my stomach. Police would raid them February 1st early morning, harassing them throughout the entire day, not even allowing them to stand still. It was open haunting season on the homeless. Press would be told that arrangements had been made with boarding facilities to waive their fees. Not one place agreed to waive their fees for two years. And none of the facilities had adequate training to handle disabled mentally ill. Another 2 winters and scorching summers, they would be forced to sleep outside and pray to survive every night. The warehouse still sits empty today.

I filmed the events that morning starting at 5AM and continued the rest of the day; police started driving these individuals out into the streets and towards south Dallas.

On this day, the City would also start to enforce the new Food Ordinance, which would cause many of these to go hungry and without food.

Headline: 2/9/06 Video captures officer's attack on homeless individual

City officials who saw the video said Officer Matlock's behavior was unacceptable. "I expect the behavior of all our employees to treat all our citizens appropriately (and) respectfully and this does not appear to be what happened," said Dallas City Manager Mary Suhm "…We will not accept that at all."

The next day, City Hall employees and City Hall police started to inquire about my schedule, when I take lunch and my whereabouts. My employer, Dallas MetroCare Services, relocated me away from the Day Resource Center due to concerns about my personal safety. My concerns about City Hall Police with reason, last till this day.

To: James Waghorne
CC: "Tulin Ozdeger"
Subject: Targeting of the Homeless in Dallas
Date: Fri, 10 Feb 2006 15:59:40 -0500

Dear Mr. Waghorne,

I saw the video clips that you had referred Ms. Ozdeger at the NLCHP to. This is exactly the type of evidence we need. Having some of the homeless who have been injured directly join in the case as parties, including Mr. Green, would be beneficial to a case brought against the City of Dallas. Do you know of any directly injured persons who would be interested in participating in a lawsuit should we be able to go forward with one?

Thank you for your assistance.

Candace Kaiser
HOWREY, LLP
1111 Louisiana, 25th Floor
Houston, Texas 77002

In Dallas though, not even God or those who served Him were safe from the City.

Reprint Courtesy Associated Press: By MATT CURRY, Associated Press Writer Thu Mar 9, 2006

DALLAS - Panhandling banned. Shopping carts prohibited on city streets. The distribution of food to the homeless restricted to designated areas.

With a series of ordinances governing its growing homeless population, Dallas is gaining a reputation as a city uncharitable toward some of its neediest citizens.

The National Coalition for the Homeless recently ranked Dallas sixth among the Top 10 "meanest" cities in the country.

Dallas officials say they are trying to steer the homeless toward help and make the streets a little safer for them. But advocates for the estimated 9,000 homeless people in Dallas say the city is pursuing a harsh and pitiless policy.

"That's like a form of social Darwinism, if you cut off food to force people to get help, and it really doesn't work that way," said Michael Stoops, acting executive director of the National Coalition for the Homeless.

"It's OK to sell someone a sandwich, but if I hand a sandwich to a homeless person, I'm committing a crime," groused Charles Wellhausen, a volunteer for the Sathya Sai Baba Center.

Boadicea White, the city's interim manager for homeless services, "We're definitely not trying to starve anyone and not trying to keep anyone from services," she said. "We're trying to do just the opposite."

James Waghorne, a 48-year-old advocate for the homeless, said the new ordinance will lead more people to eat out of the trash. He said he received food from a charitable organization during the two years he lived on the streets.

"It really wasn't so much about the food, but that someone still cared," he said.

Nationally, 28% of homeless persons say they sometimes or often do not get enough to eat, with 20% eating one meal a day or less. In the last 30 days, 40% of Americas homeless went one or more days without anything to eat because they could not afford food.

In the end, we will remember not the words of our enemies, but the silence of our friends.
                                              Martin Luther King Jr.

Even for the secular community, it is important to acknowledge the interaction between faith and poverty. Not to promote Christianity or any other faith; religion and the poor are inseparable. Every religion has doctrine and teachings concerning the poor. God and the poor are joined at the hips. Throughout our world history, as religion goes so goes human suffering and how it is addressed.

Sadly, today in Dallas, the acts of many below would make them criminals.

November 2001

I needed a lift up after my experience in the Salvation Army. Luke and Carol told me about this small ministry named, "Butterflies from Heaven", and this girl named Cindi Appleberry who I should get in touch with. After multiple misses of connecting, one day in November while I was doing my "Endless Choices" papers at an intersection, a young woman stopped at the red light, signaled me over to her little Ford Escort. Walking over towards her hoping to make a donation, she explained she didn't have any money, but wanted to let me know she works with a ministry for the homeless.

In an instant, I said, "Your name is Cindi." Here eyes got as wide as saucers.

The excerpt below is reprinted with Butterflies from Heaven and Cindi Appleberry's permission from her memoirs and accounts of those involved in the ministry.

Friday, December 21, 2001, Dallas, TX Cindi's Account

I stopped by the Compass Bank today to pick up the donations that were collected for the ministry. My best friend, Suzi followed me to the bank, and took some toys to distribute herself, to a family that is dire need. It is so good to know that there are people out there that want to help those that are so desperately in need. But the time I finished loading my car, I could not see out the back window. Praise You, Lord Jesus! You have blessed us abundantly! I headed home to get ready to travel to Shreveport. I didn't want to spend any of the holidays by myself! As I passed a corner, I saw James Waghorne standing there, distributing his papers. I did a flip, and went back to visit with him. He was so surprised to see me, as he thought I had already left town. He told me that they had a memorial service for all the homeless that had died in Dallas this year… a total of 63. He said it was a beautiful service, and if he had known I was in town he most certainly would have invited me. I left, after telling him of our plans to be back on Sunday to deliver a huge Christmas dinner to the homeless. I invited him to go along, telling him that everyone else wanted to meet him. We all anxiously await Sunday!

Pastor Todd's account of Saturday, December 22, 2001, Dallas, TX

My conclusion; Here we go again! W should have been leaving Mt. Pleasant, Texas by at least 7:00 p.m. but delays have hit me again. We had hoped to be able to shop for Christmas dinner for our friends and get ham cooked early but Satan is trying to discourage me again. I am getting frustrated because I am 2 hours late again. I have tried not to let it get to me but it is difficult because I want to be in Dallas now. But as it always does, we finally get on our way. This time Cindi is riding back to Dallas with us since she came home Friday. We are all excited about being able to gibe the homeless a good Christmas dinner. We stopped in Rockwall at the Walmart to get the food we bought: a very large ham, yams, green beans, stuffing, rolls and cranberry sauce. When we were finished we had a meal fit for a king. We rushed to Cindi's apartment to start the ham cooking. The excitement was evident in us all; we could hardly wait until morning.

Sunday, December 23, 2001

I am up early to take out the ham and begin preparing the rest of today's feast. I got the yams cooking then Cindi and I went to get some paper plates and something to serve the food in and on the way back home we got a call from James Waghorne, the man that Cindi met who lives with the homeless and spreads the Gospel to them as one of them. I was excited to meet him because I had a feeling he was going to be an important part of our ministry, and, as I would find out later this would be an understatement. James had a man with him who was homeless; his name was Bar-B-Q Bob. We told Bob that we would be right back with a wonderful Christmas Dinner for home. We were then off to the apartment to finish food preparations. When we got back, Benji, Cindi's brother and his wife Bonnie had arrived. After introductions were made we took a chance to get to know James while we finished with the food. James led us in prayer and we loaded up and headed out. James led us to our first gentlemen whose names were Jerry, Bobby and Greg; they were so surprises to see us with this huge banquet of food for them. We told them to be sure to get all they could stand because we didn't want them to walk away hungry. We next hurried to the church where Buddy went so we could meet with Rev. Walker and give him some toys that we received from Compass bank, so he could give them to some needy people, which he knew. We were then off to find Bar-B-Q- Bob. When we got there, James went to find Bob and see if there was anybody else in the area. Bob soon returned, then James with a man named Eric. They both loaded up their plates and after sharing some conversation with the two, we were off to find others. As we came to an intersection to, out left we saw our old friend Roy walking down the sidewalk. Cindi rolled down the window and told him to wait and meet us in the parking lot behind him. Roy was glad to see us and I was especially glad, because the last time I saw him he was in intensive care. The first thing Roy did was to show us with pride the Bible that we had given him. I fixed Roy a plate and helped him sit on the curb to enjoy his meal. We kept having to insist that he eat, but he was excited to see us and was afraid we were going to leave him. Cindi assured him that we were not going anywhere that we would stay and talk to him awhile. But after awhile we had to be on our way again. We stopped by a building that used to be a post office annex that James had told us about. This would make a great place to base the ministry. We all stood around for a few minutes wishing that God would somehow get us a building like this. Then from around the corner Buddy appeared and this time he had his wife Robin with him. James had said that they were back together earlier in the day so we didn't think we would get to see him today but, there he was clean shaven and looking very happy. He said robin was helping him get a job at Home Depot. It was so good to see him again and while we were talking a man named Butch walked up. I had met Butch once before and he had a big yellow dog. He fixed a plate for himself then I fixed a plate for him to take to a friend (Art) that was staying with him. We then said good-bye to Buddy and Robin and were back on the road again. We drove for a while then saw Bruce, a man Kaye and I had met the last time we were out here. Benji yelled out the window for him to meet us in the parking lot behind him. I was glad to see that he remembered us. We prepared a plate for him and again we stood and talked to him while he ate his Christmas Dinner. He told us about himself again but this time was able to tell everyone else, not just Kaye and myself. He told us Billy Glenn and Cornbread was over at another corner so we told him that would be our next stop. We drove over to where Billy Glenn and Cornbread were, Cornbread was more than ready to eat, and he loaded his plate. About this time, James brought Billy to the truck. James fixed a plate for Billy but he said he wasn't hungry. I don't feel that this was a true statement. Billy was hungry for love and for someone to talk to, for we stayed and talked to him for 30 minutes or so. Billy also gave Cindi a gift; he had found a watch in the mall parking lot. After visiting with Billy, James took us over close to where his camp was to meet Don and Cajun. As we walked down the narrow path we passed by a small tent where we met James from Sudan. We then met Don who was trying to talk to Cajun into coming out of the tent to eat some fried chicken he had just bought, but the falling temperatures was more persuasive in keeping Cajun in the warmth of his tent and covers. We told Don to save the chicken for later and come have a Christmas Dinner. We stopped by and invited James from Sudan to come and join us for dinner. Once again we loaded plates with food and as Don was getting ready to return to his camp, he told us "God Bless You" it wasn't until later when James explained that Don was a diehard atheist that we understood the importance of that statement. James from Sudan was also very thankful to have the dinner. We were off again to another place that James W. knew of, by this time we were just about out of food. We drove behind a supermarket, which was next to an overpass; James W. was off to find another one of his friends. He soon returned with Luis, a Hispanic gentleman that spoke very little English, it was time for Bonnie to help us out. She was truly an asset to us today. I think the fact that we had someone that could speak with him moved him. We gave him the last of our food and he gave each one of us several hugs as the tears ran down his cheeks. James helped him take his food to his camp while we put everything back up. With the day over, we all went to eat and get James a good meal also. We had to go by storage and we found a Christmas tree someone had thrown away. Someone had the idea of loading it up and taking it to the camp where Don and Cajun were, so after a good meal, we went back to Cindi's and helped Benji and Bonnie get ready to go back home. Then Cindi, James, Kaye, and I went to take the tree to Don's camp and take James home. James and I unloaded the tree and I found some canned food, some Bibles, and tracts to give Don and Cajun. It was after 10:00 pm when James and I went walking down the dark narrow path to the camp. As we were walking several thoughts came to mind, first was that if my mother could see me, she would have a stroke, second, the absence of fear and presence of complete confidence that God was with me. We delivered the tree and food but Don and Cajun were already in their tent trying to stay warm and didn't get up. James placed the food in the tent at their feet and told them to look for a surprise in the morning when they woke up. We then said good-bye to James as he left to go to his camp. My conclusion, Satan had me upset over delays Saturday but I see now he was just trying to discourage me. From this day forward I will look at these delays as a promise of good things to come. So Satan, next time you decide to discourage me, I know your game plan; so try very hard…I know something GREAT is coming from God.

A note from Cindi, May 7 2002

It has been such a very long time since any of us have written in the diary. So much has happened with the ministry, though we have all been so busy. We are seeing God move in miraculous ways! I don't even know where to begin. Being that my full time job is for a CPA firm, the last 4 months have been very busy and hectic for me. The ministry work had come to pretty much a screeching halt, as I began working more hours. But though the ministry was not much of an "organized effort", many things have happened.

A note from Cindi, July 8, 2002

So much has happened in the last few months, since the last entry. I have been in the hospital with pneumonia, Luke, Carol and Lee came to visit me at the hospital, and James told me that Bar-B-Q Bob and Don were praying for me. It warms my soul to know they pray for me as I do them. This past Saturday, Kaye and Todd came over, and we went searching for our friends. We had no food, no clothing, nothing but ourselves. We found Luke, Bob, don and another gentleman we had never met, under a tree. When we drove up, Bar-B-Q Bob jumped up and ran over to me first; giving me the biggest hug I had ever received. He told me he had been praying for me. Tell me that doesn't humble a soul! We had a very nice visit with everyone, and had to be on our way. A few statistics for our readers. We have now seen 19 of our friends get off the streets. Praise God for His miraculous wonders! And God bless each of you!!!

In loving memory of Roy: Where do I begin when it comes to Roy? Roy is one of the sweetest men I ever met. Though he was homeless, he had a heart so full of love and warmth and a smile that brightened any place he walked into, Roy, as many who are on the streets, was an alcoholic. I worried about him so much, especially as his belly grew bigger and bigger from the liver disease that he was fighting.

Roy survived being struck by a car, and was in the hospital for several days, unconscious to what was going on around him. We, as a group, visited him in the hospital and left him a Bible. He did not know we were there, but when he got out, and next we saw him, we all received the biggest smile as he pulled out his Bible. He told us he cried when he saw what we had left him, and he considered that Bible to be his most precious worldly possession. We had written an inscription in the very front, and he opened the Bible, caressing the pages lovingly. I'll never forget that...a man, who had nothing, taught me so much!! Roy is the one, that when we delivered Christmas dinners in 2001, instead of eating a warm dinner, he wanted to visit with us. He told us he could eat anytime, but he didn't always get to visit with people who truly cared about him, but the food we gave his soul…our time…was so much more important. We lost Roy in August of 2002. The disease finally overtook him, and he went home to be with the Lord. Oh, how Roy loved to talk about Jesus! I know one day I will be hugging him on the streets of gold!!! We held a small service on the Railroad tracks that led to nowhere, where everyone hung out. This was one of the sweetest services I have ever attended. Thank you, Roy, for sharing your life and love with me. You touched our little group so much! We will forever smile fondly on our time with you!!! Rest in peace, my dear friend. You may be gone from this earth, but you are not forgotten.

Clora Hogan was my mentor for advocacy. She was persecuted because of her love and compassion for the homeless and less fortunate. She stood against all who abused the homeless, regardless of their status or religious affiliation. When asked by a reporter, about Clora and why "Endless Choices" folded, a social worker from the Stewpot stated she had burned too many bridges. That wasn't exactly true. Clora told the truth and because of that she was feared. She would be exiled because of her passion for the homeless and her desire to change the system for those she advocated for. The homeless.

January/February 2002 - Endless Choices:
The Uncounted: Sleeping Rough in Dallas
Finding the homeless who live outside shelters is a very daunting task. Except for the obvious, downtown area, where does one look?
James Waghorne, Endless Choices vendor, is one of several homeless or formerly homeless people who serve on a committee of the Metro Dallas Homeless Alliance and is helping to conduct this year's survey of Dallas' homeless.
James and I set out with my car full of coats, donated by Holy Spirit Catholic Church in Duncanville and "Love Bags", (containing snacks, toiletries, and socks) donated by the Eddy Family and the Quality Assurance Department at Ernst and Young, Certified Public Accounts. It was cold on this day. The temperature the night before was thirty-four degrees. The people we met living in the campsites seldom, if ever, go into the downtown area or use any of the social services available. They are what are known as "service

resistant" individuals. Their stories of life before they became homeless were different. But today, many of them share the same difficulty, alcohol addiction and a place to be free from hassle and intrusion.

During my lecture, Homelessness 101, people often ask my opinion about giving to panhandlers. This quest to find the uncounted made an answer even more difficult. Most of the people we met were panhandlers.

Yes, some money is used to buy alcohol but they also buy food. They do not use taxpayer services or other free services such as eating at the Stewpot. Panhandling is their only means of survival.

Greg and Jerry work together to collect $20 a day. Once that is accomplished they retire to camp. "I always keep some money in my pocket for the next morning." Says Greg. I understood it to mean that being as alcoholic he needed to be sure he had enough money to buy a beer to help him start the day. Greg also starts everyday buying the Dallas Morning News and working the crossword puzzle.

"We don't ask for more than we need." Said Jerry. Their dog, Rufus, is given free care from a nearby veterinarian.

Getting to most of the campsites took some effort. Unlike the visible homeless seen in downtown, the campsites are well hidden and invisible to cars passing by. Near a major intersection of Dallas, we walked through the thickets to get to the tent that Luke and his friend (Carol) called home. Luke worked as a construction worker when he can get the jobs. (Most of these jobs are only given to illegal aliens) He has been homeless periodically for eight years.

Don, a friend visiting Luke, had just learned of programs at the V.A. that would help him as a homeless veteran.

They were grateful for the coats and bags they received. Carol also needed a pair of tennis shoes, but I didn't have her size. "I had a new pair but ran into someone who needed them more than I did." Says Carol, "so I gave them to her."

Meeting Hernando and Luis proved to be a little challenging since I don't speak Spanish and Hernando spoke very little English. He did say he tries to work but on this day he had no job, no money, and no family to help him. Unlike other campsites, theirs was clean and appeared to be uninhabited. They had only a cot and blankets. They live under the bridge of a very busy over-pass. Getting to them meant parking across the street from the bridge then walking through a narrow passage back up to the bridge. Knowing James, they welcomed us into their home.

Another site we visited was located along side a street I travel almost daily. Although I consider myself observant, I never saw this lean-to that was home to Buddy, (Art and Butch and his dog Freeway) Except for Art, they too are panhandlers. Art says he just can't be on the corner asking people for money. He had a good job making $15/hour until recently and hopes to find a new job soon.

The sites we visited were not near one another. Yet the homeless, even if they don't congregate downtown, have a network of friends. They watch out for each other. We asked the people we met of others in camps that may need coats and love bags. Although James already knew of the camps mentioned, they were happy to direct us to others in need. Among the names mentioned most often were those of Perry, John and Debbie.

The three of them work the intersection near my house, and I have known them for over a year. I stop frequently to talk to them and check on their needs. It was New Years Eve, 2000, when I witnessed the police arresting Perry.

They did not take his duffel bag or blankets with them. I convinced my husband to turn the car around so I could retrieve his belongings. The medication inside his bag helped me to identify him and return his things to him. It was through Perry that I met Debbie and John.

Personal changes in my life recently caused my schedule and routine to change. I did not see Perry or Debbie for weeks. Perry called the Endless choices voice mail, leaving a beautiful message of friendship and concern for me. Once again, he proved what I truly believe, "The poor and homeless, have compassion and are worthy of compassion."

I want to thank James for taking me to the campsite. And a special thanks to the people pictured here for letting me into their homes and sharing part of their lives with me. It was learning and giving experience. In the future when I see them, I will not have to wonder if they are really homeless and need my help. I will know them and they will know me as a friend.

Clora D. Hogan

February 23, 2007

At a recent presentation during the Irving Coalition Conference: The faces of homelessness. I spoke about fear. Fear that has driven our faith base communities to become fortresses against a world in need. Instead of being the tip of the sword to reach outward, a majority now coward, only ministering inwards to a small social club. A suburb of Dallas, Lake Highlands, was a prime example of that fear in our society. It was not property value or a way of life they seek to protect when signing a petition to bar Americans from their neighborhoods based on a single word, "homeless", but was instead the same historical social disease that has lead many nations and peoples into dark times. It is the same thing, which barred those of Jewish faith to live in neighborhoods, or those who were considered unworthy to have a home in a particular area based on the color of their skin. It is the same social immaturity exercised by children in high school, "who is allowed in our "cliques" and who isn't, strictly based on looks, popularity, cool clothes, cars, etc…" The great irony of fear, the birth child of ignorance and prejudice, is that eventually it will destroy the very thing people want to protect. It will destroy neighborhoods, communities and society.

It was very clear that the leadership in Dallas had poisoned parts of our community and City Hall. Trying to contain the hatred from over taking the entire city would be nothing short of a small miracle.

1/11/06 Dallas -The 'Meanest' City In Texas
Jan 11, 2006 "Blog"
Charles Ft Worth

I live near downtown Dallas, and I say hooray for the "sweeps" of the homeless and getting them out of the library. They have repeatedly sat up camps on vacant lots next to my house and covered them knee-deep in garbage that blows everywhere while dropping their 40-ounce bottles in my yard. Go to the library and you can't get near a computer because they're hogging them all, drooling over gyno-cam porn in full view of children. If you want to be treated with respect, try showing a little bit to other people around you.

Reply-   Jan13, 2006 Jesus Christ Garland

Charles wrote: I live near downtown Dallas… We know you work for the city, we can see your ip, I pity people like you who hate their fellow man instead of helping, criticizing and spreading hate with our words.

There would be many reasons to criticize this city employee listed as Charles for his blog. Using taxpayer's computers for personal use, using taxpayer time to post on web sites. Using City Hall to spread his own bias for his own purposes.

In the final analysis - "ATTITUDE REFLECTS LEADERSHIP"

Chapter 6
Silent Genocide

In today's society, we have not yet stopped the abhorrent act of human sacrifice to false gods; we just changed the methods.

June 1, 2000

The trial began this day for Mr. Robert Sanchez. On November 15, 1999 in Dallas Texas, Mr. Sanchez from the top window of his house ended the life of Mr. William Long with a shotgun blast. According to reports, Mr. Long was trying to get some copper wire from a refrigerator, which was left in Mr. Sanchez's yard. A witness, one of Mr. Sanchez's neighbors stated that he heard Mr. Sanchez yell out a racial slur before firing.

After the Not in my Yard slaying that November day, on June 6, 2000, five days after the trial had started, Mr. Sanchez was a free man and received two years probation for taking Mr. Long's life. The local media referred to Mr. Long as a vagrant and evidently so did the jury, as Mr. Sanchez did not receive jail time for killing Mr. Long. As the media referred to Mr. Long, in life as in death, he was degraded to a vagrant as oppose to a human being.

48 individuals like Mr. Long dehumanized by an economic status, were murdered in 1999.

Six months after this trial ended, I dropped off the face of the known world and entered into this alien existence called homelessness. Like some "B" science fiction movie, Soylent Green, Americas homeless were being cannibalized, feeding the class-ism and political creature of greed. "Soylent Green is homeless people!"

Dallas Soup Kitchen sets new record high in its 27-year history for daily served.
Endless Choices

October 2001

Gregory was walking one late evening down a road, heading to the place that would be out of all the external and internal insanity; he would hopefully find a safe place to sleep for the night. There are only two priorities for a homeless individual or family, the first is to survive the day and the second is to survive through the night. No one will ever know what Gregory was thinking when Chante Mallard's vehicle careened into him, impaling his body into the windshield or what he thinking as Chante continued to drive home as his life blood drained away and pain racked through every nerve as she drove around the curves and over bumps in the road. No one will ever know what Gregory was thinking as Chante parked the car in the garage with him still stuck in the windshield, crying desperately for help from the nurses aide, as she turned off the lights and went inside her home while he finally gave up his last breath sometime that night or maybe a day later. But somewhere along the line, because Gregory was homeless, maybe he thought he had become invisible.

I empathized traveling down a dark cold road both physically and mentally, only hoping to find a safe place from harm to lie down. I empathized crying out to no avail. I knew the emotions surrounding the lost of purpose and self-value. I also understood a system not set up to empower and heal, but instead, keeping you down.

The suffering of such plight creates a bond beyond the common social barriers that separate people. There are over 20 million stories in America about becoming homeless, but there is only one story of suffering.

Las Vegas, NV 2001

Ty and his other college buddies had used "chronic homeless" to shoot what became a million dollar video. "Chronic Homeless" by definition according to the U.S. Department of Housing and Urban Development, is a disabled citizen who has been homeless for at least one year or has had four episodes during a three-year period. Upwards to 80% of the "chronic homeless" are disabled with untreated mental illness and most with co-occurring disorder. With his camera crew, Ty would offer these ill and desperate individuals, money to fight each other, smash their heads into objects and perform other atrocious acts to be caught on film.

In three weeks "Bum Fights" sold over 100,000 copies and brought in 2 million dollars. The courts failed to stop their exploitation of the disabled and national stores such as Target jumped on the bandwagon to earn a sleazy buck. The Federal Government failed to protect these disabled citizens even with the American Disability Act in place.

After watching the video, two 19 year-olds grabbed aluminum bats and went to the downtown streets of Los Angeles one early morning. Finding a couple of homeless men sleeping, they beat them with the bats leaving one elderly man in critical condition with severe head wounds. The power of media to inspire evil among men was never more evident. Such heinous acts would spread across our nation and become all too commonplace.

While Ty and his cohorts would be sued and publicly chastised, even disgraced on the floors of our Nations Capital for their acts, I found nothing different in their character from that of local governments who have passed laws abusing Americans without homes in the name of revitalization projects and money.

Early September 2002

We gathered together at the top of the hill in the same place where we would regularly meet every cold morning, escaping the shroud of trees to warm up in the bright sunlight. The homeless, Luke, Carol, myself and also those who had ministered to and befriended us over the past year, Todd, a Baptist Minister, his wife Kaye and Cindi who had started Butterflies from Heaven outreach ministry. As we stood and looked at the homemade wood plank cross with a photograph of Roy tied to the middle, I couldn't help but smile as I remembered the time we had met almost a year ago.

It was last November; Roy was sitting down in the medium at the busy intersection of Lovers and Greenville Ave. A popular spot to "fly a sign". There are two different ways our poor beg. Panhandling amounts to going up to people and verbally asking for change or holding out an object for people to drop change into while "flying a sign" is a small piece of cardboard with written words on it and held out in view for passing cars to see and entice donations. It was always an irony to me that people who gave, considered it compassionate and a donation while those who did not give, considered it an ugly hassle to view such "in your face poverty" that would invade the self-conscience. I myself was guilty at onetime being the latter. We called our cardboard signs a credit card because it was small enough to fold up and placed in our back pocket for safekeeping. Also, it was a quick way to hide it when the police were around or as we called them, Po-Po or five-O. One way to tell the difference between con artists and true homeless is by the size of their sign. Homeless don't have the money to waste ink on making a big sign.

Though Roy never mentioned to me directly, his running dogs told me he was a Vietnam Veteran. Bitter by the treatment of his own government and community when he got back home, Roy's only solace now was found in a bottle of Wild Irish Rose or Cisco, cheap wines that had taken down many homeless.

Wrapped in a blanket, still wearing the hospital gown and the hospital band around his wrist; he wore a pair of ill fitting shorts tied with a rope to keep them from falling down, no shoes and a pair of crutches beside him. Roy was happily content; smacking down on the 7-11 hot dog someone had given him. He was every bit the pitiful sight that the kitten was when I first saw him.

Roy explained he had just gotten out of Baylor Hospital after having been hit by a car. He didn't know for sure but thought he had spent about ten days in I.C.U. All too often compassion at hospitals is reserved for the insured as I had witnessed many homeless patients from hospitals dumping them back out into the streets and even experienced this firsthand. Still dazed and confused, Roy was doing the only thing he had known for the last fifteen years. Survive by flying a sign to get money to eat and self medicate to dull the pain and quiet the internal demons.

Roy roamed around more than most river rats. We preferred to set up a campsite or have specific safe places scoped out to sleep every night. Not Roy, he traveled from site to site sometimes sleeping wherever that night's bottle ran dry, his mind numb to whatever pained him. Regardless of his illness and past, he was the most humble person I had ever met in my life. Whenever Butterflies from Heaven ministry would bring by hot food, unlike some other homeless who would dive into the food, Roy would put his plate aside and talk to those who came as our acting angels, letting his food even get cold. He was so appreciative of those who would accept him as he was and not judging him. What is human or patriotic that so many who had signed up to serve their nations highest calling in the time of greatest need and then are abandoned in their time of need? I Questioned.

That day as we gathered to say goodbye, I read Emma Lazarus's poem, which is place in the foundation holding up Lady Liberty.

With silent lips, "Give me you're tired, you're poor,

Your huddled masses yearning to breathe free,

The wretched refuse of your teeming shore,

Send these, the homeless, tempest-tossed to me,

I lift my lamp beside the golden door!"

For those of us who had suffered the prejudice of class-ism, those words today were mute and Lady Liberty had become nothing more than a high-class prostitute afforded to only those who could pay the asking price. The homeless that night topped-off a small bottle cap with whiskey, held it up in the air and then tossed the contents to the ground before each sharing a swig from the bottle in toast to what we called the Silent Genocide. While the official cause of death will go down as cirrhosis of the liver, Roy died from the most common death experienced in our homeless community. Hopelessness...

Goodbye Roy.

James, hands Roy and Bobby love bags. They also received coats. Unlike the other people we met this day Roy and Bobby aren't out of sight. They sleep among retail stores located just north of downtown.

November/December 2002 Endless Choices: 1 Meningitis death - 2 ill in homeless shelter. Dallas County slow reacting. 1,500 homeless to be vaccinated

March 2003

Mankind has found many ways to kill a person without actually taking their lives. Sherry asked if she could come over to my apartment and talk. Sherry wasn't a full time homeless person though. She would end up on the streets two to three times a year, running away from her spouse who would beat her regularly. I first met her when Eric brought her to our campsite when I was staying with Bar-B-Q and Don near the old Katy Trail RR. She was very attractive, long brown hair, beautiful face with full lips and a slender body with all the right curves.

She was more than just friendly and as I was shy around ladies, this made me uncomfortable. I let her stay in my hooch that night as I slept outside, even though she had invited me to sleep with her. It was rumored she had been sleeping with many of the homeless who stayed over in the Lovers and Greenville Ave. area and that sometimes for liquor, she would prostitute.

It was visually obvious why some men would be tempted. It was hard for me to understand why she didn't file for divorce and leave her husband. Maybe it was her three children, or that she didn't have a job, or yet the threats of violence. I remember the time her husband came looking for her; gun in hand.

Inviting her into my apartment, I sat down on the couch. I was a bit nervous, aware of her appetite for sex, but I wanted to help. If she would open up, maybe I could find some answers to her ghosts.

"James," she said sitting near me, her hand on my thigh, "you've known for over a year now, I've been attracted to you, why won't you have sex with me? Are you Gay?"

That question had been asked before because of my profound beliefs against casual sex. I turned a shade of red as I felt the blood rush to my head. Her boldness was unsettling.

"No." as I drop the tone of my voice two octaves sounding as manly as possible.

"What, do you have a problem, because if you do we can just have oral sex. You do like oral sex don't you?"

I started to feel trapped, as if I was surrounded by a pack of use car salesmen.

"I just want to have sex with you, not because you physically turn me on, but because of what's inside you."

Not exactly music to my ears. I knew that I wasn't a physical specimen, but this knowledge didn't make it any easier hearing it from a beautiful woman.

"Why do we have to have sex? Now angered.

"I just want to talk to you. What is it with you and sex all the time? There's more than sex. Tell me, why do you have to have sex with everyone?"

Tears filled her eyes from the sting of my words and I thought that maybe my abrasiveness would drive her away.

"Sherry, please tell me what is wrong?" I prodded softly.

She turned her head away and stared down at the floor. Moments passed.

"What?" I urged.

"I'm remembering." She answered.

"The color of my pajamas as I would stand in the hallway. My two little sisters sound asleep. I couldn't stand for him to touch them. Only eight and five years old. So, when I was 10, I would stand in the hallway every night, waiting for Dad to get home from work and from drinking. And I would offer myself to him so he wouldn't touch them. I would offer myself to him."

Her voice breaking and tears flowing freely down her cheeks, she turned her face back to mine, looking right into my eyes, "I don't know anything but sex."

My heart ached and I did the only thing I knew. I hugged her. I was not the person who could help her. I knew I was the wrong person needed for the job here.

I walked her back to Eric's and Clark's apartment, knowing well that they would take advantage of her past and that she would feel temporarily valued because of it. I haven't seen Sherry since; though I was told one day she came looking for me. The word on the street, she finally did leave her husband and is now prostituting somewhere in South Dallas, doing the only she knows to be of value and loved.

April 25, 2003

If you shipped Butch to the North Pole and dressed him in Elves clothing, you would have the perfect looking Santa helper. I wonder today why he never worked the department stores during the holiday season. He was as unthreatening as an ant to an elephant, so what happened that early morning could only be described as hate driven. Art and Butch, along with their big yellow dog, Freeway, stayed behind some apartments alongside the creek on the edge of "crack hill". They were fixtures in the area and at the intersections of Park Ln. & Central Expressway. Butch was found early morning around 2 AM in the parking lot close to their site one night. He was busted up and was unconscious. The viciousness of the attack left Butch in critical condition. The damage from the kicks to the head and face, left Butch severely brain damage and eventually we heard that he would end up in a nursing home. The police would state they didn't know if a car had hit Butch or if something else happened. Art knew it was the gang, which frequented the nightclub in the shopping center close by. Later, the same gang would stab Art in the foot before he fended them off with a club. Sadly, that's not the end to the cruelty of this story.

A women hearing about the tragedy went to Art and offered to take Freeway, their dog, for veterinarian care and have him checked out, paying whatever the bill might be. Art agreed with the plan because she was to bring Freeway back to him. The woman's generosity made for a heart-warming story in the Dallas Morning News, except for Art.

As Art was recounting what happened, tears welled up in his eyes, he called and called Ms. Chernoff to return Freeway back to him. As Art said in the article, "He's our buddy dog. He's like Butchy's son and I'm the Uncle." For all of us who knew Butch and Art, Freeway was part of their family. Crushed by the events, Butch and now Freeway lost, Art disappeared. For the homeless, the heart often dies long before the body goes.

June 2003 - Homeless man discovered murdered in posh "M" streets area. Gunshot wound to the head cited as the cause of death.

From: "Endless Choices"

To: "James Waghorne"

Subject: Re; Homeless Memorial

Date: Thu, 18 Dec 2003

James,

I got a call from the Coroners office – after I sent you the last email – My first contact retired but the new guy is faxing me a list of names (first names only) of people not claimed by families.

Dennis told me about Gerald Joiner – I'd known him for 5 years – not sure what he died of. During the service we have a time for community reflections – when anyone can speak about people they knew who died.

Clora Hogan

Every year, the Memorial would remember upwards to 50 - 60 people. These were only the unclaimed bodies and didn't include those victims who family members did claim the deceased remains of their loved ones after they had been identified.

Dallas City Hall interdepartmental email:

From: "Dave Hogan" <ci.dallas.tx.us>

Subject: Re: Did you guys see this article in this morning DMN

Date: Fri, 16 Jan 2004 19:53:07 – 0600

Boss,

I sure did see it – very, very sad. In a short period of time recently, 3 homeless men have died violently: one was murdered, one burned himself up, and now one was drunk & got squished under a Hummer. Appears homeless men are becoming an endangered species.

Thanks-Dave,

Crisis Intervention

From: "Mariana"
To: James
Date: Tue, 09 Aug 2005 15:43:21 +0000

James,

I am teaching a Death Investigation class at Baylor in Waco, Texas this semester. I would like to address some of the issues associated with Death and the Homeless population. Would you be available to speak to my class on Monday at 5pm? I know it's a little bit of a drive for you but I know the students would welcome your knowledge.

Mariana

Mariana and I had met at a public art exhibit benefiting our homeless. Certainly I was a little surprised to meet someone from the Dallas County Morgue at such an exhibit but Mariana worked as an investigator helping to find families for the nameless. I admired her dedication to help bring closure for families who had lost loved ones. From June 2003 until January 2004, I had volunteered myself with helping Julie, a social worker employed at Baylor Hospital. She often called me from the I.C.U. located in the Roberts building, asking my assistance to help the hospital in trying to locate families for those homeless who had life threatening injuries, illnesses and were incapacitated. Without fieldwork, it's almost an impossible job.

Mariana emailed me this day about the man found floating in Turtle Creek.

To: Mariana
From: Trumpetcall
Subject: Turtle Creek Man

It was a pleasure to meet you and your husband the other night at Hal's photo show. I'm going down to Turtle Creek today to ask around about the deceased individual. Did you have a cause of death? Also, I'm putting together a report impart to show the need of what we discussed that night. I'm trying to find out how many homeless were victims of "hit and run's" during the last ten months. Could you assist me in anyway on this? Thanks again and I'll let you know what I find out.

James K. Waghorne - Dallas Homeless Neighborhood Association

From: "Mariana

Date: Tue, 30 Mar 2004 15:44:41 +0000

To: trumpetcall@mail.com

Subject: RE: Turtle Creek man, Hero to Zero, Other

James,

It was great meeting you too. I asked about any abnormalities in the feet and legs of the man found in Turtle Creek. I read the autopsy report and there was no mention of anything out of the ordinary. The cause and manner of death are pending toxicology. Usually those results come back in two months. Good luck with your search today. I am off from work today and tomorrow. When I get back there on Thursday I will work on a search of "hit and run" homeless people. There should be a few for this year. I will also try to make a general list of our deceased homeless people.

Mariana

Date: Fri, 09 Apr 2004 11:48:44 -0600

To: "Mariana

Subject: RE: Turtle Creek man, Hero to Zero, Other

Hello Mariana,

Update, I found someone who says he knows the man who died in Turtle Creek. His name was Dickey. He has a sister who lives here in town (Park Cities Area). I hope to get her name tonight when I go back over there to talk to another guy. Dickey was said to be a "Coke" addict. WM 50's long stringy hair, beard, thin build. He once owned his own florist here in town. I was told his sister had taken over the business when Dickey suffer a Major Depressive Episode. If you already know please email me, otherwise I will continue to gather info and send to you.

Best Regards

James

From: "Mariana

Date: Sat, 10 Apr 2004 16:21:30 +0000

To: James Waghorne

Subject: RE: Turtle Creek man, Hero to Zero, Other

James,

I will write a supplement to the case with this info. He is still not identified. This info. is really helpful

Mariana

From: James Waghorne <trumpetcall@mail.com>
To: Mariana
Subject: RE: Turtle Creek man, Hero to Zero, Other
Date: Mon, 12 Apr 2004 12:17:25 -0600

Hello Mariana,

I hope to find Butch today or tomorrow to get Dickey's last name. While I was doing outreach, a homeless friend told me they found Debbie Townsend dead at her campsite. Have you heard anything more from her since you last saw her? It could be a rumor started by John.

James

From: "Mariana
To: James Waghorne
Subject: RE: Turtle Creek man, Hero to Zero, Other
Date: Tue, 13 Apr 2004 00:54:02 +0000

James,

I saw Debra because she was deceased. I got a call from a Dallas officer last week. He was with her friend James Seward. (AKA John) The officer was inquiring as to what Funeral Home Debra went to. She went to Indiana where her family lives. Her cause of death is pending toxicology. The officer said he was buying James a bus ticket to go to Indiana. I gave them contact info. for Debra's family. Hope to hear more about Dickey soon.

Mariana

The body of Dickey evidently had been in the water for a long time because his features were too damaged for a picture I.D. That meant going to the camps along Turtle Creek and talking with the homeless in the area.

The Turtle Creek area in Dallas is not exactly where you would think to find homeless. When the Prince of Saudi Arabia comes on a trip to Dallas, he rents a couple of floors at the famed five stars Turtle Creek Mansion. Multi-million dollar homes and multi-million dollar high-rise lofts cover the landscape. Running through the area is a beautiful stream named Turtle Creek. Wealth abounding all around, for the homeless here it must had resemble how the wayward mariner felt, "Water, water everywhere and not a drop to drink."

I spent two weeks in the area, tracking down campsites and homeless living there. My firsthand experience gave me a clear advantage on how to find those who didn't wish to be found, but even knowing the homeless language and how to act socially, I could only find out limit information. His street name "Dickey", he was from Dallas and had a sister living here. At one time he owned a flower shop. Turtle Creek man suffered severely from depression and used cocaine. That was all the information I could find out about a man who lived better than 50 years. Just over three sentences.

Debbie Townsend also was part of our tribe. She was a fixture along Walnut Hill and Central Expressway, along with John, (James Steward) her boyfriend, Maggie their dog and their cat Blue, which she kept in a baby carriage.

She was close friends with homeless advocate, Clora Hogan, who would often times bring them food and give a little money when available.

They camped in the woods, close by Presbyterian Hospital. Arguments and fighting (domestic violence) is common for those couples living on the streets. The stress mixed with mental illness and self medication lends itself for a volatile existence. John and Debbie were sadly a typical example. After such a case, John left the campsite, only to come back find Debbie dead. I didn't contact Mariana later to find out what the Coroner had said was the cause of death; it was the same cause for everyone else. We knew another had become victim to the "Silent Genocide". Debbie was one of the lucky ones. They found her family in Indiana and her body was sent to have a proper burial. Dallas County had decided to balance their budget and save $75 per human being by cremating, instead of burying the less fortunate and those unclaimed. It made for a sick logic, if were not going to provide them with housing and proper services while alive, why treat them with dignity in death.

Two years later, John (James Steward) would be found murdered in a City park. 2004 saw many multiple violent deaths among our homeless. March saw three die violently not unlike January, and while they each are tragic, questions surrounding Mr. Clarence Noble Jr.'s death have not been answered to this day. He died after being released from police custody at the detention center.

Marianna was able to provide me with the information I was looking for. It not only proved that an average of 50 homeless individuals were found dead on the streets every year, but when combined with the deaths in the hospitals, the number would be closer to 150 and 175. City Hall would not be able to hide this human tragedy and shame forever.

DCME #	Age/Race /Sex	Last name	First name	Date of Death	Place Found	Cause of Death	Manner of Death
0023-04		Unknown		01.02.04	100 S. Stemmons	Blunt Force Injuries	Accident
0041-04	47WM	Guess	Michael	01.02.04	5119 Lawnview	Acute ethanol intoxication associated with thermal injuries	Accident
0182-04	51BM	Bell	Felix	01.13.04	2100 Block Market Center Blvd.	Multiple Blunt Force Injuries	Accident
0188-04	22BM	Bluitt	Harold	01.14.04	1500 N-IH35	Blunt Force Injuries	Accident
0248-04	47WM	Hamman	Larry	01.17.04	5302 Harry Hines Blvd.	Cardiac Hypertrophy of unknown origin	Natural
0348-04	64WM	Durant	Fredrick	01.25.04	5203 Harry Hines Blvd.	Critical coronary athersclerosis	Natural
0441-04	50BM	Coffey	Bobby	02.03.04	300 S. Marsalis Ave.	AIDS	Natural

0768-04	48BM	Nobles	Clarence Jr.	03.03.04	1600 Chestnut	Spontaneous"stroke" due to HT & ASCVD II Hep B and C; chronic alcoholism	Natural
0869-04	50-60M	Unknown		03.10.04	3400 Block of Turtle Creek	Undetermined	Undetermined
0873-04	38WF	Avant	Robin	03.11.04	5500 Maple Ave.	Sharp force injuries	Homicide
0898-04	26WF	Peden	Tiffany	03.12.04	8900 Block of East RL Thorton	Acute pyelonephritis II Chronic alcoholism	Natural
0937-04	30-30WM	Unknown		03.16.04	7100 Block of John Carpenter	Multiple Blunt Force Injuries	Accident
0996-04	54WM	Cook	James Allen	03.20.04	4318 Harry Hines Blvd. #2	Peritonitis due to perforation of duodenum due to peptic ulcer	Natural
1160-04	47WF	Townson	Debra	04.01.04	8000 Block of Walnut Hill	Acute pyelonephritis II Chronic alcoholism	Natural
1194-04	47BM	Morgan	Michael A.	04.04.04	3511 E. Kiest Rm 219	Toxic effects of Cocaine, II HT & ASCVD and smoking	Accident
1354-04	45LF	Gonzalez	Bonny	04.16.04	800 N. Stemmons	Blunt Force Injuries	Accident
1359-04	37WM	Aleshire	John	04.16.04	800 N. Stemmons Frwy.	Blunt Force Injuries	Accident
1364-04	53BM	Gillins	Robert	04.17.04	3011 Park Row Ave. #164	Toxic effects of Heroin	Accident
1399-04	42BF	Erhabor	Michele Sharese	04.19.04	5455 Blair Rd.	Toxic effects of cocaine in combination with HT &ASCVD	Accident
1584-04	34LM	Saenz	Norberto Ochoa	05.07.04	12000 CF Hawn Frwy	Multiple Blunt Force Injuries	Accident

| 1767-04 | 51BM | Chatman | Leon | 05.22.04 | 4130 Gaston Ave. (on street) | Multiple stab wounds | Homicide |
| 1300-04 | 45WM | Sanford | Donald | 05.25.04 | 2936 Rolinda Dr. | Hanging | Suicide |

To: "James Waghorne"
Subject: RE: Homeless Victim
Date: Wed, 24 Mar 2004 10:10:54-0600
James,
Found out about Clarence Noble. They are awaiting toxicology tests before making a ruling. Unfortunately these things take quite a while when law enforcement isn't pushing for it. The tests usually take about 6-12 weeks to come back. I have it on my list to start checking in early April. Michael – DallasMorningNews

Headlines: 5/11/04 MD. Man sentenced in homeless deaths
Harold "Jay" Waterbury, 20, was convicted to life in prison without parole for his part in the death of three homeless individuals. Mr. Waterbury stated he was doing "Bum stomping" and was involved in a systematic cleansing…to kill homeless people in and around south Baltimore.

October 28, 2004
I first met Bill outside the Stewpot, the only soup kitchen located in Dallas. Gingerly walking with his cane, he stopped, leaned against the brick wall and slowly slid down to a seat. Bill was a puzzle to me. He harbored great anger against the government that had turned its back on him, yet he loved to talk about his military career and his fondness of electronics he had honed while serving. He dreamed of a day when he would be able to open his own shop. Unfortunately such dreams and hopes while homeless can be more a hindrance, than a motivating factor.
Most of our downtown homeless now would take refuge and sleep on the sidewalks outside the City ran Day Resource Center Unable to pay the shelter prices and a lack of available beds in Dallas, up to 300 stayed in the downtown area at night, while the other

700 found more isolated areas. Bills declining health didn't afford him to travel far, so Bill became a downtown fixture, using his wheelchair as both a walker and a carrier for his belongings.

That evening Bill and David (another veteran) had taken their spot for the night at the corner of the building, near the entrance to the Resource Center. The nights in downtown were the prime business hours for the drug dealers to come and prey on the homeless taking their Social Security or day labor money. The Dealers set up shop just around the corner in front of the old synagogue. For as little as one dollar, you could relieve the suffering and mental illness. One of the greatest challenges for an outreach counselor was the fact the drug dealers outnumber us, 100 to 1. Ninety percent of those sleeping outside just wanted to wake up in the morning alive. Bill and David were one of the innocent but that is not protection in the world of desperation and hopelessness, which the homeless live in.

Bill and David were settling in, going through the routine of laying down cardboard and blankets on the hard unforgiving pavement. Rolling a last cigarette and sharing the small talk that takes up most of the homeless day. David was standing while Bill had settled himself down leaning against the brick wall.

Shouts erupted across the street as a small pickup pulls up to another homeless man. Two people, a women and a man, wanted their $5.00 for the drugs they had sold to the homeless individual. Threats were hurled; a knife brandished and the homeless man fled. The woman, Lydia Marie Kelly, jumped behind the steering wheel and her cohort, Dennis Keith Moore, in the passenger seat order her to run the homeless man over. The homeless man ran down the street with the truck racing behind him, the passengers' inside the vehicle intent on ending his life. Trying to dodge, the homeless man veered over towards the sidewalk where Bill and David had sought refuge. The truck turned hard right trying to capture their prey.

According to witnesses, the front bumper hit Bill square in the face and David was struck in the upper chest. The impact pushed both Bill and David through the brick wall and into the security offices inside the building. Another victim, Edward Strickland laid under the truck, trapped. Other homeless who witnessed the tragedy rushed over to try and help their friends in futility while some started to pull the drug dealers out of the truck to beat them. I was told David was almost virtually cut in half and Bill didn't even look human.

David died instantly while Bill agonized until the following day. Mr. Strickland trapped under the vehicle, lived.

At the trial for Mr. Moore, who was sentenced to life for his involvement, Prosecutor David Alex told the jury what 3.5 million Americans know first hand, "These people in our society are invisible. We don't see them in our everyday lives. These people are living, breathing human beings with the right to live in our society. For whatever reason, they were out there on the street when this happened."

It was only when Bill's daughter addressed Mr. Moore about her father that some light of truth about homelessness was shed.

"He helped more people than you can ever hope to redeem yourself with. He was not a nameless nothing on the street. He was not a criminal. He raised children. He had a life. I hope you use some of this time to reflect on that."

Maybe we all could use a little bit of time to reflect on that, because our American landscape has become bloodied with such needless atrocities.

Just A Day in Time – For me Eternity: By Lowell Smith 10/28/04 -Homeless

Well it's another day living on the streets, but this one is different. Yesterday was my birthday. It was cool. I was able to witness a lunar eclipse. I was telling my friends, Bill Banks and David Decker that God must be cool because look at what He showed me on my birthday. It was something that was only visible every many, many years and it was on my birthday.

I was happy and they were happy for me. I shared my whiskey with them and we fell asleep. I remember a thought that came to me to write about, it was "You know something, I thank God, cause I'm learning, even though a lot of the times you get screwed, there's a lot of heart and caring for each other out here on the streets. We come from different cultures and beliefs, but in reality we're all the same." Deep down we all believe in God or something like it. I really believe that's what keeps us alive. A belief in hope, a belief we are worthy of love, respect and the grace of that God, that keeps us going. That's the secret that keeps us all alive for another day!!!

We have all been hurt in one way or another, sometimes we hurt ourselves. This life is sometimes a lot of torture, but it gives a lot of satisfaction. What I'm trying to say, is if you work 9 to 5, you get into a humdrum repetition way of life and even if you go to church, you don't get as close; you don't understand what is being given to you everyday.

Hey, I know I started this writing with 10/28/04; the reason is my friends died on that day. Just sitting against the building talking, when a truck ran over them and took them into the building. I helped another one named Edward that I didn't know. But I couldn't help my friends. That's just how easy it is to lose a friend out here on the streets.

Bill Banks

October 12, 2005 Texas Homeless Network Annual Convention

Mr. Southrey's quote, "Such attacks are not unusual." should send chills down the spine of a normal human being. How is it to be burned alive?

In June 2004, Lucas Wiser, 21, was sleeping on the bench outside Metro Ministries, an agency that helps the homeless. He would have been inside, but all the beds had been taken. During the evening, 7 youths in two vehicles pulled up to where he was sleeping and lit him on fire. Caught on video, Mr. Wiser is seen failing his arms and running trying his best to put the flames out. He survived; suffering third degree burns and is marked with the scares of hate forever.

I admired his courage and that of his family as he stood before the group to tell his story. The tears could not truly define the external pain and internal suffering they had gone through. Still wearing bandages and facing more operations to patch back the mangled burnt skin, I wonder if we could ever patch back humanity.

Rev. Robert Trache, director of Metro Ministries, said Mr. Wiser's incident was the third in a 24 hr. period that day. One other homeless individual had been dragged along the street and the other beaten with a belt buckle.

How many are dieing? The Bush Administration appointed Homeless Czar Phillip Mangano acknowledges the number is over 2,400 citizens in 2005, but advocates estimates are 5 times greater. Upwards to 10,000 American citizens without homes die every year in America.

The wholesale slaughter of Americans has occurred in the darkest annuals of American history and we will never truly know how many Americans without housing have died since 1980. Still it is logical to say the death toll stands at a minimal of 64,000 to a maximum of 250,000 Americans. This is Americas Silent Genocide.

Chapter 7
Dark Secrets of the Social Club

The real heroes are those people who are friends to the poorest of the poor.

Nelson Mandela

The compassion movement to address homelessness in our Nation is unlike any other social movement in our history. Other movements involved just two populations, the victims of injustice vs. the perpetrators. Homelessness has 3 parties involved, the victims (homeless), Social Service Agencies and Government public policy. In Dallas, our homeless social service agency industry accumulates over $60 million dollars per year making status quo very attractive. The human suffering trade business pays some people a nice income and they didn't like the idea of closing it down and ending homelessness. The money spent on homelessness in Dallas equated to $10,000 per homeless individual per year. There was a lot of incentive to keep people homeless and no wonder agencies would fight each other for turf and even dehumanized different segments of the homeless and poor populations in hopes of economic gain for their own nonprofit.

Daniel had been in an dormitory boarding facility for a reported 15 years while the shelter was taking his disability income; sadly it wasn't unusual for such places to take peoples' disability checks as a fee. Those who could work; would pay $5 - $7 per night and those who didn't have a job were forced to work up to 3 hours (less than $2.35 per hr.) in the facility to pay the fee. The homeless seeking refuges in these places were under the constant threat of eviction, as employees use terror tactics. Human maltreatment continues to be reported from these types of facilities across America today and there is a great need to have federal investigations of these places for violations of the American Disability Act and the Fair Housing Act. Local politicians cowered about protecting the rights of the homeless in these places because many advertise themselves as faith based organizations. There are some quality general population shelters but these kinds of organizations are few and far between. Seeing "general population shelters" in America closed down and eventually becoming museum pieces of needless human suffering should become a top priority in our country.

May/June 2001 Shelter denies homeless journalist "Freedom of Speech" – Endless Choices

"Harry Dailey, co-director of Austin Street Shelter, told a reporter that Mr. Hilgers was not barred because of the events of April 11th but rather because of negative press he'd given Austin Street Shelter in the Endless Choices paper."

The first thing I noticed with the shelter system in Dallas was the restrictions of American freedoms. Forget the U.S. Constitution and the Bill of Rights.

Once inside one of these places, be it a shelter or one of the boarding facilities, you belong to them. Freedom of Speech – gone. Freedom of Religion – gone. Freedom of the Press – gone. The second thing I noticed was that if you try to exercise any of these freedoms, out the door you go. Barred from their collectivism charity, they called it "street therapy".

I had a serious problem with those who use threats and terror to proselytize. It didn't match my Christianity as much as my own definition of religious and human abuse. The homeless in Dallas desperately needed an alternative.

Jim Shultz, writer for the Dallas Observer asked the question, "We don't want to build a concentration camp. Right? Not even for ugly, smelly people." Many facilities could already fall under the definition as "re-education camps." Would this carry over to the new Homeless Assistance Center?

The battle to find a location for the new Homeless Assistance Center raged across our entire city. "Not in my Backyard" was flying out of everyone's mouth, from neighborhoods, churches, and developers and of course politicians. The type of people you would expect to have major concerns due to the promoted myths and fears, which surrounded the homeless.

What many people might not understand was why agencies, whose mission it was to help the homeless, didn't want the new center anywhere near them. The Director of the Austin Street Shelter was one of those individuals, becoming crosswise with the Mayor at a public meeting about the purposed location near the shelter. Bubba Dailey would use the same argument as neighborhoods, that undesirable homeless would be attracted to the area.

Dallas lagged behind the rest of the country, when it came to proven innovated services and even more so when it came to social justice and compassion.

The new center would offer a menu of services, a clearinghouse. Services that would help people get out of homelessness and not extend it. Services, which the shelters did not offer. The truth started to emerge that the main issue was "competition".

The Mayor had to tell our homeless service agencies that the City wasn't going into competition with them, trying to calm their nerves. That is how competitive and greedy Dallas services had become, service agencies worried about their own piece of the pie more than the homeless. Of the $60 million coming into agencies, only 14% or $8 million was actually being used to end homelessness and this was one of the primary reasons for the continued growth of homelessness. Dallas shelters only had a 15-20% success rate compared to housing programs that had an 80-85% success rate. Regardless of how a first class Homeless Assistant Center would benefit the entire homeless population and our community; agencies were going to protect their turf, money, and existence. The one City that was leading the way towards eliminating homelessness, Philadelphia, found it necessary that to achieve the goal; they would have to shut down some shelters and forced others to change. The main challenge with many of the agencies is to find quality people who know how to empower others, instead of exercising their own power over others.

The definition of homeless: without a home or haven: should be used as the guide to end homelessness. $60 million dollars per year spent on housing would virtually end homelessness in Dallas and in other major cities in a humane manner, the problem was that it would also end 80% of the agencies, whose programs perpetuated homelessness and benefited them economically. HUD knew this and started to require that 80% of grants monies received by applicants go towards housing. If foundations and donors would make the same demand with their money, homelessness would end in Dallas in less than 48 months.

To: "Vince Golbeck" <vgolbec@ci.dallas.tx.us>
From: "James" trumpetcall
Subject: Could use your help.
Date: Wed, 03 Sep 2003
Hello Vince,
Hope everything is going well with you.

Would like to set up meeting about new policy concerning handing out warnings for "sleeping in public ordinance", also have concerns raised about a particular officers actions towards the homeless. His name is Officer Cephus Gordon III. Would like him to attend the meeting also if possible.

Working hard to get a good communication line opened between Police and homeless; feel addressing issues in an open and in a personal matter will go a long way. What do you think? Please let me know when it would be convenient for you.

James Waghorne

A meeting was held upstairs in the Americorps offices, on the request of Ben Johnson, the VISTA who replaced my position. We needed information about the treatment of the 150 –200 homeless who were sleeping outside the Soup kitchen. Over ninety percent on the Dallas Police Department wanted to improve the community by enforcing laws aimed at the serious crime, which had conquered our City, but instead they were enforcing the new Jim Crow "inequality of life" laws. Not long after the meeting, police and city employees swept into the area throwing away the belongings of our homeless, forcing them from the area. This abuse was unique compared to other 'sweeps' because the orders didn't come from the Castle on the Hill.

October/November 2003 Police raid homeless sleeping in front of area Soup Kitchen, Homeless have their belongings thrown away and are told not to return – Endless Choices

I received the first call from Clora; editor for "Endless Choices" which housed out of the Stewpot about the 'sweep' happening at the location and rushed over. Before leaving my office at the day resource center, I received another call from Ben Johnson, the Americorps VISTA who had taken my place. By the time I had arrived, much of the damage had already been done, without warning; city personnel were throwing away peoples belongings into dump trucks. Park Ave. in front of the Stewpot was where 150 – 200 disabled individuals slept on the sidewalks and the area had been a 'safe haven' for years. They couldn't afford the boarding facilities and were too sick to go to shelters. I didn't have the power to stop what was happening but the one thing I needed to do was to document this cruelty. I asked who called for the sweep and two sources including the police lieutenant in charge told me it was someone from the Stewpot itself who had asked for the sweep.

Certainly, such acts were hidden from the general public by those homeless agencies involved in these actions.

The five intangibles, dignity, empowerment, equality, justice and "Quality of Life", which every human being strives for in life, were nonexistent in Dallas and in many of our services for the homeless.

Dallas Association of Services to the Homeless

DASH Meeting Minutes: 9/28/2000 1:30 the Salvation Army:

Presentation on Safe Haven: It is a form of supportive housing with the following criteria; 1) serves hard to reach homeless adults with severe mental illness, are on the streets and been unable or unwilling to participate in supportive services; 2) provides 24 hour residence for unspecified duration 3) provides private or semi private rooms; 4) has overnight capacity limited to 24 persons.

This coalition of service agencies decided that supportive housing would not be appropriate, but decided it would be better to write HUD instead, to get assistance for purchasing coin operated restrooms for the homeless. No housing but instead pay toilets for those who don't have money. That was the mentality of the Service Agencies.

Paige Flink, Chair for the Homeless Consortium

Guest included: Karen Boudreaux, City manager of the homeless services program; Mary Kay Vaughn, Director City of Dallas Environmental and Health Services Department; Kathy Reid, Director of the Texas Homeless Network

Kathy Reid was asked by the Federal Government to consult how the Consortium should be organized, help with the Continuum of Care process and also input into a merger with DASH and build an effective coalition.

The Homeless Consortium Meeting Minutes: 7/17/01 Kathy Reid

In 1995, the consortium was created to meet quarterly and bring together coalitions. Each year, it became more and more money-driven. Too much emphasis has been placed on funding, she added…

She stated that successful coalitions had it "all together". She believed that we should all come together to plan a way to effectively organize…

A simple political correct way for Kathy to express that the homeless and community was getting "mislead" by the agencies and City Hall. Unfortunately Kathy's recommendation of joining two poisoned coalitions into one just created one large poisoned coalition with the same issues of greed, deceit and arrogance.

Homeless Consortium Meeting: 12/13/01 Chair, Paige Flink

II. Paige provided an update on the OIG Audit recommendations; the work products that OIG will require to clear the audit; the various roles and responsibilities of HUD, City of Dallas staff, Consortium members and Texas Homeless Network; and establishment of appropriate timeframes. A concern from the audit was that the consortium was not allowed an opportunity to address issues during the process of the audit.

IV. The Lead Organization for Supernova on the table and suggested that City of Dallas continue to be the Lead Organization. It is a concern as to who should write Exhibit 1 of the Supernova and it was motioned and seconded that City be Lead Organization and write Exhibit 1. The Consortium voted unanimously that the City of Dallas would write and prepare Exhibit 1.

So DASH and the Dallas Homeless Consortium would merge and our homeless would continue to suffer from a broken system and arrogance.

Headlines: 2/2001 Continuum of Carelessness – Homeless Service Providers struggle to understand loss of $3.2 million in HUD Money – Endless choices

The lack of management and coordination between services, HUD would virtually force a change.

On November 19, 2002, DASH and the Consortium became Metro Dallas Homeless Alliance. Sitting on the committee for the new bylaws, we agreed to have three-homeless/formerly representation on the new board.

May 1, 2003 MDHA Board Meeting - Minutes

It was agreed to stricken Karen Bradford (Rayzer) from the board due to her inability to be present at the meetings.

There were suggestions about the open spot on the board. Mr. Miller suggested a representative of an area hospital. Ms. Flink suggested filling the open with a businessperson. James Waghorne pointed out that according to the by-laws the spot needed to be filled by a homeless or formerly homeless person. The obligatory composition of the board is found on pg. 6 of the by-laws.

The homeless/formerly homeless would be guaranteed to have a voice for the first time in Dallas among the service agencies and issues surrounding homelessness. We also agreed that the new Alliance would be a membership organization with each agency having one vote. My experience in the past with a school board taught me how important it was to have a board, which could not exercise unlimited power. Still, the agencies had control and the same mismanagement was evident almost immediately when it was discovered the proper paper work was never filed for the name change with the State until the following year, ten months later.

For the homeless in Dallas it came down to this, when you have two sour lemons, choose one and try to make some lemonade. The homeless could never move forward without the agencies and dealing with the City in a practical manner was out for now. The big challenges facing the homeless were how to deal with a old regime and old mentality from the service providers who had proven ineffective while trying to build a legitimate organization to address and eliminate homelessness. The answer: Image, image, image.

June 2002

I was eager to visit our Nations Capitol. Washington D.C. had always been one of the places I wanted to visit during my lifetime. Boarding the airplane and passing through 1st class, on my way for the "peon" section, I wondered what the response would be if everyone knew I was homeless. Would 1st class demand that I be removed because I'm bringing down the value of their seats and would the business class section say if I stayed, I would harm their profits and stop the progress to our final destination. A small grin crossed my face at the thought of how people can act because of a single term, "homeless". It would probably be even worse if I told people on the plane I live with mental illness. It never occurred to me that one day, I would have to keep secrets because of others prejudice.

The National Alliance to End Homelessness annual conference in the U.S. is the largest of its kind. I spent the first day of the conference going to different seminars, which focused on ending homelessness. This was different than what I heard in Dallas. I learned about "housing first", SRO's (single room occupancy), safe havens, and most importantly, civil rights. Everything we didn't have in Dallas. I gathered all the information I could to study, the "what, who, how and where", when it came to homelessness. I spoke with as many people possible about the success going on in their programs and cities. Dallas at best was ten years behind the curve.

The next day was spent visiting Capitol Hill seeking out politicians interested in the plight of America's suffering. We spoke primarily with staffers who graciously handed us business cards and nodded their heads up and down about our concerns.

The last day made the most impact on me emotionally and was the most insightful. I first went to visit the Vietnam Wall Memorial, then over to the holocaust tour, next the Lincoln Memorial. I traveled up and down the National Lawn going from one place to another, gathering up our history, sacrifice and battles against hatred and prejudice. America's greatness came as much from withstanding aggression from foreign nations as it did from changing aggression within its own society. I looked forward towards giving my report to the Metro Dallas Homeless Alliance board about what I had learned concerning homelessness and how it could be addressed, but what I gained personally could never be given in some report.

The Metro Dallas Homeless Alliance had not yet found a home and our next board meeting was held at the Nonprofit Center in Dallas. How ironic I thought that the main proclaimed advocacy agency for our homeless could not find a home for themselves, much less for those on our streets. When I saw our agenda, I knew something was up. I was not listed to give a report. It proved my token position on the board.

Later I would resign. The homeless could not get any support for their projects, nor were they taken seriously. You can't move an issue ahead serving in a token position but this was O.K., because there wasn't anything this organization was going to do to advocate for the homeless and bring the issue to the public. I could leave and put my path in the Hands of someone I trusted. Another homeless/formerly homeless could take my seat on the board. Certainly the board would at least respect the by-laws. I was wrong.

**Metro Dallas Homeless Alliance
Special Board Meeting
April 7, 2005**

Members Present

Michael Anderson
Kathleen Beathard
Paige Flink
Don Maison
Bennett Miller
Lee Schimmel
Bill Thompson
Jennifer Ytem

NOTE: The April Board Meeting was a special meeting called in order for the full board to review and approve the by-laws which had been edited by the Executive Committee.

Bennett Miller called the meeting to order at 4:00 P.M.

The Board members had been previously provided a copy of the By-laws as approved by the Executive Committee. Each article was reviewed for suggested corrections or additions.

Don Maison made a motion to approve the by-laws as amended during this special session. Lee Schimmel seconded the motion. All were in favor; the motion carried. Cindy will make the edits as outlined during the board meeting discussion and distribute the newly adopted By-laws via email.

Don made a motion to postpone the next Board meeting until June 2nd so that the rankings for the SuperNOFA could be approved. Lee seconded the motion. All were in favor, the motion carried.

The Board also noted a desire to thank legal counsel from Methodist Health System for preparing the new by-laws, as well as Kathleen Beathard for arranging to have the work done.

The meeting was adjourned at 4:45 P.M.

Even though the minutes reflected that an email would go out with the new changes, it was almost 16 months later that the Dallas Homeless Neighborhood Association had discovered what had been done.

From: James Waghorne
To: MDHA Board
Sent: Wednesday, August 2, 2006
Subject: Action

In light of recent discoveries, the Dallas Homeless Neighborhood Association feels it necessary to address this Board urging immediate change for the benefit of the Metro Dallas Homeless Alliance, the membership, Dallas Community and most importantly our homeless population, which this organization claims to advocate for. While we hope that the changes done to the by-laws which cut homeless/formerly homeless representation on the Board from 3 down to 1 (eliminating the homeless committee completely) and limited the entire membership into an advisory role giving full power to the Board without any accountability to the membership was done strictly due to poor judgment and not with malice, regardless, our organization has contacted the National Coalition for conference and we are seeking possible legal remedies. (National Law Center is reviewing for us). The deception and betrayal of trust of not allowing the membership or the homeless/formerly homeless a voice in, neither changes nor even notification of said changes is unacceptable and will be challenge with all means.

Dallas Homeless Neighborhood Association

Dear James,

Thanks for letting me know about this.

I think you can file a lawsuit over the issue of the by-laws being changed without proper notice. Sad that they made second-class citizens of homeless people and membership regulating them to an advisory role. This same thing happened in Nashville. Homeless people picketed, boycotted and went to the media. They won.

Sincerely,

Michael Stoops

Acting Executive Director

National Coalition for the Homeless

Washington D.C.

A majority of the membership within Metro Dallas Homeless Alliance revolted and representatives of the Mayors Homeless Task Force became involved to help settle the dispute. It was important because the Mayors Task Force was seeking to join the organization and unite both groups.

It was my fervent prayer that with the Mayors Task Force combined with Metro Dallas Homeless Alliance, progress could be made to address the continued criminalization of our homeless and that the missions of advocating for equality, justice and dignity for our homeless once again became the top priority.

In September 2006, the two groups made plans to merge and the Dallas City Council appointed the new Metro Dallas Homeless Alliance to be the "Homeless Authority". Mike Rawlings, former C.E.O. for Pizza Hut would be Executive Chair. I was worried as many from the get-go, because Mr. Rawlings had chaired the committee ultimately responsible for the "Food Ordinance".

2/1/2007 Publication: THE DALLAS MORNING NEWS reprint with permission
Headline: Suit challenges limits on feeding homeless Dallas: Ministries say distribution rules violate religious rights
Byline: KIM HORNER

Rip Parker's Ministry and Don's Big Heart Ministries filed a federal lawsuit claiming that city restrictions on where charities can feed the homeless violate the groups' right to practice their religion. Mike Rawlings, Dallas' homeless czar, told the paper he believes the city has "bent over backwards" to work with charitable groups,

From: Liam Mulvaney [mailto:lmulvaney@lifenettexas.org]
Sent: Friday, May 25, 2007 2:58 PM
To: Jesse Aguilera
Subject: MDHA Membership Meeting

Jesse, I want to thank you very much for attending and speaking at the City Council Meeting! Your support and interest is very much appreciated.

As you know however, I am very unhappy with the decision of the MDHA Executive Committee to remain neutral on the question of utilizing the Army Reserve Center for homeless assistance purposes. While Cindy, Mike Faenza, and you have been very supportive, I feel that I cannot ignore what I think is a serious dynamic, which is striking at the core of MDHA's history and mission.

I had planned to make a statement to the membership at the meeting of June 1st, but unfortunately I will be out of the country on vacation on that day. I don't feel that it's fair to Tras to make him stand up and speak on my behalf on such a controversial subject so I wonder if you would feel comfortable reading the attached statement on my behalf at the meeting?

If not, perhaps you could at least announce to the membership that I have a concern that I want to express at the July membership meeting and just leave it at that.

Even though I'll be away I'll be staying in touch by e-mail so we can correspond back and forth if you wish.

Thank you.

Liam <<...>>

TO THE MEMBERSHIP OF MDHA:

We all engaged in a healthy debate last fall about the profound changes to the organizational structure, which we knew would occur if and when MDHA "merged" with the Mayor's Task Force on Homelessness. Following that debate, we decided to move ahead with the reorganization and the first few months from my perspective had been going well.

However, my experiences in May have left me with grave concerns about what the new structure may have done to the heart and soul of MDHA. It seems to me, while still relatively new to MDHA that we have always been, first and foremost, and advocate for the needs of the homeless. We all know that tragically, the homeless themselves have little effective voice in the political and governmental process. It is my understanding that for years MDHA has been a powerful and effective voice for the homeless and we can proudly point to a growing list of accomplishments that have been achieved through that advocacy. I am afraid that the new organizational structure has resulted in that strong voice being at worst silenced, and at best, censored.

Last year, the federal government declared the Army Reserve Center on Northwest Highway to be "surplus" and announced that it will be closing. There is Federal law, which governs how such surplus property is to be disposed of. In its wisdom, the federal law requires a diligent process of determining whether and how the property in question could be used for homeless assistance purposes. If, and only if, the outcome of that due diligence is that there is no conceivable way for the property to be used for the purpose of assisting the homeless, then the law allows for a "public benefits conveyance for a non-homeless assistance purpose.

LifeNet last year submitted a Letter of Interest (LOI) on the property and we stated that we would consider using the property for SRO housing for the homeless. Several other entities submitted LOI's also. No one from the City of Dallas (which was designated as the "Local Redevelopment Authority (LRA) ever contacted LifeNet for more information about our plans. It is my understanding that no one from the City talked to MDHA about their thoughts on any possible homeless assistance use for the property. Nonetheless, in May the staff of the City of Dallas disclosed that they are recommending that the property be given to themselves (through the Parks and Recreation Department). At the same time we learned that a public hearing was scheduled so that City Council could receive input on the issue.

I approached MDHA and asked that MDHA appear at the hearing and speak on behalf of utilizing the property for homeless assistance services. To my dismay and disbelief, **the MDHA Executive Committee met and voted to remain silent on this issue!**

Is anyone besides me horrified that the Metro Dallas Homeless Alliance would choose to not recommend that the intent of the federal government be upheld and ask that the property be used to help the homeless? If not the Homeless Alliance, who will be the voice for the homeless? What does this say about what this organization has become?

Second handedly, it is my understanding that the MDHA Executive Committee did not want to upset the City of Dallas by advocating for the homeless in this situation. From what I understand, there was concern that the city's funding of the HAC could be adversely effected.

Is this what MDHA has become? Have we become an organization that puts the desires of bureaucrats and politicians before the needs of the homeless? Have we sold out to the special interest dollars that flow through city hall? Can we be effective in meeting the needs of the homeless if we now have other masters to serve?

I urge the membership of MDHA to discuss this and reexamine our mission and our purpose. Who will speak for the homeless?

Liam Mulvaney

To placate government, is to sacrifice liberty, justice, equality and most importantly, democracy.

May 23, 2007 – Dallas adds new restrictions and seeks to banish panhandling in Downtown.

SEC. 31-35. SOLICITATION BY COERCION; SOLICITATION NEAR DESIGNATED LOCATIONS AND FACILITIES.

Solicitation by coercion; solicitation near designated locations and facilities; solicitation anywhere in the city after sunset and before sunrise any day of the week. (Exception can be made on private property with advance written permission of the owner, manager, or other person in control of the property.)

A person commits an offense if he conducts a solicitation to any person placing or preparing to place money in a parking meter.

The ordinance specifically applies to solicitations at anytime within 25 feet of:

Automatic teller machines;

Exterior public pay phones;

Public transportation stops;

Self service car washes;

Self Service gas pumps;

An entrance to a bank, credit union or similar financial institution;

Outdoor dining areas or fixed food establishments.

Chapter 8
Homeless acquire a voice

Resolution

Let then our first act every morning be to make the following resolve for the day:

I shall not fear anyone on earth.

I shall fear only God.

I shall not bear ill will toward anyone.

I shall not submit to injustice from anyone.

I shall conquer untruth with truth.

And in resisting untruth I shall put up with all suffering.

Mahatma Gandhi

5/5/03 Publication: THE DALLAS MORNING NEWS reprint with permission
Headline: Homeless acquire a new voice, Association run by those on streets seeks to address their issues
Byline: KIM HORNER

The City of Dallas was full of self-proclaimed homeless advocates. No one elected them to be their voice, and most of the homeless didn't even know who they were. The individuals just one day decided that they would be the voice for someone else without seeking approval first and very few of these individuals truly comprehended that advocacy meant a willingness to sacrifice for the cause. Only five such people in Dallas who I had met, truly had put their lives on the line and suffered, John Fullinwider, Sandy Rollins, Dorothy Masterson, Ben Johnson and my mentor Clora Hogan. Each one was also eventually quieted in some manner. Pushed out or pushed away.

I found out early on that after Clora, the only true advocates I could count on were the National Organizations. They weren't bound by company policies or local politics. Prince, the only on the street homeless – homeless advocate had been murdered. If the victims don't have a voice, they stay the victim. If arrogance and ignorance were allowed to win, status quo and needless suffering would continue. Only the homeless themselves could lead and take on such a challenge and only God could see it through.

From: Ron Cowart: rcowart@ci.dallas.tx.us
To: James: trumpetcall@mail.com
CC: Dave Hogan dhogan@ci.dallas.tx.us
Subject: Downtown Homeless
Date: Thu, 22 May 2003
Reply Requested When Convenient
James:

As you know, the Downtown Homeless Neighborhood Association is having its 2nd meeting on the 28th at 2PM at the Dallas Life Foundation. Even though we cannot "Appoint" chairpersons, it would be advantageous for you to consider heading this up. Can you meet with us tomorrow afternoon? Oliver can pick you up, and maybe we could go to Café Brazil or something. Sorry to be late getting back to you, but would be grateful to discuss this with you. In addition, the Metro Alliance will have you on the agenda to talk about the association, and maybe see where you think it might head. Thank you!

Ron Cowart

May 28, 2003

Regardless of popular belief, there isn't anything glorious about true advocacy for human rights. Homeless advocacy first and foremost is not about saving lives. Instead its about going into the mud pits to help those who wish to save themselves and staying in those same mud pits to befriend and show human compassion to those whose flame of hope has extinguished until they themselves are no longer. Advocacy is about exposing the truth and abuse; it is a drain in many ways and eventually known as a "Hell Raiser" even from those, whose work benefited from your efforts, many will turn their backs on you. The path of advocacy is littered with unsung heroes, trashed after individuals and organizations profit from their efforts.

Fighting against prejudice is also a suffering proposition. Each time a decision is made to expose the atrocities by those in control, there is the profound knowledge that additional abuses could be committed for revenge. Advocacy is the constant revolving door of love and heartache; it is the courage to care and the emotional suffering that comes with it.

I despised being called a "Homeless Advocate". I disliked cameras, speaking engagements and I disliked being recognized publicly and I feared leadership, something I had failed at miserably during my lifetime.

The meeting with the City Crisis Intervention Department, it was clear they wanted this organization for a puppet. A public relations win by giving a voice to the homeless.

The City employees did their best to push me to chair this new group. I wanted a true election giving anyone who desired to take on the tremendous burden, carrying the weight of 6,000 homeless, to be able to run for the position.

I was pleased to see two individuals stand up for the challenge, both African American females. I had studied hard on social movements and learned women normally stand up before men during times of hardship. History never gives them their just due. The 400 in the chapel were 80% African American which gave me hope that I would not be elected. They knew the women; they didn't know who I was. Fact is, I should not had been elected, but with a show of hands, over 250 elected me to become the first President of the Dallas Homeless Neighborhood Association.

Why a majority of African Americans would put their trust in a small bald headed white man I don't know, but I was truly humbled and overwhelmed. I was a lousy Christian, suffered from anxiety, I was a lousy speaker and not long ago, I had crawled out of the pits of society. There wasn't a worst choice on the planet and I would carry the homeless cross as far as God would allow, but many times, He would have to drag me kicking and screaming. If I had known about the challenges, the battles and the personal cost, which would face me, I would not have accepted the nomination.

The attributes and advantages I did have, was the deep love for the suffering, the empathy I carried upon my heart and the burning anger I had witnessing such cruelty in my own city. Immediately, I asked my two opponents to become Vice President and Secretary. Then we proceeded to list our top 5 primary concerns as homeless and planned for the first march on City Hall in over 8 years. We would not be puppets.

7/1/03 Homeless march to City Hall with concerns about services, housing and jobs

With City Hall working a skeleton staff because of the summer break and the 4th of July, twenty-five homeless and formerly homeless marched in the sweltering heat, calling for access to jobs and housing. It was an important moment in history, though overlooked and minimized by most; it was the beginning of active advocacy once again in the City of Dallas. It had been almost a decade since the homeless had challenged the local Government.

The courage exercised this day started the turning point for our homeless in Dallas. It was also the first day I worked with the reporter, Kim Horner of the Dallas Morning News who turned out to be the ultimate professional and was instrumental in bringing our side of the story to the community.

North American Street Newspaper Association Conference- July 18th 2002

Clora Hogan, and "Endless Choices" street newspaper, helped us raise money and sponsored three homeless to go to the conference.

This would be my second trip on a plane as a homeless person, this time to Boston for a three-day conference to meet with other homeless individuals from all across the country and Canada. Being homeless, I didn't have the normal worries most people have. What to pack and what to leave behind? My options were limited.

The weather was sweltering in Boston when we arrived and the dorm rooms we stayed in at Boston College didn't have air conditioning; so most of the time was spent outdoors. Boston is a magnificent city. Vibrant, with 23 colleges surrounding the area, one could feel the youth and energy. It was here where I had the good fortune of meeting Michael Stoops for the first time. Current Executive Director of the National Coalition for the Homeless. He would prove invaluable in our fight for social justice and practical solutions for our homeless. Our second day there, all the homeless went to the famed Harvard Square and had a sell-off to see who could earn the most donations from their papers, each individual representing their local City. Instead of participating, I spent the time sight seeing around this amazing little Square, enamored by the people, the atmosphere and most importantly how they treated the homeless. It was a complete different attitude and social consciousness than what I had experienced.

The homeless were treated as part of the community as oppose to third-class citizens and the homeless in return showed dignity and respect for others. No harsh panhandling or inappropriate behavior.

I met three young homeless individuals outside a storefront, where they were sitting down, and asking passerby's for change in a courteous and humble manner. The two young men were in their early twenties and the girl in her late teens. They were train jumpers. A small group of young people in America who travel across the country, jumping trains for exploration and site seeing.

In town for three days, I asked them if they could compare other cities, which they had been to, as far as the treatment they received.

New York, Dallas, Atlanta and Las Vegas was on their "never go again list".

Having been homeless in Dallas for over 16 months, I had first hand knowledge.

It was simply amazing to watch the homeless in Boston get treated with compassion versus terror and heartlessness.

Dallas was once one of the friendliest cities in the south. It was that reputation which helped Dallas after the J.F.K. assassination. It was that reputation which built Dallas.

The last day in Boston, I went on a trip, which will remain forever burned into my soul. The Freedom Trail. Faneuil Hill, Park Street Church, King' Chapel burial grounds, the Boston massacre site, Old North Church, Paul Revere's house, Bunker Hill memorial and the U.S.S. Constitution. Three miles past 16 historic sites, covering the very beginning of democracy and the fight for freedom, equality and independence. The very place where individuals tired of being treated as third class citizens, changed world history forever. It was ironic how a Nation built on such sacrifice would one day treat some of their own as third class citizens, turning their backs on what made this Nation. The common cause of justice, freedom, and a hope for a brighter future.

I left Boston overflowing with the inspiration of our forefathers to fight against the brutality happening in Dallas; aimed at the least fortunate of America's society. They might be the least fortunates, but they were still Americans and still the rightful heirs of the sacrifices that had been made by many.

From: James Waghorne

Sent: Monday, August 23, 2004 8:54 AM

To: Kleinknecht@downtowndallas.org

Subject: Private Security, Downtown Ambassadors

Hello Patty,

Since reading the article in the Dallas Morning News about the new duties for the Downtown Ambassadors, I have been extremely concerned. I have contacted the National Law Center on Homelessness & Poverty (See Attached) about my concerns primarily the violation of individuals' civil rights. If you would like to speak about this, please don't hesitate to call. I will be meeting with Chief Kunkle today to also express my concerns.

James K Waghorne - President

Dallas Homeless Neighborhood Association

From: Ron Cowart (City of Dallas)

To: Dallas Life Foundation, David Hogan, Vincent Golbeck, James Waghorne

Subject: Dallas Homeless Neighborhood Association

Date: Tues, 02 Dec 2003

Greetings All,

There are two volatile issues effecting our homeless population:

1. The Shopping Cart Ordinance: Schedule for Jan 2004

2. The Homeless Intake Facility: (Site Location, services, transportation, safety issues, etc…)

I am proposing that the Dallas Homeless Neighborhood Association host a community event featuring city leaders, police administrators, homeless advocates and members of the site committee who will discuss these relevant issues, and to gather needed input to enable the City to be more responsive to the needs of the homeless. The event will be moderated by the elected Association President, James Waghorne following introductory remarks by the Dallas Life Foundation director, Rev. Bill Bailey.

We are currently working to invite Mayor Miller and members of the Dallas City Council along with other respected committee members to participate.

Regards,

Ron Cowart

The first priority for any movement is to organize. The next step is to go straight to the people with the issues at hand. News drives public opinion but public opinion can also drive the news.

Advocates for Change - Meeting Notes – October 8, 2002

The October 5th rally to celebrate UN Habitat Day and National Tenants Day was held. Reporters from Channel 4 and Channel 8 TV news covered the event. Speakers included Ben Johnson, a homeless volunteer and activist. Mr. Johnson is a member of the "Advocates for Change" speakers' bureau.

James Waghorne announced that he would be speaking October 20th at the Preston Hollow Presbyterian Church. He also said that members of "Advocates for Change" speakers' bureau would be presenting a talk for the League of Women Voters and Church Women United at the First Presbyterian Church of Dallas on October 29th.

I had given a presentation to only one large group of people in my life, it was to an auditorium full of children at Nathan Adams Elementary School and I was nervous even then. It was not important what I said to this group or any other group, as much as it was to allow people to see an American whose homeless suffering had caused great pain. Most conversation and conferences about homelessness didn't include the homeless themselves. It was equivalent to having a conference about African American history without any African American speakers. Not only was it degrading, but it also cheated the audience from hearing the intimate knowledge of homelessness. Speaking from the heart is often better than speaking on the issues and speaking from experience is more factual then facts.

The 3 homeless who spoke this day must have had some impact, because Council Member Veletta Forsythe Lill came in late after we had finished speaking and was bomblasted by some of the audience for the way City Hall was acting towards our homeless. Afterwards, the Council Member became a champion in City Hall for the homeless and the issues.

It proved to me that our citizens did care, compared to what I had heard from service providers and other homeless. It was just a matter of putting a true face, to go with the message.

May 12, 2004

Honorable Mayor Laura Miller and Dallas City Council Members
Ref: Ten-Year Plan

The Advocates for the Dallas Homeless and Dallas Homeless Neighborhood Association have some grave concerns with the final draft of the ten-year plan to end chronic homelessness. These two homeless and formerly homeless organizations represent over 450 individuals in Dallas. Language in the original draft that guaranteed their voice (that of the homeless) and participation was stricken from the final plan. It should be ensured that homeless and formerly homeless individuals would have the opportunity to serve on every task force and also participate in the new economic benefits that will arise from this plan.

Secondly, model Mobile Outreach programs in Miami and New York has formerly homeless individuals employed to do this work. The success rate is well documented. Each of the Four proposed Outreach Teams should employ a minimum of one trained formerly homeless individual per team. If new jobs are to be created to address homelessness, it is only logical to hire the homeless and those with street experience. To hire individuals otherwise and not make an effort to help the homeless with employment is counterproductive to the stated goals.

We believe it is important to us, HUD, service providers, MDHA and the City of Dallas, for the homeless themselves to support the Ten-Year plan to end chronic homelessness. In its current form we cannot but are willing to meet at your convenience to discuss viable solutions.

Respectfully,

Mr. James Blount – Executive Chair   Mr. James K Waghorne – President
Advocates for Change   Dallas Homeless Neighborhood Association

Our letter never received an answer from the Mayor.

There was going to be a 3-prong counteroffensive to combat City Hall. Grassroots advocacy needed to be established and counter what so called experts and false advocates were saying. People needed to hear from the victims themselves. Until now, the homeless had been pushed to the back of the bus. Civil disobedience was one option, but because people in charge were more worried about their image and would use civil disobedience as a tool to justify their own actions to persecute, instead we would go after what they held most precious. I would have to face my greatest fear; public speaking and reconcile with it.

We had to use Churches, Schools, Colleges, Internet, Blog sites, media, and every aspect of communication to offset the damage and propaganda by City Hall and the old media. We could not change everybody's heart; this was not the goal, the goal was to reach out to those who cared about their fellow citizens and to inspire them to act. The church seemed to be the natural place to start.

To: James Waghorne
Subject: Class Etc. Sunday school
Date: Fri., 4 Apr 2003
James,

Thank you for agreeing to speak to our class Sunday May 25.

We are looking forward to hearing about the Dallas Homeless Alliance and how the various organizations work together or not. Our class has many Cross Roads volunteers.

Thanks Again,

Pat Rodgers

To: James Waghorne

Subject: Tex. Women's University Homeless Forum

Date: Thurs, 4 March 2004

James, I don't know if you remember me from the meeting in Dallas City Hall with Mayor Laura Miller or not? I am emailing you to ask if you would consider coming to the University here in Denton and addressing the social welfare class.

Galynn Lindemann TWU

From: "Singleton, Natasha"
To: "James Waghorne"
Subject: RE: Leadership Dallas
Date: Tue, 8 Feb 2005 12:38:38 -0600

Hi James,

THANK YOU for speaking to our Leadership Dallas class. You were AWESOME. We did pass out the CD's; people were interested in getting one so that is good news! You and Dave gave a very clear picture of the homelessness issue and it sparked a great deal of discussion. It is always good to keep people in touch with issues facing our community and if that does not work, maybe they will at the least, see how blessed they are...

May You Stay Blessed!!

Natasha

The following week I received a call from CNN in Dallas and was asked to do an interview with Anderson Cooper on his show 360. Unfortunately tragedy struck in Israel. Ariel Sharon had a stroke and the interview was canceled. But it remained a fact that the maltreatment of the homeless by City Hall had gather both National and International attention.

From: "Jason Hiatt"
To: James Waghorne
Subject: Interview Request
Date: Thu, 16 Mar 2006 16:32:14 -0800

Hi Mr. Waghorne,

I'm writing to request an interview with you on The Mike Gallagher Show (we're a radio program on 660 KSKY) tomorrow morning regarding your position that the film version of "Dallas" should be shot in another city. If you receive this tonight, please contact me at the number below. Thank you for your time and consideration.

Jason Hiatt

The Dallas Homeless Neighborhood Association or someone representing the organization would be quoted in the Dallas Morning News 44 times over the next 4 years and the issue of homelessness in our community would be mentioned twice that number in the local media, giving us a voice to challenge the one-sided discrimination of those who sought to victimize us and to counter the false advocates, but it was also vital to have our voice heard on a national and international level, bringing pressure on those in power. Achieving this, we would have to document and expose the horrors of homelessness and the brutality of those who sought to do us harm.

In every stage of these Oppressions We have Petitioned for Redress in the most humble terms: Our repeated Petitions have been answered only by repeated injury.

Thomas Jefferson – Declaration of Independence

Chronological Events

January 2003: Census count reveals 363 homeless individuals and another estimated 10 individuals are locked up in County facilities for Class C misdemeanor offenses making the Dallas County jails the third largest homeless shelter in the City of Dallas.

January 20 2003: Time Magazine article cites police harassment and abuses aimed at the homeless in the City of Dallas.

February 4 2003: DART transit officers attack homeless individuals in front of City Hall with clubs and mace. Incident was caused when an individual "who isn't homeless" was arrested for jaywalking. The individual known by some of the homeless is legally blind and suffers due to brain damage from an accident. DART officers handcuff him and slam his head on their car, causing the man's mouth to bust open. The homeless, who witness the action, complain about the treatment of the man and are attacked by Police resulting in the beatings and use of mace. Incident is verified by witness accounts including a City employee but is not reported in media. One officer involved had a history of disciplinary actions while he was serving for the Dallas Police Dept.

March 2003: Dallas City Council passed City Ordinance 25213 effective April 15th• The new solicitation ordinance is directly aimed at homeless individuals. Penalty: Jail or up to a $500 fine.

April 2003: New solicitation ordinance goes into effect.

April 25 2003: Mr. Robert "Butch" Strickland is attacked by gang and beaten near death. His friend Art is quoted, "All he was doing was panhandling. There's no reason for anyone to do this to him." (DMN 5/10)

May 2003: Police write 112 citations to homeless individuals for solicitation (panhandling). (DMN 11/11)

May 2003: Citizens of Dallas pass $3 million (Prop 17 is the last item on the bond package) for a New 24 hr homeless assistance center. Initially, it was purposed by the then Director of EHHS to the City Council that the amount of $6 million be put on the proposition citing studies and evidence this would be the cost. Amount is cut in half while at the same time over $11 million is passed for an animal shelter.

May 2003: Same individuals who beat Mr. Strickland two weeks before attack Arthur McClanahan. Mr. McClanahan escapes with knife wound to the foot.

June 3 2003: Homeless man discovered murdered. Gunshot wound to the head citied as the cause of death. (DMN 6/3)

June 6 2003: Representative from the Dallas Police Dept. confirms no statistics are kept as to crime committed against the "Homeless" or by the "Homeless" yet public officials continually blame homeless for crimes. Hate Crimes go unpunished. (Email Doc. 6/6)

June 26 2003: Article titled "Make Yourself at Home: Want to know why the city is making plans for the homeless downtown? Visit the library, but don't take the kids." appears in the Dallas Observer

July 1 2003: Homeless march for housing, jobs and against civil rights violations. Continuous "Sweeps" conducted by the Dallas Police Dept. end with the destruction of homeless belongings including, medicines, clothes, family photos, bibles, etc ... All Public Officials refuse to comment. (DMN 7/2)

September 2003: The J. Erik Jonsson Central Library starts enforcing new rules aimed at keeping the homeless off of property and out of the library. Rules include no sitting outside and limit size of bags allowed inside. (DMN 10/8)

September 22 2003: City Employee reveals plans to purposely provoke homeless individuals with mental illness and or those with addictions to commit crimes during Police conducted "Sweeps", so police can arrest and incarcerate homeless individuals on the spot.

September 29 2003: The night before the Mayor is to help feed the homeless at the City's only Soup Kitchen; Dallas Police confiscate bottles of syrup out of a shopping cart and pour the liquid on the sidewalk in front of the Soup Kitchen where homeless individuals sleep forcing them elsewhere.

October 2003: Carload of individuals drive by Soup Kitchen shooting homeless with Paint Guns.

October 27 2003: Police conduct sweeps in front of Soup Kitchen and close off area permanently which has long been used as a place by the homeless to sleep.

November 2003. Police shoot mentally ill homeless man wounding him in the stomach.

November 6, 2003: Crime initiatives, Panhandling crackdown and new Shopping cart ordinance. (DMN 11/6)

November 11 2003: Article in DMN reveals 450 citations have been issued for solicitation since new ordinance went into effect. In same article the Mayor of Dallas is quoted, "For a while I would roll down my window and yell and scream at them (the homeless) to get off the streets." Also, article reports 258 arrests and the destruction and forced relocation of 6 campsites. City officials for use to report homeless panhandlers recommend calling 311.

December 2003: A report conducted by the City of Dallas which was not released publicly, titled" Homeless: Crime, Victimization and Fear." is discovered. The report shows among other things that out of the 312 homeless people surveyed 59 had become victims of violent crime. Statistically, 1 out of every 6 homeless individuals in Dallas will become a victim of crime. (25 times higher than the National rate) Taking all data into account, logic and hypothesis, over 50 "Hate Crimes" are committed against homeless individuals in Dallas every year. City employees initially deny having such a report when first asked for a copy by a local reporter.

December 2003: New "Shopping Cart" ordinance is passed effective January 15th 2004. Dallas ties New York City as having most ordinances criminalizing the homeless.

December 25 2003: Article titled: Savage Breasts: Do the homeless hate classical music? The Dallas Observer. Public Service Administrator at Library denies using "Classical Music" as a physiological weapon aimed at driving off the homeless.

January 8 2004: Internal email document shows City Hall had designed plans to use physiological warfare against homeless to drive them away from certain areas in Downtown Dallas. "Clear Cutting" in wooded and wetland areas is also discussed with environmental groups and parks.

January 11 2004: Those who feed the homeless are harassed and issued citations by police and city code enforcement. (DMN 1/11)

January 16 2004: Internal City Hall email documenting homeless ~ deaths.

January 20 2004: Mill Creek Homeowners Association forces service provider to close doors and move. (DMN 1/20)

January 21 2004: Census count reveals over 360 homeless individuals locked up in County facilities during a one day period for the second year in a row costing tax payers over $4 million per year.

February 4 2004: Neighborhood Associations show up in force at City Hall to voice their opposition against a new Assistance Center being located in their areas. (DMN 2/4)

February 25 2004: City Council unanimously votes to not allow the Annette Strauss Family Gateway Center to apply for tax-credits to build permanent housing units for homeless families. This occurs on the same day when the Executive Director for the Interagency Council on Homelessness, Mr. Philip Mangano is in Dallas to attend the announcement of the "Ten year plan to end chronic homelessness" in Dallas.

February 26 2004: Article "Homeless Cleansing: Proposed "intake center" for homeless looks scary." Dallas Observer

March 12 2004 (week of): Three homeless people die. One found in a creek, another stabbed to death and one while incarcerated.

March 13 2004: Downtown group wants to use employees paid with tax dollars to spy on and harass the homeless. (DMN 3/13)

March 29 2004: EMS paramedics deny assistance or treatment to a homeless man. The V.A. outreach workers are told he can get himself to the hospital. No vital signs are even taken. Homeless man whose leg was swollen from his ankle to his kneecap and was using a walker could not get to the hospital. A Dallas MetroCare outreach worker provided transportation to Baylor Hospital where the homeless man was taken in immediately due to a possible severe infection.

From: James Waghorne
To: Michael Stoops
Date: 03/25/04
Subject: Homeless Report
Hello Mike,

I was wondering whom I should fax information to about what has gone on in Dallas this past year since the last National Homeless Report. We had 3 homeless people die the week of the 8th. By unnatural causes, two murdered and one died in County Detention, The Dallas County Medical Examiner's office are dragging their feet as to the cause of death. I have kept fairly good records of most reported and unreported violent deaths. Also, a report done by the City but hidden from the public, titled… "Homelessness: crime, victimization and fear" should be released soon after I told a friend reporter about it. They have stalled her for a month, but have told her she will get it this Thursday. One of the things it shows is that a homeless person here in Dallas is 25 times more likely to be a victim of violent crime as oppose to the National average. Thanks for your help.
James

From: Michael Stoops
To: James Waghorne
Subject: FW: Illegal to be Homeless '04 report; "mean" city designation
Date: Thu, 21 Oct 2004
Dear Homeless Advocate:

Your City and/or State will be included in our Top 20 Meanest Cities and 4 Meanest States ranking in our forthcoming report called, Illegal to be Homeless: The Criminalization of Homelessness in the U.S.

We will be deciding on a final, final release date on Thursday, Oct 28.

Sincerely,

Michael Stoops - National Coalition for the Homeless

11/10/04 Dallas breaks the top 20: The National Coalition for the Homeless ranks Dallas 15th meanest city in America

Dallas City Hall started to get a national notoriety for the inhumane treatment of its citizens. They had failed in their primary governmental obligation to protect human life, promoting liberty and ensuring justice for all. Like many local governments in America the main focus centered on catering to the elite and special interest. "Quality of Life" meant building doggie parks while people went hungry, it meant hundred million dollar projects for bridges while people went homeless and it meant giving away millions of tax payer dollars to millionaires and billion dollar corporations while citizens were dieing on their streets.

It was what the library did though which brought Dallas to International infamy.

Houston Chronicle (TX) - December 30, 2005: Homeless advocates cry foul over Dallas library's new rules, They say public facility's code of conduct reeks of discrimination

December 2005 - Dallas City Library new rule run's a foul.

If you have an odor don't come to the library according to their new rules.

I haven't met anyone in my 47 years who didn't have odor since it is a natural function of the human body. Some odors are pleasant to me and some aren't. Who's to decide what is the right odor for the library? There are thousands of perfumes and colognes because not everyone can agree on the perfect odor. Some cultures find masking ones natural odor offensive. Then there's cultures whose food causes a different body odor. Do we ask them not to eat their food because someone thinks it makes them stink? How about those individuals who take life saving medicine, which might alter their odor, or those who have had medical procedures, which could also cause a possible offensive smell to the new "stink patrols"? Do babies get tossed out? They stink to high heaven many times, as do children. Also, there are those people who deal with obesity and might perspire more in 100-degree heat. No entrance during summer for them…right? Of course let's be honest here. This new rule is aimed at denying the less fortunate equal access to a public tax funded facility. The main city library has crossed the stinking line with this rule. There are many different types of stink in our society that are offensive but the most putrid odor is the foul character of prejudice.

James K Waghorne – President

Dallas Homeless Neighborhood Association

The Nationalist News Network endorsed the City's actions against the homeless and the new policies targeting them. When the Libertarian Nationalist Socialist Green Party starts to support a Mayor and City Council for the ill treatment of others, maybe sanity had left the City of Dallas. Prejudice brings together strange bedfellows.

From: Theopi Skarlatos @ bbc

To: James Waghorne

Subject: BBC Interview

Hi James,

I am a journalist working for BBC Five live in London. We have come across a story about a ruling in Dallas, which will allow public libraries to ban people who smell. As an advocate for the homeless, I am aware you may feel strongly against this ruling and we would like to talk to you on the programme Up All Night tonight. If you are interested in having your say please give me a call when you get this message.

Look forward to hearing from you.

Theopi Skarlatos

Broadcast Journalist

12/30/05 No 'odor' allowed in Dallas Libraries. Benjamin Franklin rolls over in grave

Naturally many supported the 'odor' rule for the library but it was also this move, which really brought to light just how far Dallas City Hall would go to segregate and persecute those who they had abandoned. This new rule was aimed at denying the less fortunate equal access to a public tax funded facility without recourse. The first libraries opened in America were meant to serve those who could not afford books. As a Librarian would write regarding the homeless, "it is then the library's responsibility to look for ways in which to serve the homeless. Information dispersal is our specialty and we as librarians need to broaden our knowledge of area services by extending our relationships with community organizations that aid the homeless…we can be catalysts of social awareness in our communities. Recognizing the multiple origins of homelessness is the first step in allowing ourselves to emerge from a defensive, angry attitude toward the homeless. Regardless of how weary we are of this situation, it is our problem, and we must respond to it. Let us respond with care and thoughtfulness." Judy Silver

From Asia to South America and into Europe, articles appeared about the brutality of Dallas City Hall. Even www.nazi.org supported the moves made by Dallas against the poorest of the poor. Dallas City Hall had made Dallas one of the most prejudice cities in America. It had to be exposed.

Ron Cowart, a city employee would reveal to me that my nickname in City Hall was "Frankenstein." It didn't bother me because many of the homeless had a different name for me "Uncle." I was family.

July 24, 2005

"The most despised man in America is Saddam Hussein, and he'll sleep in a bed tonight," But our homeless ... they're sleeping on pavement. How can you say we're truly treating them humanely and civilized?"

James K Waghorne
Dallas Homeless Neighborhood Association

"Mis" treating our Homeless 2006 Dallas, Texas U.S.A.
Report prepared by: Dallas Homeless Neighborhood Association

Within just the last 4 years, the issue of homelessness in our City has become increasingly National and International news. No longer allocated to just warm fuzzy stories around the holiday season, the reality of the brutal and inhumane treatment of the poorest and neediest citizens in our society plays across our televisions and is reported almost weekly in the print media. Some elected officials and non-elected individuals have responded with increasingly harsh tactics including but not limited to; curtailing civil liberties, exercising control by limiting food resources leading to additional hunger, malnutrition and other health problems and increased laws sugarcoated in the term, "Quality of life" to punish the less fortunate.

This supercilious landlord mentality has not lead one single individual towards improved services, treatment, recovery, employment or housing but instead has increased the barriers and challenges of survival for our estimated 11,000 homeless every year in our city, (estimated 6,000 daily).

A one-sided punishment ideology to manipulate and control a free people of society has long been viewed by a civilized world and by civilized people to be nothing short of tyranny. The justification to act accordingly evolves from a philosophical and social hierarchy.

For the 2nd year straight, citizens of Dallas graded the City and the Department of Environmental & Health Services, a failing grade of 32 out of 100 when it came to services for our poor, showing zero improvement over the previous year and also homelessness was one of the top five issues facing our City according to the survey.

On a partial improvement, "Sweeps" included social service agencies offering assistance. The shortage of treatment beds and housing though were dismal giving few options to those in need. The first new "Sweep" was aimed at an estimated 180 individuals.

See Dallas Morning News article May 18th 2006

Only 8 treatment beds and 5 housing beds were made available.

More collaboration and beds need to be made available.

It cost $27,285.00 per person, per annum, to have a disabled individual live on our streets without proper treatment and housing. "Housing First" with 24 hr. available treatment for the same person cost $20,000.00 per year.

August 2005, Hurricane Katrina left over 12,000 homeless in Dallas. Without prejudice, we were able to place all. It didn't matter if one had been homeless before, was an ex-offender, unemployed or had a disability. The question I ask; "Why does it matter with our own homeless and why must we end homelessness differently for them." Whether a person is homeless due to a natural disaster or unnatural disaster, it is still a human crisis. While 2005 ended on a high note, with the citizens of Dallas passing a 23 million-bond package to build a new Assistance Center; 2006 started with more broken promises from City Hall and more tragedy for the homeless.

January 18, 2006

Jason Trahan from the Dallas Morning News called me to ask about a homeless individual who had been doused in gasoline and lit on fire. He told me the location of the incident and I went to gather some information. The Fire-Rescue stated that it had been one of those accidental incidents in which the person had set himself on fire. After arriving at the crime scene, even as a novice, it was easy to tell Mr. Ramirez had been purposely set on fire in an attempt to murder him.

It was January and all the grass and weeds in the area were bone dry. The campfire was over 50 feet away from where the grass fire had started due to Mr. Ramirez trying desperately to put himself out. Dry weeds between the campfire and where the grass fire started were as high as my shoulders in many places. It would've been impossible for Mr. Ramirez to have accidentally set himself on fire without the surrounding area also catching on fire.

Until the story ran in the newspaper, there wasn't any investigation and police had not been called. The family started their own inquiry and had the assailant identified in less than 24 hours, but due to the slow investigation by authorities, the person responsible had escaped.

In addition to the continued injury and loss of life on the streets; new rules and laws have placed up to 300 homeless lives in danger when they evicted them from the current Day Resource Center without the promise assistance that these individuals would have vouchers to live in other shelters or in other living arrangements. Most of these 300 individuals were the most venerable among our population as a majority suffered from disabilities.

(See Dallas Morning News article dated March 26, 2006.)

It is important to note that the City Council were briefed in August 2005, that with only $95,000.00, a warehouse which will be part of the new Assistance Center could be used instead to allow these disabled citizens a place to sleep instead of throwing people out onto the streets. In August 2006, 7 homeless became victims of violence. 4 dead, 3 shot.

January 30th 2006: Meeting at City Hall. Department of Environmental & Health Services decide not to provide for the up to 300 individuals sleeping at the Day Resource Center. Disabled are forced to the streets.

Employees attending: tape record meeting where Supervisors are heard stating their unconcern.

February 1st 2006: 5:00 a.m. Dallas Police in 4 squad cars show up at Day Resource center and start to harass our homeless sleeping there. Throughout the entire day, homeless are harassed and driven away from the Day Resource Center, threatened with (invalid) tickets.

February 1st 2006: Dallas institutes new rule allowing security at main library to throw out anyone they believe to have a bad odor. Reports of harassment start immediately. Libertarian National Socialist Green Party support Dallas City Hall's move.

February 1st 2006: Dallas starts to enforce new law making it illegal to give food except in City approved locations. Small faith base and Good Samaritan organizations are forced from practicing their "freedom of religion" in fear of getting a $2,000 fine. Some homeless, many disabled have to walk miles to get a meal. Many are seen eating from trashcans for survival. Current Dallas "Homeless Czar" Mike Rawlings chaired committee on the Mayor's Homeless Taskforce in which this new ordinance evolved from.

February 1st 2006: Metro Dallas Homeless Alliance offers no protest for harsh treatment, eviction, rules or new law. Excessive tickets are given to many of the 300 homeless evicted for Sleeping in Public.

January 2006   Meanest Cities – "A Dream Denied"

While most cities throughout the country have either laws or practices that criminalize homeless persons, some city practices or laws have stood out as more egregious than others in their attempt to criminalize homelessness. The National Coalition for the Homeless and the National Law Center on Homelessness & Poverty have chosen the following top 20 meanest cities in 2005 based on one or more of the following criteria: the number of anti-homeless laws in the city, the enforcement of those laws and severities of penalties, the general political climate toward homeless people in the city, local advocate support for the meanest designation, the city's history of criminalization measures, and the existence of pending or recently enacted criminalization legislation in the city. Although some of the report's top 20 meanest cities have made some efforts to address homelessness in their communities, the punitive practices highlighted in the report impede true progress in solving the problem.

1. **Sarasota, FL**
2. **Lawrence, KS**
3. **Little Rock, AR**
4. **Atlanta, GA**
5. **Las Vegas, NV**
6. **Dallas, TX**

Bucks County Courier Times (Levittown, PA) - March 9, 2006
Dallas accused of taking hard line on homeless

Kansas City Star, The (MO) - March 10, 2006
Dallas climbs ranks of 'meanest' cities

Miami Herald, The (FL) - March 12, 2006
DALLAS CRITICIZED FOR STRICT HOMELESS LAWS

Thanks to the National Organizations, from coast to coast and worldwide, the cruelty and inhumanity of Dallas City Hall was exposed and our P.R. campaign started to turn the tide. The pressure on the Mayor and City Hall persuaded some Council Members to start advocating for projects to help the homeless. It also brought new advocates into the mix and many of the current agencies would start to collaborate on projects to build housing. New leadership came to the Metro Dallas Homeless Alliance and they chose to focus on "Housing First." Putting homeless into housing and delivering the services to help them maintain a roof over their head.

Having won the P.R. campaign, the battle for a location to build the new Homeless Assistance Center would still be one of our greatest challenges, achieving a system that would start the end of homelessness with practical solutions. Lines in the sand were drawn. Developers wanted to force the homeless far outside the city center, eight miles away, and would do anything to make their push.

To: "Karen Boudreaux" City Manager Homeless Services
From: "James Waghorne"
Subject: Re: Day Resource Center Task force
Date: Mon, 25 Aug 2003
Hello Karen,
I wish to get the names of those who serve on the Day Resource Center Task Force and also would like to know who the representatives are for the homeless/formerly homeless.
Thank you – James

To: James
There isn't a meeting task force. There is a site selection committee – I'll take the names from power point for you. - Karen
Attached is the list.
Site Committee - Judith Sturrock – Chair
Financial Advisor - Jim Depetris Attorney/Property Owner
Jonathan Vickery - MDHA – Metro Dallas Homeless Alliance
Bennett Miller - Developer/MDHA – Metro Dallas Homeless Alliance
Larry Berkley - Formerly Homeless

Greta Minkin VA – Veterans Administration

David Kellogg - MHA – Mental Health Association

Larry Berkley, the formerly homeless person, was a City plant on the site selection committee. He was housed in a city program and worked for the City through their Americorp VISTA program. Federal law made it clear that VISTA's could not sit on committees, which could influence political decisions. Dallas City Hall wasn't grand on obeying Federal law, if they could get away with it. Judith Anne Sturrock, the chair for the committee, was upset that I had exposed this violation. She would later take employment advocating for the developers. It was all part of the city's conspiracy to segregate and relocate homeless citizens 8.5 miles outside downtown to a location on Harry Hines Blvd.

Date: Thu, 9 Sep 2004
From: Jackson Fulgham1
To: Judith Anne Sturrock, herschel@att.net, rweisfeld@hotmail.com
Subject: Re: Updating on Service Providers for 9713 Harry Hines

Judith,

You agreed with Don Cass and I (Don Blanton has been urging you to do this for months) to go get "letters of interest? How many do you have?

Congratulations on what you are doing, but you need to do what you have been asked to do at the same time.

How about James Waghorne also?

How many of those named below operate either out of or in conjunction with the Day Resource Center'? How many of them are, or would be 'key' users at HH? (We need to make sure that we are spending our last few 'precious' days going after 'only' the 'key' tenants, I would think. Can you report to all of us after today as to those who either have or would sign a 'letter of interest? Don Cass told you he needs something that something needs to be on paper…What Don and all the group are desperately trying to get your efforts to accomplish is to have 'signed expressions of interest' from as many as possible…

    Jackson Fulgham

Letter to Council Member Steve Salazar,

Every Tuesday evening from 3PM to 6PM at Dallas City Hall, Mr. Dunning and the committee to address homelessness and where the new Homeless Assistance Center should be located in Dallas, meet. These are opened to the general public. Last nights' meeting ended in a frightening revelation. Mr. Dunning revealed he had been informed that North Dallas and the Harry Hines location had 8 votes on the City council. He also warned the committee members that they would be lobbied hard to take tours of the Harry Hines site. The past site selection chair has even gone so far as to threaten a Service Provider that if their organization did not move, they would open direct competition aimed at them.

From: Mankins, Greta (Veterans Affairs)
To: James Waghorne
Subject: Petition
Date: Tues, 5 Jan. 2004
James,
If you have a copy of your petition about the location of the Homeless Assistance Center, I have some homeless veterans who would be happy to sign.
Thanks - Greta

The first site selection committee proposed 3 different locations all outside of downtown. Each of the 3 choices faced major challenges from neighborhoods and business interest. Our organization allowed each homeless individual to have a voice and a vote. Over 425 individuals voted with their signature for the location they preferred, voting for the location closest to downtown. I knew it would be hard for any politician to deny Americans their right to vote, regardless of having a home or not. The Mayor, instead of making a decision for a location, disbanded the first site selection and formed her own Task Force.

It meant more time for us to wait, but it also meant the ultimate defeat of those who sought to segregate us out of downtown. It was one of many bittersweet victories for the Dallas Homeless Neighborhood Association and our family without homes. The fight for a location would drag on for another three years.

"Where justice is denied, where poverty is enforced, where ignorance prevails, and where any one class is made to feel that society is an organized conspiracy to oppress, rob and degrade them, neither person nor property will be safe."

Fredrick Douglas

"There is one thing the rich and poor have in common, they never have enough."

William Pettet – homeless

From the Offices of Hamilton Properties Corporation

June 3, 2005

Honorable Mayor and Honorable Members of the Dallas City Council

Ladies and Gentlemen:

We the undersigned property owners and stakeholders in downtown, urge the Dallas City Council to reconsider its proposed Homeless Assistance Center site for the following reasons:

4. The presence of numerous vagrants panhandling, loitering, sleeping on laying on sidewalks, gaining entry to corridors and stairwells for the night, the debris left in their wake, and their other negative consequences have a regrettable effect on this livability. Residential property management professionals identify the presence of large numbers of homeless as one of the biggest negative factors to downtown living. It is a major cost in terms of security, custodial, maintenance and management that is significantly less of a problem in outlying areas. Horror stories abound of offensive tasks arising out of their presence.

5. An assistance center may indeed be a way for the City to act compassionately to address the social problems of homeless persons so that they can become productive members of society. It is not likely, however, to be a panacea that cures all those who utilize its services and facilities. Moreover its CBD location will encourage the continued presence of the homeless in and around the downtown area whether they are legitimate candidates for help or chronic cases unlikely to be made under any circumstances.

6. Even if the intent of the center is to ultimately cure and eliminate homelessness and vagrancy, such outcome cannot be guaranteed, and therefore we would urge caution in the selection of a location.

9. Some of us have received City incentives for our projects (over 250 million in their pockets). This is not an expression of ingratitude...

Thank you for your efforts to resolve a vexing community issue. Those of us undersigned would be happy to become more involved in finding an appropriate location for this Center and regret the extent of our involvement to date has not been greater.

Usually, terrible things that are done with the excuse that progress requires them are not really progress at all, but just terrible things.   Russell Baker

The list of this letter and those who would later donate money to defeat Proposition 14, which would build a new Homeless Assistance Center for the homeless along with money to be used for housing, read like something out of the who's who in Dallas. Fresh Choice, Inc. a subsidiary of Starbucks, The Staubach Company, representatives from the Adolphus Tower and Magnolia Hotel supported the move. $160,000 dollars was raised for their cause. The two advantages the homeless had; first, was their voice and secondly, a secret weapon, those individuals and companies who campaigned to defeat Prop 14, called The Heart of Dallas Partnership.

November 04, 2005

Kim Horner called me about a booklet she had gotten from a downtown grocery store. What few called to be a satirical book aimed at the homeless was nothing more than degrading and hateful. It was the same type of literature one would expect from a white supremacist group targeting a minority. David Millet, part owner of Millet the Printer and contributor to the Heart of Dallas Partnership, printed the booklet, revealing the hatred and prejudice within their group. The campaign philosophy was based on spreading fear and mistruths about the homeless. Secondly, the political consultant hired also used such tactics as denying the $23 million new Homeless Assistance Center would even help the homeless. The mailer sent out to the community quoted a Dallas Independent School District official, making reference that the new place would jeopardize the safety of young ladies attending an alternative school. It did not say that the current Day Resource

Center, which had been opened since 1988, was directly across the street from the school and the new center would be further away.

The David Millet booklet contained even more disturbing material. Titled to confuse people as to who the publisher was, Millet combined the names of the two well know groups, Dallas Homeless Neighborhood Association and the Metro Dallas Homeless Alliance, to make up the name, Homeless District Neighborhood Alliance. The production cost of the booklet was projected to be over $12,000 and was a violation of State laws.

It included a membership application to be filled out and encouraged people to break the litter laws by throwing it on the ground for City crews to pick up. A homeless walking guide to downtown, respect for wildlife including not eating the local domestic animals or squirrels, tips for disposing of human waste, minimizing campfires, etc… The publicity of this booklet and the obvious slander mailers, fired up voters who would normally stay at home. People were tiring of campaigns ran on lies and they certainly did not want these type of people to represent the morals of our community. I spent most of November 8th 2005 in prayer at the Cathedral of Guadalupe.

11/9/2005 Publication: THE DALLAS MORNING NEWS reprint with permission
Headline: Gay-marriage ban coasts; **Dallas rejects strong mayor; DOWNTOWN HOMELESS CENTER PLAN PASSES EASILY, FOR 59% AGAINST 41%**
Some say second defeat in 6 months signals lack of trust in Miller
Byline: EMILY RAMSHAW
Credit: Staff Writer

When I arrived at work the next morning, there were plenty of hugs and plenty of tears. For the homeless, and myself it was a bittersweet victory. So many of our friends had died before seeing that a majority of citizens in Dallas did care and had a heart. The percentages didn't reveal what really happened the day of the vote. Proposition 14 passed in every district and won in over 93% of the voting precincts. Twice the amount of voters went to the polls as projected by political analysts and Prop. 14 was only second to the Strong Mayor proposal in the amount of votes cast. It was a trifecta win for the homeless. Mayor Laura Miller lost her bid to become a "Strong Mayor", the homeless won the bond and the site location for the new Homeless Assistance Center in downtown was already firm. Groundbreaking for the new Homeless Assistant Center would take place on -

February 25, 2007

The politicians took their bows, clamoring for the cameras, making speeches all the while leaving the people who had sacrificed their lives for this day to come, off to the side. The homeless and the community were responsible for the bond money being past. It was the true advocates of the past who had paved the way with their own sacrifices that deserved credit. I was reminded of the tragic time when politicians from D.C. came out patting themselves on their backs in front of cameras because they had passed additional funds to FEMA, while people in New Orleans were dying and the bodies laid everywhere from Hurricane Katrina. I could never understand how people claim glory when being forced to do the right thing. Politics in Dallas might not ever change but people with conviction and a willingness to sacrifice can move it to one side or the other.

The projected completion for the new center is spring of 2008, almost 5 years after the first initial bond election. It would come to late for some 400 homeless who had died the most of horrible deaths since 2000. Their bodies found on the streets in Dallas.

J.C., a double amputee and veteran had been staying in an abandon parking garage at 500 S. Ervay (100 yards from City Hall) just a few days after the official groundbreaking. The City of Dallas, Crisis Intervention Team found J.C. shaking with tremors. He had tied two garbage bags to his stumps to collect the drainage from the infection and gangrene, which had formed. Calling EMS, the paramedics tried to refuse giving assistance and transportation to the hospital. City representatives virtually had to threaten the EMS personnel to transport him. J.C. would be taken off of life support the next day.

It's hard living with the fact that not everybody will have an opportunity and in fact die in such a grizzly way. But it's the ones that do make it, which keeps an advocate going.

A young tall African American male dressed in a suit and tie, came into my office when I was working for Dallas MetroCare. He asked if my name was James, which I answered yes. "You might not remember me," he said. "But I came to you three months ago asking for help and you took me to the hospital I just wanted to come by and tell you thank you."

I shook his hand and told him he was welcomed. His eyes started to glisten up. "When I came in, I had reached the lowest point in my life. My crack addiction had gotten so bad; I was living underneath a bridge and was giving myself to other men to do as the pleased just so I could get a $5 rock." (Crack cocaine). Tears were now flowing down his cheeks. "Today I have my own place and a full time job." He hugged me as he thanked me again. It was stories like this that kept me motivated through the worst of times. It was seeing the courage people that had to change their lives and to face their demons, making our community and nation a better place for all. Maybe people needed a second chance, a third chance or even a fifth chance but with these types of results, how could I ever turn aside anyone.

My mother had taught me never to reveal anything negative about someone unless it will help others. I had an obligation to the homeless after they voted and gave me their confidence to be their voice and advocate, I would fulfill that obligation to all ends. My work and goals had been completed. The homeless would have a new Homeless Assistant Center in downtown. Over 300 million dollars had poured into agencies in 5 years of advocacy. "Housing First" was adopted as the top priority. It was rumored that the City of Dallas entered into negotiations with Corporate Supportive Housing for 1,200 SRO housing units. Homelessness became the third most important issue in Dallas and a majority of the citizens supported us. Still I had some serious concerns.

Mr. Waghorne,

My name is Jason Gerig and I'm currently interning at the National Coalition for the Homeless for Michael Stoops. He provided me with your name and e-mail address so that I could contact you regarding an update to our bi-annual "Criminalization of Homelessness" report. As you know, Dallas ranked #6 on our "Meanest Cities" list in the 2006 report. The next full report won't be released until 2008, but we're issuing an update on the '06 "20 Meanest Cities" next month as an interim report.

That being said, we would like your observations and opinion in three areas:

1. What has happened in Dallas regarding homelessness since the publication of "A Dream Denied?"
2. What positive actions have occurred since then?
3. What negative actions have occurred since then?

If you would like to e-mail your responses, that would be great. We can also set up a time to speak on the phone this week if you would prefer.

Jason Gerig –

National Coalition for the Homeless

As far as the City of Dallas treating Americans without homes as citizens and individuals with medical, social and economic needs in a manner befitting humane treatment, they have yet to do so in my opinion and instead continue to use criminalization tactics to punish the least fortunate due to politicians own failures to address social issues.

Still today, the City of Dallas continues to violate Federal Law and the U.S. Constitution by the illegal seizure of property and its destruction. Maybe the most telling of all about Dallas City Hall and how it operates is contained in this letter:

August 4, 2007

Go Get A Job

Certainly one of the most often heard expressions when discussing homelessness has the words in some form or variety stating, "Go get a job". In the last seven years I cannot count how many times I have heard these words spoken from every part of society; even from some homeless themselves.

It is my personal belief that if an individual can work and be self sufficient contributing to mainstream society, then that should be the goal not only for the individual but also for our entire community.

Many remember the fight over Proposition 14 last year; bond monies to be used to build a new Homeless Assistance Center and the almost $200,000 which was spent by both sides of the issue seeking passage or its defeat. Proposition 14 was so emotionally charged, that it received the most votes on the ballot that day, second only to the strong Mayor proposal. While many thought they were defeated with the passage of the bond monies, I saw an opportunity for everyone to come out a winner.

With the official groundbreaking held last February, I watched as Politicians and Guests of Honor take their bows, patting each other on their backs and give speeches of a grand

and bright future for not only our homeless but also for Dallas and Downtown revitalization which this new project would help bring. I also heard one thing that would make this project truly a win-win for everyone. This new Center would be built by hiring homeless individuals. Building a Homeless Assistance Center without hiring qualified homeless is equivalent to building a Latino Cultural Center without hiring any Latinos, or building the memorial in Washington D.C. for Martin Luther King Jr. without hiring African Americans. The next day many homeless went to the location told to them by the politicians to apply, only to be told the Construction Company wasn't hiring.

Now I know for certain there are homeless who can dig a ditch. I know there are some who can hammer a nail. I know that there are those in need of a job who are trained bricklayers, plumbers, electricians, etc… I know these things because I talk with them on a daily basis. One more thing I know. Regardless of how a person voted on Proposition 14 and regardless if a person even did vote. An overwhelming majority of our citizens would like to see homeless individuals in our community get a job and become self-sufficient.

So the big question is why did this Construction Company put the "screws" not only to our homeless but also to every citizen in Dallas by not hiring homeless individuals?

Do they not understand that the millions in profits they are going to make are because of the homeless and the citizens of Dallas? Is it about prejudice? Is it about greed?

Did the Citizens of Dallas and the homeless in our community; just get railroaded again by City Hall and greedy Developers?

Whatever the answers are to these questions, it was a sad day three weeks ago as I watched homeless individuals pile into a pick-up truck to go hang flyers on peoples doorknobs for $40 that day, when just down the street, a great opportunity to help the very people this Center was intended for, is instead giving all of us a reason not to trust the local government or any bond money Proposition for projects in the future.

James K Waghorne
Dallas Homeless Neighborhood Association

The homeless in Dallas will have a new center in 2008 and hopefully receive appropriate services, employment and housing and as humans; treated with dignity and respect.

The evolution of the Metro Dallas Homeless Alliance is the most positive thing to happen for our Americans without homes. This organization under new guidance will once again have inclusion of homeless individuals and now can fulfill its promise to not only fight for services but more importantly to those in the midst of surviving and dieing in the worst depredation in America today, and that being equality, dignity, justice and the most important aspect of advocacy; allow the victims a voice and to give these the support needed to carry their message of suffering and injustice. As Executive Director, Mike Faenza, of the Metro Dallas Homeless Alliance recently stated, "the central value of advocacy is for consumers, not organizations, governments, businesses or neighborhood associations."

With local, state and national support, this newly reformed organization can actually bring about the end of homelessness in Dallas while also ensuring our Americans without homes are treated humanely on a daily basis.

While the issues surrounding homelessness will be widely debated, the solution to end someone's homelessness should not be. That solution is a home and if need be, the means of support to maintain it. Unfortunately social movements historically in America have had to trudge through a slow process time and time again before the solution of moral maturity and correctness is achieved. Until then men, women and children suffer unjustly and are needlessly persecuted only because they do not conform to a personal political ideology.

The solutions surrounding social issues and doing what is morally right for the people of our Nation and even the world lies solely within the human consciousness. Everything else is just "smoke and mirrors".

July 3, 2007 Laversha Johnson, a 40 year-old homeless woman was dragged 25 feet and killed by speeding driver. The driver of the green Ford Explorer fled the scene.

August 30, 2007

Hi James,

Thank you for responding to my email.

Joe was born in Mexico, he was brought to West Texas by my father (who raised him as his own) and has lived here all his life. He was in the Army during the Vietnam era. While in the Army, stationed in Germany, he lost his best friend in Vietnam (wasn't given leave to come to his funeral), Our father was very ill during one of his leaves and we requested that he be given an extension, which was denied. Upon his return to Germany, he was told to return to the US, as our father had died. During the his tour, he also lost his wife to (her) infidelity.

When Joe was discharged he was very different, bitter, cold and was smoking pot. Not that he perfect before.

To make a long story short: Joe eventually moved to the Dallas area around 1988. Since then it has been down hill. Drugs-pot-homeless. During this time he lost his SS card, never renewed his drivers license and has become scared that he will be deported since he never became a US citizen.

I'm sure there have been brushes with the law. Some years we haven't heard form him at all, this last time it was four years.

Right now my sister (whom he calls when he is in dire need of money) knows where he is. Living in some building behind a warehouse in South Dallas, where he has worked and lived off and on for years. (not the warehouse, Dallas)

What he needs is direction and help to get his ID's and citizenship. (and drug rehab)

My sister and I don't have the answers, funds, or he can't seem to stay in communication with us long enough to help him. I'm hoping an outside party could.

I take care of our mother who has Alzheimer's and my sister's husband is terminally ill. And we work monster hours to take care of our families.

There it is in a nutshell.

What do you think?

Thanks for taking the time to read this email. It was good for me just to put this huge problem (guilt) in writing.

Lydia

This is my report of the crime.

Chapter 9

Facts and the numbers...

Why Are People Homeless?

NCH Fact Sheet #1

Published by the National Coalition for the Homeless, June 2006 – reprinted with permission:

Two trends are largely responsible for the rise in homelessness over the past 20-25 years: a growing shortage of affordable rental housing and a simultaneous increase in poverty. Below is an overview of current poverty and housing statistics, as well as additional factors contributing to homelessness. A list of resources for further study is also provided.

POVERTY

Homelessness and poverty are inextricably linked. Poor people are frequently unable to pay for housing, food, childcare, health care, and education. Difficult choices must be made when limited resources cover only some of these necessities. Often it is housing, which absorbs a high proportion of income that must be dropped. Being poor means being an illness, an accident, or a paycheck away from living on the streets.

In 2004, 12.7% of the U.S. population, or 37 million people, lived in poverty. Both the poverty rate and the number of poor people have increased in recent years, up from 12.5% in 2003, and up 1.1 million from 2003 (U.S. Bureau of the Census, 2005). 36% of persons living in poverty are children; in fact, the 2004 poverty rate of 17.6% for children under 18 years old is significantly higher than the poverty rate for any other age group. Two factors help account for increasing poverty: eroding employment opportunities for large segments of the workforce, and the declining value and availability of public assistance.

Eroding Work Opportunities

Media reports of a growing economy and low unemployment mask a number of important reasons why homelessness persists, and, in some areas of the country, is worsening. These reasons include stagnant or falling incomes and less secure jobs which offer fewer benefits. While the last few years have seen growth in real wages at all levels, these increases have not been enough to counteract a long pattern of stagnant and declining wages. Low-wage workers have been particularly hard hit by wage trends and have been left behind as the disparity between rich and poor has mushroomed. To compound the problem, the real value of the minimum wage in 2004 was 26% less than in 1979 (The Economic Policy Institute, 2005). Although incomes appear to be rising, this growth is largely due to more hours worked – which in turn can be attributed to welfare reform and the tight labor markets. Factors contributing to wage declines include a steep drop in the number and bargaining power of unionized workers; erosion in the value of the minimum wage; a decline in manufacturing jobs and the corresponding expansion of lower-paying service-sector employment; globalization; and increased nonstandard work, such as temporary and part-time employment (Mishel, Bernstein, and Schmitt, 1999). Declining wages, in turn, have put housing out of reach for many workers: in every state, more than the minimum wage is required to afford a one- or two-bedroom apartment at Fair Market Rent. A recent U.S. Conference of Mayors report stated that in every state more than the minimum-wage is required to afford a one or two-bedroom apartment at 30% of his or her income, which is the federal definition of affordable housing. In 2001, five million rental households had "worst case housing needs," which means that they paid more than half their incomes for rent, living in severely substandard housing, or both (Children's Defense Fund, 2005). The primary source of income for 80% of these households was earnings from jobs (U.S. Housing and Urban Development, 2001). The connection between impoverished workers and homelessness can be seen in homeless shelters, many of which house significant numbers of full-time wage earners. A survey of 24 U.S. cities found that 15% of persons in homeless situations are employed (U.S. Conference of Mayors, 2005). Surveys in past years have yielded the percentage of homeless working to be as high as 26% (U.S. Conference of Mayors, 2000). In a number of cities not surveyed by the U.S. Conference of Mayors - as well as in many states - the percentage is even higher (National Coalition for the Homeless, 1997).

The future of job growth does not appear promising for many workers: a 1998 study estimated that 46% of the jobs with the most growth between 1994 and 2005 pay less than $16,000 a year; these jobs will not lift families out of poverty (National Priorities Project, 1998). Moreover, 74% of these jobs pay below a livable wage ($32,185 for a family of four). Thus, for many Americans, work provides no escape from poverty. The benefits of economic growth have not been equally distributed; instead, they have been concentrated at the top of income and wealth distributions. A rising tide does not lift all boats, and in the United States today, many boats are struggling to stay afloat.

Decline in Public Assistance

The declining value and availability of public assistance is another source of increasing poverty and homelessness. Until its repeal in August 1996, the largest cash assistance program for poor families with children was the Aid to Families with Dependent Children (AFDC) program. The Personal Responsibility and Work Opportunity Reconciliation Act of 1996 (the federal welfare reform law) repealed the AFDC program and replaced it with a block grant program called Temporary Assistance to Needy Families (TANF). Current TANF benefits and Food Stamps combined are below the poverty level in every state; in fact, the current maximum TANF benefit for a single mother of two children is 29% of the federal poverty level (Nickelson, 2004). Thus, contrary to popular opinion, welfare does not provide relief from poverty.

Welfare caseloads have dropped sharply since the passage and implementation of welfare reform legislation. However, declining welfare rolls simply mean that fewer people are receiving benefits -- not that they are employed or doing better financially. Early findings suggest that although more families are moving from welfare to work, many of them are faring poorly due to low wages and inadequate work supports. Only a small fraction of welfare recipients' new jobs pay above-poverty wages; most of the new jobs pay far below the poverty line (Children's Defense Fund and the National Coalition for the Homeless, 1998). These statistics from the Institute for Children and Poverty are particularly revealing: In the 2001 Institute for Children and Poverty study, 37% of homeless families had their welfare benefits reduced or cut in the last year. More strikingly, in Bucks County and Philadelphia, PA, and Seattle, WA, more than 50% had their benefits reduced or cut…Among those who lost their benefits, 20% said they became homeless as a direct result. Additionally, a second study of six states found that between 1997 and 1998, 25% of families who had stopped receiving welfare in the last six months doubled-up on housing to save money, and 23% moved because they could not pay rent (Institute for Children and Poverty, 2001). Moreover, extreme poverty is growing more common for children, especially those in female-headed and working families. This increase can be traced directly to the declining number of children lifted above one-half of the poverty line by government cash assistance for the poor (Children's Defense Fund and the National Coalition for the Homeless, 1998).

As a result of loss of benefits, low wages, and unstable employment, many families leaving welfare struggle to get medical care, food, and housing. Many lose health insurance, despite continued Medicaid eligibility: a study found that 675,000 people lost health insurance in 1997 as a result of the federal welfare reform legislation, including 400,000 children (Families USA, 1999). Moreover, over 725,000 workers, laid off from their jobs due to the recession in 2000, lost their health insurance (Families USA, 2001). According to the Children's Defense Fund, over nine million children in America have no health insurance, and over 90 percent of them are in working families.

In addition, housing is rarely affordable for families leaving welfare for low wages, yet subsidized housing is so limited that fewer than one in four TANF families nationwide lives in public housing or receives a housing voucher to help them rent a private unit. For most families leaving the rolls, housing subsidies are not an option. In some communities, former welfare families appear to be experiencing homelessness in increasing numbers (Children's Defense Fund and the National Coalition for the Homeless, 1998).

In addition to the reduction in the value and availability of welfare benefits for families, recent policy changes have reduced or eliminated public assistance for poor single individuals. Several states have cut or eliminated General Assistance (GA) benefits for single impoverished people, despite evidence that the availability of GA reduces the prevalence of homelessness (Greenberg and Baumohl, 1996). People with disabilities, too, must struggle to obtain and maintain stable housing. In 1998, on a national average, a person receiving Supplemental Security Income (SSI) benefits had to spend 69% of his or her SSI monthly income to rent a one-bedroom apartment at Fair Market Rent; in more than 125 housing market areas, the cost of a one-bedroom apartment at Fair Market Rent was more than a person's total monthly SSI income (Technical Assistance Collaborative & the Consortium for Citizens with Disabilities Housing Task Force, 1999). Today, only nine percent of non-institutionalized people receiving SSI receive housing assistance (Consortium for Citizens with Disabilities, 2005).

Presently, most states have not replaced the old welfare system with an alternative that enables families and individuals to obtain above-poverty employment and to sustain themselves when work is not available or possible.

HOUSING

A lack of affordable housing and the limited scale of housing assistance programs have contributed to the current housing crisis and to homelessness.

The gap between the number of affordable housing units and the number of people needing them has created a housing crisis for poor people. Between 1973 and 1993, 2.2 million low-rent units disappeared from the market. These units were either abandoned, converted into condominiums or expensive apartments, or became unaffordable because of cost increases. Between 1991 and 1995, median rental costs paid by low-income renters rose 21%; at the same time, the number of low-income renters increased. Over these years, despite an improving economy, the affordable housing gap grew by one million (Daskal, 1998). Between 1970 and 1995, the gap between the number of low-income renters and the amount of affordable housing units skyrocketed from a nonexistent gap to a shortage of 4.4 million affordable housing units – the largest shortfall on record (Institute for Children and Poverty, 2001). According to HUD, in recent years the shortages of affordable housing are most severe for units affordable to renters with extremely low incomes. Federal support for low-income housing has fallen 49% from 1980 to 2003 (National Low Income Housing Coalition, 2005).

More recently, the strong economy has caused rents to soar, putting housing out of reach for the poorest Americans. After the 1980s, income growth has never kept pace with rents, and since 2000, the incomes of low-income households has declined as rents continue to rise (National Low Income Housing Coalition, 2005). The number of housing units that rent for less than $300, adjusted for inflation, declined from 6.8 million in 1996 to 5.5 million in 1998, a 19 percent drop of 1.3 million units (U.S. Department of Housing and Urban Development, 1999).

The loss of affordable housing puts even greater numbers of people at risk of homelessness. The lack of affordable housing has lead to high rent burdens (rents which absorb a high-proportion of income), overcrowding, and substandard housing. These phenomena, in turn, have not only forced many people to become homeless; they have put a large and growing number of people at risk of becoming homeless. A 2001 Housing and Urban Development (HUD) study found that 4.9 million unassisted, very low-income households – this is 10.9 million people, 3.6 million of whom are children -- had "worst case needs" for housing assistance in 1999 (U.S. Department of Housing and Urban Development, 2001). Although this figure seems to be a decrease from 1997, it is misleading since, in the same two-year span, "the number of units affordable to extremely low-income renters dropped between 1997 and 1999 at an accelerated rate, and shortages of housing both affordable and available to these renters actually worsened (HUD Report on Worst Case Housing Needs, 1999).

Housing assistance can make the difference between stable housing, precarious housing, or no housing at all. However, the demand for assisted housing clearly exceeds the supply: only about one-third of poor renter households receive a housing subsidy from the federal, state, or a local government (Daskal, 1998). The limited level of housing assistance means that most poor families and individuals seeking housing assistance are placed on long waiting lists. From 1996- 1998, the time households spent on waiting lists for HUD housing assistance grew dramatically. For the largest public housing authorities, a family's average time on a waiting list rose from 22 to 33 months from 1996 to 1998 - a 50% increase (U.S. Department of Housing and Urban Development, 1999). The average waiting period for a Section 8 rental assistance voucher rose from 26 months to 28 months between 1996 and 1998. Today the average wait for Section 8 Vouchers is 35 months (U.S. Conference of Mayors, 2004). Excessive waiting lists for public housing mean that people must remain in shelters or inadequate housing arrangements longer. For instance, in the mid-1990s in New York, families stayed in a shelter an average of five months before moving on to permanent housing. In a survey of 24 cities, people remain homeless an average of seven months, and 87% of cities reported that the length of time people are homeless has increased in recent years (U.S. Conference of Mayors, 2005). Longer stays in homeless shelters a result in less shelter space available for other homeless people, who must find shelter elsewhere or live on the streets. A housing trend with a particularly severe impact on homelessness is the loss of single room occupancy (SRO) housing. In the past, SRO housing served to house many poor individuals, including poor persons suffering from mental illness or substance abuse. From 1970 to the mid-1980s, an estimated one million SRO units were demolished (Dolbeare, 1996). The demolition of SRO housing was most notable in large cities: between 1970-1982, New York City lost 87% of its $200 per month or less SRO stock; Chicago experienced the total elimination of cubicle hotels; and by 1985, Los Angeles had lost more than half of its downtown SRO housing (Koegel, et al, 1996). From 1975 to 1988, San Francisco lost 43% of its stock of low-cost residential hotels; from 1970 to 1986, Portland, Oregon lost 59% of its residential hotels; and from 1971 to 1981 Denver lost 64% of its SRO hotels (Wright and Rubin, 1997). Thus the destruction of SRO housing is a major factor in the growth of homelessness in many cities. Finally, it should be noted that the largest federal housing assistance program is the entitlement to deduct mortgage interest from income for tax purposes. In fact, for every one dollar spent on low income housing programs, the federal treasury loses four dollars to housing-related tax expenditures, 75% of which benefit households in the top fifth of income distribution (Dolbeare, 1996). In 2003, the federal government spent almost twice as much in housing-related tax expenditures and direct housing assistance for households in the top income quintile than on housing subsidies for the lowest-income households (National Low Income Housing Coalition, 2005. Thus, federal housing policy has not responded to the needs of low-income households, while disproportionately benefiting the wealthiest Americans.

OTHER FACTORS

Particularly within the context of poverty and the lack of affordable housing, certain additional factors may push people into homelessness. Other major factors, which can contribute to homelessness, include the following:

Lack of Affordable Health Care: For families and individuals struggling to pay the rent, a serious illness or disability can start a downward spiral into homelessness, beginning with a lost job, depletion of savings to pay for care, and eventual eviction. In 2004, approximately 45.8 million Americans had no health care insurance. That equates to 15.7% of the population (U.S. Bureau of the Census, 2005). Nearly a third of persons living in poverty had no health insurance of any kind. The coverage held by many others would not carry them through a catastrophic illness.

Domestic Violence: Battered women who live in poverty are often forced to choose between abusive relationships and homelessness. In a study of 777 homeless parents (the majority of whom were mothers) in ten U.S. cities, 22% said they had left their last place of residence because of domestic violence (Homes for the Homeless, 1998). In addition, 50% of the cities surveyed by the U.S. Conference of Mayors identified domestic violence as a primary cause of homelessness (U.S. Conference of Mayors, 2005). Studying the entire country, though, reveals that the problem is even more serious.

Nationally, approximately half of all women and children experiencing homelessness are fleeing domestic violence (Zorza, 1991; National Coalition Against Domestic Violence, 2001).

Mental Illness: Approximately 22% of the single adult homeless population suffers from some form of severe and persistent mental illness (U.S. Conference of Mayors, 2005). Despite the disproportionate number of severely mentally ill people among the homeless population, increases in homelessness are not attributable to the release of severely mentally ill people from institutions. Most patients were released from mental hospitals in the 1950s and 1960s, yet vast increases in homelessness did not occur until the 1980s, when incomes and housing options for those living on the margins began to diminish rapidly. According to the 2003 U.S. Department of Health and Human Services Report, most homeless persons with mental illness do not need to be institutionalized, but can live in the community with the appropriate supportive housing options (U.S. Department of Health and Human Services, 2003). However, many mentally ill homeless people are unable to obtain access to supportive housing and/or other treatment services. The mental health support services most needed include case management, housing, and treatment.

Addiction Disorders: The relationship between addiction and homelessness is complex and controversial. While rates of alcohol and drug abuse are disproportionately high among the homeless population, the increase in homelessness over the past two decades cannot be explained by addiction alone. Many people who are addicted to alcohol and drugs never become homeless, but people who are poor and addicted are clearly at increased risk of homelessness. During the 1980s, competition for increasingly scarce low-income housing grew so intense that those with disabilities such as addiction and mental illness were more likely to lose out and find themselves on the streets. The loss of SRO housing, a source of stability for many poor people suffering from addiction and/or mental illness, was a major factor in increased homelessness in many communities. Addiction does increase the risk of displacement for the precariously housed; in the absence of appropriate treatment, it may doom one's chances of getting housing once on the streets. Homeless people often face insurmountable barriers to obtaining health care, including addictive disorder treatment services and recovery supports. The following are among the obstacles to treatment for homeless persons: lack of health insurance; lack of documentation; waiting lists; scheduling difficulties; daily contact requirements; lack of transportation; ineffective treatment methods; lack of supportive services; and cultural insensitivity. An in-depth study of 13 communities across the nation revealed service gaps in every community in at least one stage of the treatment and recovery continuum for homeless people (National Coalition for the Homeless, 1998).

Reprinted with permission from the National Coalition for the Homeless.

National Coalition for the Homeless
2201 P. St. NW Washington, DC 20037
Phone: (202) 462-4822 Fax: (202) 462-4823
Email: info@nationalhomeless.org |Website: www.nationalhomeless.org

FOOTNOTES

1. FMRs are the monthly amounts "needed to rent privately owned, decent, safe, and sanitary rental housing of a modest (non-luxury) nature with suitable amenities." Federal Register. HUD determines FMRs for localities in all 50 states.

2. The poverty line for a family of three is $12,750; for a family of four, the poverty line is $16,813. See http://www.census.gov/hhes/ww w/poverty.html for details.

3. "Worst case needs" refers to those renters with incomes below 50% of the area median income who are involuntarily displaced, pay more than half of their income for rent and utilities, or live in substandard housing.

4. The Section 8 Program is a federal housing assistance program that provides housing subsidies for families and individuals to live in existing rental housing or in designated housing projects.

National Alliance to End Homelessness – Summary – visit www.naeh.org for full report – reprinted with permission

RESEARCH REPORTS ON HOMELESSNESS

Homelessness Counts

How community approaches to homelessness are changing dramatically, what we should be doing to track progress, and how many people are homeless in your community.

JANUARY 2007

Homelessness Counts

JANUARY 2007

Authors

The Homelessness Research Institute of the National Alliance to End Homelessness prepared this report. The primary authors of the paper are Mary Cunningham and Meghan Henry.

Acknowledgements:

The authors thank Samantha Batko and Webb Lyons of the National Alliance to End Homelessness for providing careful editing. Any errors or omissions are, of course, the responsibility of the authors.

The National Alliance to End Homelessness is a nonpartisan, mission-driven organization committed to preventing and ending homelessness in the United States.

Our work

The National Alliance to End Homelessness is a leading voice on the issue of homelessness. The Alliance analyzes policy and develops pragmatic, cost-effective policy solutions.

We work collaboratively with the public, private, and nonprofit sectors to build state and local capacity, leading to stronger programs and policies that help homeless individuals and families make positive changes in their lives. We provide data and research to policymakers and elected officials in order to inform policy debates and educate the public and opinion leaders nationwide. Guiding our work is A Plan, Not a Dream: How to End Homelessness in Ten Years. The Ten Year Plan identifies our nation's challenges in addressing the problem and lays out practical steps our nation can take to change its present course and truly end homelessness within 10 years. To learn how to end 20 years of homelessness in 10 years, please visit www.endhomelessness.org.

Homelessness Research Institute

The Homelessness Research Institute at the National Alliance to End Homelessness works to end homelessness by building and disseminating knowledge that drives policy change. The goals of the Institute are to build the intellectual capital around solutions to homelessness; to connect with researchers across the country to ensure that policy-makers, practitioners, and the caring public have the best information about trends in homelessness demographics, research, and emerging solutions; and to engage the media to ensure intelligent reporting on the issue of homelessness.

Homelessness Counts

JANUARY 2007

Summary

A movement to end homelessness is underway. Thousands of stakeholders—policymakers, advocates, researchers, practitioners, former and current homeless people, community leaders, and concerned citizens—from across the country are involved in efforts to end homelessness at the local and national level. Today, hundreds of communities are re-tooling their homeless assistance systems and have committed to ending homelessness through local plans. At the federal level, the U.S. Department of Housing and Urban Development's (HUD) homelessness assistance programs are targeting resources to permanent housing, and the Congress and the Bush Administration have committed to ending chronic homelessness by developing 150,000 units of permanent supportive housing for people who have been homeless for long periods. The private sector, through major philanthropic organizations, is engaging and funding efforts that focus on permanent solutions for homeless people. And new research and imaginative policies at the state and local level are paving the way. Taken together, these efforts represent a nationwide effort to end homelessness.

Homeless Estimates

Chronic - 23%

Non-chronic - 77%

Total Homeless: 744,313 people

Sheltered - 56%

Unsheltered - 44%

Individuals - 59%

Persons in Families - 41%

How will we know if these efforts are successful? This report lays the groundwork for measuring efforts to end homelessness by establishing a baseline number of homeless people from which to monitor trends in homelessness. We use local point-in-time counts of homeless people to create an estimate of the number of homeless people nationwide. As with all data, the counts included in this report are not perfect and have numerous limitations, but they are the best data available at this time.

In January 2005, an estimated 744,313 people experienced homelessness.

56 percent of homeless people counted were living in shelters and transitional housing and, shockingly, 44 percent were unsheltered. 59 percent of homeless people counted were single adults and 41 percent were persons living in families.

Today, thousands of people—policymakers, advocates, researchers, practitioners, former and current homeless people, community leaders, philanthropist, and citizens—from across the country are working to end homelessness.

In total, 98,452 homeless families were counted.

23 percent of homeless people were reported as chronically homeless, which, according to HUD's definition, means that they are homeless for long periods or repeatedly and have a disability.

A number of states had high rates of homelessness, including Alaska, California, Colorado, Hawaii, Idaho, Nevada, Oregon, Rhode Island, and Washington State. In addition, Washington, DC had a high rate of homeless people.

These statistics show that far too many people are homeless. There is, however, reason for optimism. During the past five years, community approaches to homelessness have changed and thousands of people are working toward the shared goal of ending homelessness.

Measuring their success or failure will depend on collecting and analyzing outcome data, monitoring changes in homelessness populations, and understanding which interventions lead to different outcomes. Yet, up until now, we had no recent data on how many people are homeless in the United States. The data in this report represent the first effort to count homeless people nationwide in 10 years. We hope to make this report an annual report, tracking progress on the efforts to end homelessness nationwide. It is our belief that what gets measured, gets done.

Ending Homelessness in America

Can we really end homelessness? In 2000, the National Alliance to End Homelessness issued a challenge to American communities to end homelessness in 10 years. Our Ten Year Plan provides a road map: (1) strengthen prevention; (2) focus on permanent housing; (3) support long-term, data-driven strategies at the community level; and (4) rebuild the support system for low-income Americans.

Today, thousands of people—policymakers, advocates, researchers, practitioners, former and current homeless people, community leaders, philanthropists, and citizens—from across the country are working to end homelessness. They are dramatically changing the landscape for homeless people and leading communities in a new direction that reaches for results. Their efforts are striking:

Over 200 communities across the country are undertaking planning efforts to end homelessness; 90 of these communities have completed plans. Answering a challenge from the U.S. Interagency Council, the National League of Cities, National

To read the National Alliance to End Homelessness' Ten Year Plan, A Plan, Not a Dream: How to End Homeless-ness in Ten Years, please visit www.endhomelessness.org.

See "A New Vision: What Is in Community Plans to End Homelessness," National Alliance to End Homelessness (2006).

Association of Counties, and U.S. Conference of Mayors have committed to the goal of ending chronic homelessness at the local level.

Policy changes at the U.S. Department of Housing and Urban Development (HUD) are ensuring that Continuums of Care (CoCs), the local or regional bodies that coordinate services and funding for homeless people and families, focus on permanent housing. Many communities are re-tooling their homeless assistance systems using Housing First approaches that help people exit shelter and access affordable housing faster.

President Bush made ending chronic homelessness in 10 years an administration-wide goal and, each year since 2004, the President has requested an increase in homelessness assistance funding. Congress, on a bipartisan basis, committed to creating 150,000 units of permanent supportive housing for chronically homeless people. The 90 community plans completed to date call for creating 80,000 permanent supportive housing units.

Major foundations and corporations came together with the Corporation for Supportive Housing and the National Alliance to End Homelessness to form the Partnership to End Long Term Homelessness (PELTH), committing $36 million to the problem and pledging to engage the philanthropic sector in the effort. New research on chronic homelessness crystallized effective solutions, highlighting the need for permanent supportive housing. Research on how to get families back into housing faster is emerging.

Taken together, these efforts represent a national effort to end homelessness. Today, homelessness is a problem with a solution, instead of something that will always exist no matter what we do or how much money we throw at it. Challenges remain formidable, but these efforts have the potential to translate into nationwide declines in homelessness. How will we know if they are successful? The purpose of this report is to create a baseline from which to measure progress in ending homelessness. To do so, we compiled local point-in-time counts of homeless people taken in 2005. This report discusses the importance of setting a baseline, provides a brief history of counting homeless people, and then presents our findings from this analysis, including a national estimate and counts of homeless people by state and community.

In 2003, at the annual meeting of the U.S. Conference of Mayors, U.S. Interagency Council on Homelessness

Executive Director Philip Mangano challenged 100 cities to create plans to end chronic homelessness and the U.S. Conference of Mayors adopted a resolution in support of this challenge. The National League of Cities and the National Association of Counties also adopted resolutions in favor of plans to end homelessness.

HUD has renewed the department's public commitment to providing permanent housing through the homeless assistance program. The percentage of HUD homeless assistance funding that goes to housing has increased substantially.

In 2005, 58 percent of funds supported housing activities versus just 43 percent in 1998. See HUD (2006c).

For more information on communities making progress in ending homelessness, please see our Community Snapshot series available at www.endhomelessness.org.

The first commitment came from HUD Secretary Mel Martinez in his remarks at the National Alliance to End Homelessness' annual conference. See "Taking on the Problem that 'Cannot Be Solved.'" Remarks prepared for delivery by Secretary Mel Martinez, Friday, July 20, 2001. President Bush later made a commitment in the FY 2003 Federal Budget.

See "A New Vision: What Is in Community Plans to End Homelessness," National Alliance to End Homelessness (2006).

For more information on PELTH, visit www.endlongtermhomelessness.org.

Some of the most important research on permanent supportive housing has been conducted by Dr. Dennis Culhane of the University of Pennsylvania. See Culhane (2002) for details on findings and Gladwell (2006) for a description of how the research can be applied and why it is revolutionizing approaches to homelessness.

This report discusses the importance of setting a baseline, provides a brief history of counting homeless people, and then presents our findings from this analysis, including a national estimate and counts of homeless people by state and community.

Collecting data on homelessness and tracking progress can inform public opinion, increase public awareness, and attract resources that lead to the eradication of the problem.

Now that the goal of ending homelessness is set—and supported by the President, Congress, and community leaders—measuring progress is the next critical step.

"What gets measured gets done" is a popular adage that rings true. If we do not measure progress, we will not know if efforts to end homelessness are showing results. To measure progress, stakeholders must establish a baseline to record how many people are currently homeless. Next, numeric targets and a time line to meet the goal of ending homelessness should be developed. The final step in measuring progress is collecting data on specific performance measures and monitoring outcomes. Data are critical to measuring and tracking progress over time. Unfortunately, collecting data on how many people experience homelessness is a costly endeavor fraught with methodological, logistical, and political challenges.

Setting a National Baseline: Estimating the Number of Homeless People

How many people are currently homeless in the United States? The answer to this question is important because it establishes the dimensions of the problem and helps policymakers and program administrators track progress on the goal of ending homelessness. Collecting data on homelessness and tracking progress can inform public opinion, increase public awareness, and attract resources that lead to the eradication of the problem. Notwithstanding the critical role of data in crafting solutions to end homelessness, the task of estimating the number of homeless people and collecting data on their characteristics is considerably difficult.

The challenges associated with estimating the number of homeless people are not new. Since the mid-1980s, advocates, policymakers, and researchers have struggled with the Counting the number of homeless people in the United States is methodologically challenging and highly political—a dangerous combination with an interesting history. Past estimates of the number of homeless people range from 250,000 to 3 million homeless people (see Table 1). The 3 million estimates were put forth in 1983 by Mitch Snyder and Mary Ellen Hombs of the Community for Creative Non-violence (CCNV). Hombs and Snyder arrived at the number by asking service providers in 14 cities how many people were homeless and then extrapolated, using an unknown method, to get a figure of 2.2 to 3 million. Although generally viewed as a "guestimate," the numbers were used repeatedly by the media, eventually becoming ubiquitous.

In 1984, HUD conducted a similar study that also involved local informant estimates as well as enumeration and reported a figure a fraction of the size. The HUD report estimated 250,000–350,000 homeless people at a point in time. Despite the fact that the HUD number was arrived at by professional social scientists; the estimate was "greeted by advocates, media pundits, and sundry members of Congress with fury." HUD was accused of having a "hidden agenda" and of "rig[ging] the numbers." The political implication of the difference between the activist's counts and the HUD counts are still felt and provide good reason to approach homelessness counts with care and caution. The Census Bureau attempted to include individuals living on the street and in places not intended for human habitation in the 1970, 1980, and 1990 decennial censuses. In 1980, the Census conducted a "casual count" of the homeless population by selecting urban areas over a two-week period. This count took place six weeks after the Decennial Census and involved shelter counts during evening hours and public places sampling during the day. Enumerators interviewed people at employment offices and welfare and food stamp offices, as well as street locations and parks until 8:00 p.m., to identify individuals who had not been included in the original count. Due to methodological problems, the count was not released. In 1987, the Urban Institute conducted a study providing one-day and one-week estimates on the number of homeless people in the country. This month-long project counted clients of shelters as well as soup kitchens. Enumerating at soup kitchens allowed the researchers to count the often difficult-to-count street population. This study estimated 229,000 homeless adults and children on any given day in cities of over 100,000 people.

In 1990, Census enumerators again performed the shelter count during the late evening and early morning hours, but decided to use a nighttime street enumeration instead of the day count for the 1990 decennial census. On March 20–21, 1990, the S-Night count resulted in about 228,000 homeless persons enumerated. The Bureau believed that the 1990 S-Night count procedures enabled them to resolve any concerns about double-counting. In 1996, the U.S. Interagency Council on Homelessness contracted the Urban Institute to conduct the last national count of homeless people in the United States. The National Survey of Homeless Assistance Providers and Clients had a number of methodological variations from previous counts. It did not include a street count, but counted clients at soup kitchens, shelters, and other homeless service providers. The study found that between 444,000 and 842,000 people in the United States are homeless. This study, conducted more that 10 years ago, is the last national count.

A Brief History of Counting The Homeless Population

a See Estimates and Public Policy: The Politics of Numbers (Kondaratas, 1991).

b Ibid, p. 635.

c See Helping America's Homeless: Emergency Shelter or Affordable Housing (Burt et al., 2001).

d See Counting the Homeless: Limitations of the 1990 Census Results and Methodology (U.S. General Accounting Office, 1991).

. . . estimates of the number of homeless people are highly controversial and are often met with skepticism. Counting the number of homeless people has been described as a "high-stakes numbers game." Defining who is homeless, essentially identifying who to count, even with an official definition, is a complicated task. By attempting to count a population that is without a home or, as some say, "without place," enumeration efforts must overcome problems that are inherent to the question they seek to answer. Finding homeless people—notably homeless people living on the street rather than in emergency shelters— is often the biggest challenge. For all of these reasons and many more, estimates of the number of homeless people are highly controversial and are often met with skepticism. Counting the number of homeless people has been described as a "high-stakes numbers game."

The last nationwide count, and the most rigorous national estimate, of homeless people—the National Survey of Homeless Assistance Providers and Clients (NSHAPC)—was taken over 10 years ago in 1996. This research was sponsored by the U.S. Interagency Council on Homelessness and conducted by the Urban Institute. Based on counts of homeless people from a sample of homeless service providers from across the country, the study found that between 444,000 and 842,000 people in the United States are homeless. At the time, the lead researcher of the study, Martha Burt of the Urban Institute, estimated the actual number of homeless people to be around 800,000.13 The NSHAPC study estimate provides data on how many people are homeless at a specific point in time. The reality is that the homeless population is quite fluid—people move in and out of homelessness and

See Homelessness in America (Baumohl, 1996) for a historical review of efforts to enumerate homelessness in the United States.

See "Counting the Homeless Is a High Stakes Numbers Game" (Rivenburg, 2006).

See America's Homeless II: Populations and Services (Urban Institute, 2000) for more on the study, estimates ,and sampling methods. See What Will It Take to End Homelessness? (Burt, 2001).

To create an annual estimate of homelessness, Burt and colleagues extrapolated this number, estimating that between 2.3 and 3.5 million people per year experience homelessness.

Although this landmark study revealed a wealth of information on homelessness, national enumeration efforts like the one described above are logistically difficult, methodologically challenging, and expensive. To overcome these challenges, HUD has undertaken two strategies to improve the availability of the data: (1) requiring CoCs to develop administrative data systems; and (2) requiring CoCs to conduct point-in-time counts every other year. Both of these strategies focus on collecting data locally and then aggregating to obtain a national estimate. The first strategy was initiated in 2001, when Congress required all CoCs to create Homeless Management Information Systems (HMIS).

These administrative data systems collect data on the characteristics of homeless people entering and exiting the homeless assistance system. Progress on HMIS has been slow, but steady. Today, almost 75 percent of CoCs have implemented HMIS systems. HMIS is a critical tool, but it only collects data on homeless people inside the system. To overcome this gap, in 2003, HUD required CoCs to collect data on the number of people who are homeless—both sheltered and unsheltered—in their community. The quality of these point-in-time counts is uneven, with some jurisdictions using more rigorous methods than others. There have, however, been significant efforts from HUD to provide guidance and increase technical assistance to help local communities collect accurate estimates.

About the Data in This Report

The purpose of this report is to establish a nationwide baseline—an estimate of how many homeless people sleep in shelters and on the streets—so that we can measure progress toward the goal of ending homelessness. The data in this report are estimates of how many people experience homelessness in communities across the United States.

The report tabulates and summarizes data from 463 CoC point-in-time studies conducted in 2005.

The purpose of this report is to establish a nationwide baseline— an estimate of how many homeless people sleep in shelters and on the streets—so that we can measure progress toward the goal of ending homelessness.

No data are without flaws and limitations. As such, these counts are not perfect and should be used as rough guidelines rather than precise estimates. The data limitations for the local point-in-time counts in this report are similar to all counts of homeless people.

The limitations include definitional issues, finding homeless people, data collection and enumeration methods, sampling and extrapolation, de-duplicating, and differing time frames. In addition, because it is up to CoCs to design data collection methods that meet local needs, each CoC uses different methods to collect and assemble an estimate. This means that in addition to general limitations, each local point-in-time estimate holds its own unique data limitations. Because communities used varying methods for collecting point-in-time data, we caution the users of these data against comparing the data by jurisdiction because doing so runs the risks of the "apples and oranges" problem. Additional information about the methodology that CoCs use to assemble estimates can be found in an appendix to this report.

National Estimate

By tabulating local point-in-time estimates, we found that 744,313 people in the United States experienced homelessness in January 2005. This number is adjusted for data summation errors and inaccurate outliers.19 We provide both the adjusted total and the unadjusted total for the reader (see Table 1). The total adjusted estimate for January 2005 (744,313) falls within the parameters of the 1996 estimate; however, it is difficult to say if the 2005 estimate is an increase, decrease, or no change from the 1996 estimate.

In 10 years, it is worth noting that the size of the U.S. population, something that could affect the size of the homeless population, increased dramatically during this period. Further, while we do make comparisons to the general population and poor population, point-in-time estimates only tell us how many people are homeless at a given time; the reality, however, is that many more people experience homelessness annually—people move in and out of homelessness and most people are homeless for only a short period of time. The NSHAPC study estimated that between 2.3 and 3.5 million people are homeless in a given year—nearly 1 to 2 percent of the total population.20 In short, point-in-time counts, like the estimates in this report, will always represent a smaller percentage of the population when compared to annual estimates.

Sheltered or Unsheltered

The CoC estimates enumerate how many homeless people are living in shelters (this can include emergency shelters and transitional housing) and how many homeless people are literally sleeping and living on the street. The estimates show that 56 percent (407,813) of homeless people were living in shelters and 44 percent (322,082) of homeless people were unsheltered (see Exhibit 1). These point-in-time surveys were taken in January, so it is shocking that more than 300,000 people were sleeping on the street. These data suggest two possible explanations for the high number of people living on the streets: the lack of capacity of the emergency shelter system and the system's inability to bring people in from the street (either because they do not want to stay in a shelter or because the shelter does not have an adequate number of beds).

Exhibit 1 Percentage Sheltered vs.
Unsheltered N = 729,895
Sheltered - 56%
Unsheltered - 44%

Household structure is an important factor in responding to homelessness because single adults and families with children may have different needs. Approximately 59 percent (437,710) of the homeless population counted in 2005 were individuals and 41 percent (303,551) were persons in families with children (see Exhibit 2).

In total, there were 98,452 homeless families counted. These data represent a slight shift from the 1996 data in the percentage of individuals versus persons in families with children. The NSHAPC study showed that, at a point in time, 35 percent of homeless clients were persons in families and 65 percent were single adults. This increase in the percentage of persons in families with children can be explained by a number of possible factors, including differences in methodology between the studies, a decrease in the single adult population, or an actual increase in the percentage of homeless persons with families.

Chronic Homelessness

Chronically homeless people represent an estimated 23 percent (171,192) of the total homeless population counted in 2005 (see Exhibit 3). This estimate is similar to previous estimates of 150,000 to 200,000 chronically homeless people. It According to HUD's definition, a person who is ''chronically homeless'' is an unaccompanied homeless individual with a disabling condition who has either been continuously homeless for a year or more, or has had at least four episodes of homelessness in the past three years. In order to be considered chronically homeless, a person must have been sleeping in a place not meant for human habitation (e.g., living on the streets) and/or in an emergency homeless shelter. A disabling condition is defined as a diagnosable substance use disorder, serious mental illness, developmental disability, or chronic physical illness or disability including the co-occurrence of two or more of these conditions. A disabling condition limits an individual's ability to work or perform one or more activities of daily living.

Past estimates of the number of adults who experience chronic homelessness from the National Alliance to End Homelessness and the Millennial Housing Commission range from 150,000 to 200,000. See Millennial Housing Commission (2002).

Should be noted, however, that counting the number of chronically homeless single adults using point-in-time methods has inherent difficulties. Chronically homeless adults are by definition those who have been homeless for long periods or who experience repeated episodes of homelessness. Identifying chronically homeless people at a point in time means asking homeless people to self-identify as chronically homeless or asking service providers to identify who is chronically homeless. Both of these methods suffer from obvious reliability problems. As HMIS systems increase their coverage rates, program administrators will be able to estimate more accurately the number of people who experience chronic homelessness.

A number of states had high rates of homelessness per capita, including Alaska, California, Colorado, Hawaii, Idaho, Nevada, Oregon, Rhode Island, and Washington State. In addition, Washington, DC had a high rate of homeless people.

* Please note that these homeless estimates are point-in-time and do not fully capture the number of people who experience homelessness over the course of a year. The percentage of people who experience homelessness in the general population would be much higher if annual estimates were available.

Conclusion

The data in this report represent the first effort to count homeless people nationwide in 10 years. Much has changed since that time in terms of data and research on homelessness. HUD and local communities are overcoming technical inertia, despite lack of funding and scarce resources, and are putting more emphasis on collecting data, tracking how many people are homeless, and understanding the characteristics of homeless people. These data will help policymakers understand the scope of the problem and identify communities that are making progress and communities that are struggling to find effective responses to homelessness Data will also help garner national attention to the issue. Taken as a whole, the efforts to end homelessness from across the country are striking, but despite efforts to end homelessness, and some progress in a handful of communities, this report shows that far too many people remain homeless in America.

National Alliance to End Homelessness
1518 K Street, NW
Suite 410
Washington, DC 20005
www.endhomelessness.org

State of the Nation's Housing 2007 Finds:
June 13, 2007
WASHINGTON, DC – Affordability remains the nation's largest housing challenge, according to The State of the Nation's Housing 2007, an annual report by the Harvard University Joint Center for Housing Studies and supported by the National Low Income Housing Coalition (NLIHC) and several other organizations.

"Affordability problems remain the nation's fastest-growing and most pervasive housing challenge," states the report, released June 11. The number of American households spending more than half their incomes on housing is rising rapidly, and one of every seven households is severely housing cost-burdened, which means it pays more than half its income for housing, according to the report. In 2005, the number of severely cost-burdened households jumped by 1.2 million to 17 million. This brings the increase since 2001 to an astonishing 3.2 million households.

The State of the Nation's Housing 2007 can be found here: www.jchs.harvard.edu/son

National Low Income Housing Coalition
727 15th Street NW, 6th Floor
Washington D.C. 20005
www.nilch.org

Author Profile
By David Bass – Southern Methodist University

James Waghorne Profile 5/10/05

Had it not been for Barbecue Bob, Little Billy and Don, James Waghorne might not be here today. Waghorne says the three men taught him to survive outdoors when he became homeless over four years ago.

He became an advocate for the homeless while still living on the streets, largely by writing for *Endless Choices*, a newspaper homeless people can sell for money. That led to a job through Americorps, researching the services available to the homeless population. After saving for months, he finally purchased an apartment. In the two and a half years since, he has devoted his life to advocacy and forming groups such as the Dallas Homeless Neighborhood Association.

He said it is never easy to admit that you can't rescue everyone from homelessness. "When I go home, I feel like I still have someone out here suffering."

Waghorne now works for Dallas Metrocare Services. His office is in the Day Resource Center, a 24-hour downtown facility providing services to the homeless. His office is decorated with mementos of the people he has helped since becoming an advocate. One prominent letter is addressed to "Uncle," Waghorne's nickname among many of his homeless friends.

Jesse Aguilera, who also works with Dallas Metrocare Services, said Waghorne is as successful as anyone at finding suffering people. "He's very effective at going into the nooks and crannies of the city and finding those that are forgotten," Aguilera said.

David Kellogg, the public policy director for the Mental Health Association of Greater Dallas, according to Kellogg, Waghorne's passion helps him cope with the downsides of advocacy.

Waghorne graduated from W. T. White High School in 1976. He attended Tyler Junior College and North Texas State University, and then worked in sales. He lived comfortably in a home until December 2000. He found himself jobless, and eventually homeless, after a wave of mental depression attacked him.

On the streets, Waghorne began to see homeless people as individuals, rather than as he previously saw them: faceless components of a bothersome population. After about a month, he was finally welcomed into the "Tribe," a homeless group camped near White Rock Lake. He later moved to an area near Skillman Street at Abrams Road. That former campsite is now littered with playing cards, shoes, plastic spoons and human waste. Waghorne remembers sitting beside a tent labeled the "Tramp Motel" while eating day-old food from the dumpster behind Albertson's.

Waghorne said he spoke up about homelessness at a time when politicians did not want to hear it. Thanks to his efforts and the efforts of other homeless advocates, the City Council decided to build a new facility for the homeless, twice as large as the Day Resource Center. He said this is important because the non-profit and faith-based shelters he tried while homeless offered him religion and regulations at a time when he needed a place to live.

Still, Waghorne's faith is an important part of his life and mission. "On the day Christ was crucified, he picked the thief to spend the first day in paradise with," Waghorne said. "That keeps me humble to the people whom I serve. You can't doctrine people to love but you can love people to doctrine."

That's not the only thing keeping him humble. Most advocates are not well liked, he said. They don't get rich and they don't always make everybody happy. He has received plenty of hate mail, too. "I had to accept that I would always be uncomfortable doing advocacy work," he said. Despite the pressures of his job, it still consumes most of his time. He used to work 12 to 18 hours a day, but his health suffered. Now he turns the phone off at 10 p.m. and takes off at least one weekend per month.

Waghorne is driven not by his own aspirations, but rather by his belief that "housing is a right, not a privilege."...

References

REFERENCES – National Coalition for the Homeless

Children's Defense Fund and National Coalition for the Homeless. Welfare to What: Early Findings on Family Hardship and Well-being, 1998. National Coalition for the Homeless,
2201 P St NW, Washington, D.C., 20036; 202/462-4822.

Children's Defense Fund. "Bush Administration Policies Exacerbate Growing Housing Crisis For Families With Children", 2005. Available at www.childrensdefense.org.

Daskal, Jennifer. In Search of Shelter: The Growing Shortage of Affordable Rental Housing, 1998. Available from the Center on Budget and Policy Priorities, 820 First Street, NE, Suite 510, Washington, DC 20002; 202/408-1080, center@center.cbpp.org.

Dolbeare, Cushing. "Housing Policy: A General Consideration," in Homelessness in America, 1996, Oryx Press. National Coalition for the Homeless, 2201 P St NW, Washington, D.C., 20036; 202/462-4822.

The Economic Policy Institute. Minimum Wage: Frequently Asked Questions, 2005. Available from www.epinet.org.

Families USA. Losing Health Insurance: The Unintended Consequences of Welfare Reform,1999. Available from Families USA, 1334 G Street, NW, Washington, DC 20005; 202/628-3030.

Federal Task Force on Homelessness and Severe Mental Illness. Outcasts on Main Street: A Report of the Federal Task Force on Homelessness and Severe Mental Illness, 1992. Available, free, from the National Resource Center on Homelessness and Mental Illness, 262 Delaware Ave., Delmar, NY 12054-1123; 800/444-7415, nrc@prainc.com..

Greenberg, Mark, and Jim Baumohl. "Income Maintenance: Little Help Now, Less on the Way," in Homelessness in America, 1996, Oryx Press. National Coalition for the Homeless, 2201 P St NW, Washington, D.C., 20036; 202/462-4822.

Homes for the Homeless. Ten Cities 1997-1998: A Snapshot of Family Homelessness Across America. Available from Homes for the Homeless & the Institute for Children and Poverty, 36 Cooper Square, 6th Floor, New York, NY 10003; 212/529-5252.

Institute for Children and Poverty. A Shelter is Not a Home: Or is it? April 2001. Available online at www.homesforthehomeless.com/ or from the Institute for Children and Poverty, 36 Cooper Square, 6th Floor, New York, NY 10003.

Koegel, Paul, et al. "The Causes of Homelessness," in Homelessness in America, 1996, Oryx Press. National Coalition for the Homeless, 2201 P St NW, Washington, D.C., 20036; 202/462-4822.

Mishel, L., Bernstein, J., and Schmitt, J. The State of Working America: 1998-99, 1999. Available for $24.95 (paper) from the Economic Policy Institute, 1660 L Street, NW, Suite 1200, Washington, DC 20036; 202/331-5510.

National Coalition for the Homeless. Homelessness in America: Unabated and Increasing, 1997. National Coalition for the Homeless, 2201 P St NW, Washington, D.C., 20036; 202/462-4822.

National Coalition for the Homeless. No Open Door: Breaking the Lock on Addiction Recovery for Homeless People, 1998. National Coalition for the Homeless, 2201 P St NW, Washington, D.C., 20036; 202/462-4822.

National Low Income Housing Coalition. Out of Reach: Rental Housing at What Cost?, 1998.
Available from the National Low Income Housing Coalition at 1012 14th Street, Suite 610, Washington, DC 20005; 202/662-1530.

National Low Income Housing Coalition. The Crisis in America's Housing, 2005. Available from www.nlihc.org.

National Priorities Project and Jobs with Justice. Working Hard, Earning Less: The Future of Job Growth in America, 1998. Available from the National Priorities Project, 17 New South Street, Suite 301, Northampton, MA 01060; 414/584-9556.

Nickelson, Idara. "The District Should Use Its Upcoming TANF Bonus To Increase Cash Assistance and Remove Barriers to Work", 2004. D.C. Fiscal Policy Institute. Available at www.dcfpi.org.

Santos, Fernanda and Robet Ingrassia. "Family surge at shelters." New York Daily News, August 18th, 2002. Available at www.nationalhomeless.org/housing/familiesarticle.html.

Technical Assistance Collaborative, Inc. and the Consortium for Citizens with Disabilities Housing Task Force. Priced Out in 1998: The Housing Crisis for People with

Disabilities, 1999. Available from the Technical Assistance Collaborative, One Center Plaza, Suite 310, Boston, MA 02108; 617/742-5657.

U.S. Bureau of the Census(a). Poverty in the United States: 1997. Current Population Reports, Series P60-201, 1998. Available, free, from U.S. Bureau of the Census, Income Statistics Branch, Washington, DC, 20233-0001; 301/763-8576, or at http://www.census.gov/hhes/www/poverty.html.

U.S. Bureau of the Census(b). Health Insurance Coverage: 1997. Current Population Reports, Series P60-202, 1997. Available, free, from U.S. Bureau of the Census, Income Statistics Branch, Washington,DC, 20233-0001; 301/763-8576, or at http://www.census.gov/hhes/www/hlthins.html.

U.S. Bureau of the Census. Income, Poverty and Health Insurance in the United States: 2003,2004,2005. Available at www.census.gov.

U.S. Conference of Mayors. A Status Report on Hunger and Homelessness in America's Cities: 2001. Available for $15.00 from the U.S. Conference of Mayors, 1620 Eye St., NW, 4th Floor, Washington, DC, 20006-4005, 202/293-7330.

U.S. Conference of Mayors. A Status Report on Hunger and Homelessness in America's Cities: 2005. Available from http://www.usmayors.org/uscm/home.asp.

U.S. Department of Health and Human Services. Blueprint for Change, 2003. Available through National Resource and Training Center on Homelessness and Mental Illness, www.nrchmi.samhsa.gov.

U.S. Department of Housing and Urban Development, Office of Policy Development and Research. Rental Housing Assistance -- The Crisis Continues: 1997 Report to Congress on Worst Case Housing Needs, 1998. Available for $5.00 from HUD User, P.O. Box 6091,Rockville, MD, 20850, 800/245-2691.

U.S. Department of Housing and Urban Development, Office of Policy Development and Research. Waiting In Vain: An Update On America's Housing Crisis, 1999. Available for $5.00 from HUD User, P.O. Box 6091, Rockville, MD 20849-6091, 800/245-2691, or free from the HUD User web site at www.huduser.org

U.S. Department of Housing and Urban Development, Office of Policy Development and Research, A Report on Worst Case Housing Needs in 1999: New Opportunities Amid Continuing Challenges, 1999. Available from HUD User, P.O. Box 6091, Rockville, MD 20849-6091, 800/245-2691, or free from the HUD User web site at www.huduser.org

Wright, James and Beth Rubin. "Is Homelessness a Housing Problem?" in Understanding Homelessness: New Policy and Research Perspectives, 1997. Available, free, from the Fannie Mae Foundation, 4000 Wisconsin Avenue, NW, North Tower, Suite One, Washington, DC 20016-2804; 202-274-8074 or email: fmfpubs@fanniemaefoundation.org.

Zorza, J. "Woman Battering: A Major Cause of Homelessness," Clearinghouse Review, 25(4)

(1991). Qtd. In National Coalition Against Domestic Violence, "The Importance of Financial

Literacy," Oct. 2001.

Consortium for Citizens with Disabilities, Administration's Section 8 Voucher Proposal Closes National Low Income Housing Coalition.

References – National Alliance to End Homelessness

Baumohl, Jim. 1996. Homelessness in America. Phoenix, Ariz.: Oryx Press.

Burt, Martha R. 2001. What Will It Take to End Homelessness? Washington, D.C.: Urban Institute.

Burt, Martha R. 1996. "Homelessness: Definition and Counts." In Homelessness in America, edited by Jim Baumohl. Phoenix Ariz.: Oryx Press.

Burt, M., L. Y. Aron, and J. Valente. 2001. Helping America's Homeless: Emergency Shelter or Affordable Housing? Washington, D.C.: Urban Institute.

Culhane, Dennis P., Stephen Metraux, and Trevor Hadley. 2002. Public Service Reductions Associated with Placement of Persons with Serious Mental Illness in Supportive Housing. Housing Policy Debate 13(1): 107-63.

Kondratas, Anna. 1991. "Estimates and Public Policy: The Politics of Numbers." Housing Policy Debate 2(3): 631–47.

Hombs, Mary Ellen, and Mitch Snyder. 1982. Homelessness in America: A Forced March to Nowhere. Washington, D.C.: Community for Creating Non-violence.

Gladwell, Malcolm. 2006. "Million-Dollar Murray." The New Yorker, February 13.

Millennial Housing Commission. 2002. Meeting Our Nation's Housing Challenges. Washington, D.C.: Author.

Rivenburg, Roy. 2006. "Counting the Homeless Is a High Stakes Numbers Game." Los Angeles Times, June 24.

Urban Institute. 2000. America's Homeless II: Populations and Services. Washington, D.C.: Author.

U.S. Department of Housing and Urban Development. 2003. Continuum of Care Homeless Assistance Programs SuperNOFA 2003. Washington, D.C.: Author.

U.S. Department of Housing and Urban Development. 2006a. A Guide to Counting Homeless People. Washington, D.C.: Author.

U.S. Department of Housing and Urban Development. 2006b. Report to Congress: Fifth Progress Report on HUD's Strategy for Improving Homeless Data Collection, Reporting, and Analysis. Washington, D.C.: Author.

U.S. Department of Housing and Urban Development. 2006c. "HUD Perspective" presentation of Mark Johnston, Acting Deputy Assistant Secretary for Special Needs, September 20, 2006 CoC Forum.

U.S. General Accounting Office. 1991. Counting the Homeless: Limitations of the 1990 Census Results and Methodology, GAO/T-GGD-91-29. Washington, D.C.: Author

National Low Income Housing Coalition & Harvard University Joint Center for housing Studies – June 13, 2007

Associated Press – March 9 2006

National Center for Injury Prevention and Control

Marcia Purse – Internet About.com

African American News and Issues – Darwin Campbell

Bucks County Courier Times (Levittown, PA) - March 9, 2006

Dallas Morning News Headlines - 6/10/94, 1/20/01, 5/05/03, 7/24/05, 11/09/05, 2/01/07

Ft. Worth Star Telegram - 4/14/91, 12/20/94

Houston Chronicle (TX) - December 30, 2005

Kansas City Star, The (MO) - March 10, 2006

Miami Herald, The (FL) - March 12, 2006

www.ingramcontent.com/pod-product-compliance
Lightning Source LLC
Chambersburg PA
CBHW080244170426
43192CB00014BA/2560